"DO SOU

"In *Soulmates* Jess St⋯⋯⋯⋯⋯⋯ ⋯ ⋯eries of romantic adventures about real people from all walks of life with a common denominator—they have sought and found their soulmates.

"Jess Stearn investigates and illuminates these provocative and moving stories of lovers past and present, lost and found. He shows that life is stranger than fiction and that love and the human spirit are our most enduring gifts."
—Susan Strasberg, actress and author of *Bittersweet*

JESS STEARN, a world-renowned authority on spirituality and reincarnation, is the bestselling author of many books, including *Edgar Cayce: The Sleeping Prophet* and *Yoga, Youth and Reincarnation*. In *Soulmates* he reveals how love and spirituality can merge—beyond the limits of space and time, of life and death—to create a perfect union of body and soul.

ABOUT THE AUTHOR

JESS STEARN is the bestselling author of *Edgar Cayce: The Sleeping Prophet* and *Yoga, Youth and Reincarnation.* He is also the author of *The Door to the Future; The Search for the Girl with the Blue Eyes; The Search for a Soul: Taylor Caldwell's Psychic Lives; I, Judas;* and *In Search of Taylor Caldwell.*

QUANTITY PURCHASES

SOULMATES

Jess Stearn

And so it seems that we have met before,
And laughed before and loved before
But who knows where or when,

  Richard Rodgers & Lorenz Hart

BANTAM BOOKS
TORONTO · NEW YORK · LONDON · SYDNEY · AUCKLAND

SOULMATES

Bantam Hardcover edition / December 1984
2nd printing . . . March 1985
Bantam rack-size edition / October 1985

Library of Congress Cataloging in Publication Data

Stearn, Jess.
  Soulmates.

  1. Psychical research.   2. Occult sciences.
3. Stearn, Jess.   I. Title.
  BF1031.S765 1984   133.8   84-45181
ISBN 0-553-25150-3

Published simultaneously in the United States and Canada

PRINTED IN THE UNITED STATES OF AMERICA

H   0 9 8 7 6 5 4 3 2 1

Contents

By Way of Introduction

I had thought of love as an ideal seldom if ever realized. I had been told that love, like faith, could move mountains, conquer evil, and put adversity to shame. Yet even when I seemed to be experiencing it, I found it transient, fragile, possessive, often cruel, consuming itself with the very passion that set it apart.

This was something that had always been, and would always be. Or so I thought. And then, suddenly, I began to hear about an unlimited love, of soulmates, people of all ages and descriptions talking about their soulmates with a glow in their eye.

They spoke of the Aquarian Age, the New Age, of the time for an outpouring of universal love which would ignite a flame that would spread through a stricken world.

As I examined the phenomenon—I could think of it as nothing less—I was struck by the growing awareness that there must be more to life than grinding out a living and propagating offspring. There was a recognition that I—whoever that I was—am a very special person created by an all-knowing God for a very special reason, which I will get to know about through a very special love.

Since all this was new, very few existing relationships

seemed touched by its special magic. For even with those who already had a satisfactory mate, there was a deep-down searching, a restlessness, that seemed to cry out, "Should I not have more?"

I had seen people in love before, and known that state myself. So what was it that set soulmates apart? There was, I found, one telltale sign. This was its delicious urgency, a feeling of warm and instant familiarity, an overpowering impression of having known one another before.

It was often confusing, yet always exciting. And it seemed a communicable state, intriguing others who wanted as much for themselves.

Because of my interest in the metaphysical I was besieged by those who thought I might have greater knowledge of the properties of the soul—and soulmates.

But I was as much in the dark as they, and had to go quietly to the dictionary. There I found, as I had surmised, that the soul was the intangible psychical and spiritual essence of the Universe and the individual, the animating and actuating foundation of life. So a soulmate was a spiritual partner, whose love was tied somehow to a universal love. It was more instinctual, hence closer to the Creation, since originally man was more instinctual than rational.

This instinctual yearning for a soulmate was deep and sometimes obsessive, transcending any and all other relationships. The realization of love's dream often became its own justification, with normal prudence abandoned and convention ignored.

"How," I asked one beauty who had disrupted another's marriage for a love she considered eternal, "how can you build happiness on another's unhappiness?"

"When love ends," she replied, "marriage ends. It cannot sustain itself."

"But how about the wife?"

A gleam came to the woman's eyes, and she recited from the Reverend Gladys Jones's ode to soulmates:

I am known as the other woman,
A statement to which I disagree.
I did not steal what is already mine,
I'm not second but first, you see.
Though I'm known as the other woman,

Our love's ruled by destiny.
It all began many lives ago,
That is why he belongs to me.

Whenever the subject of soulmates came up, there was an interest surpassing even nuclear weaponry in its hold on the imagination. There was something intensely reassuring about the mating process, however mysteriously it worked, as opposed to the impersonal and incomprehensible immensity of universal annihilation.

The questions put to me were naturally related to the individual interest:

- Firstly, what is a soulmate?
- How do you recognize him or her?
- Can one program a soulmate?
- How and why does it transcend any other human connection?
- Why is so much of it happening now?

The questions were new, and I had no answers, and so I turned to mystics, psychics, counselors, psychologists, and sociologists, who had been familiar with the new phenomenon before I was even aware of it.

In the final analysis, the greatest authorities were the principals in this ongoing saga of love. This is their story, delving into the nature of a love that is as inevitable as it is deep and heartfelt, recasting lives in a moment of truth as it brought a depth and breadth of understanding they had never before achieved.

"It was as if I had never lived before," recalled one middle-aged woman, "for I saw love not only with new and brighter eyes, but the world around me as well, giving me a unity with God I had never known before."

"It brought me a new dimension of feeling," said actress Susan Strasberg, "permitting me to look back and understand better the nature of my father's love for me, making me realize what gaps there were did not come from lack of caring, but from fear of rejection."

She knew then that fear was love's greatest adversary, for it closed off not only what was natural to man, but what was inspiring and enhancing, that which made him aware of his potential.

I soon learned that in speaking of soulmates, people were telling me of an eternal love out of a misty past that had only to be remembered to be renewed.

But where did this memory come from? How were we to judge its validity? Some spoke of reincarnation, others of genetic memory, some of universal racial consciousness, akin to instinctual recall, or some other form of recollection we had no explanation for. As a skeptic, a former newspaperman, it gave me a lot to think about. Even so, if there was an effect, didn't this establish a cause, however hidden or obscure that cause? Was a Universe boundless in its vastness, to be bound by the petty limitations of our own limited experience? If the soul was a spiritual essence, an energy force that never died, why could it not have shared and remembered a love as deep and meaningful as the soul itself? Thinking of all this, had not the brilliant Voltaire provocatively pointed out: "It is just as remarkable to have been born once as twice."

And indeed it is.

I had half-expected to find that soulmates had clear sailing on their voyage to a deathless love. Instead, I found they had as many, if different, obstacles as the rest of us. But there was still a difference. There were relationships as beautiful and poignant as anything in history or literature. But even these were no more beautiful and exalting than those that fell short of the perfection I had assigned to an eternal love. There was an enduring quality, which exalted the individual, even when the relationship itself did not endure. For in that interlude, many memories were invoked and many lessons learned that prepared soulmates for even greater excursions into life and love. And the greatest lesson was that true and abiding love was the strongest force of all. It had no limitations. For where there were limitations, it was not love. It was then other things— friendship, sex, affection, companionship. But not love. For love, it became clear, was a giving for love's sake alone, enhancing not only he who received, but, more, he who gave.

All this was self-evident as I came to know the people in this book. Theirs was indeed a special kind of love, bringing growth to themselves and those they loved. A true mating of heart and mind and soul. In other words—soulmates.

CHAPTER 1

Getting to Know You

"Did you know," said Nikki Schevers, "that this is the Age of Soulmates?"

I eyed her curiously as she took my breakfast off the tray and settled it on the restaurant table.

"You should look into it," she said, handing me my orange juice. "You know, there are classes on finding your soulmates."

I had known Nikki for years, without knowing too much about her private life, except that she seemed a reasonably well-balanced young woman, with a fresh, fragile loveliness.

"And what is your idea of a soulmate?" I asked.

She looked around the tiny restaurant in Pacific Palisades— Ronald Reaganland—to make sure the handful of people there needed no immediate attention, and her brow furled into a thoughtful frown.

"It's more than just compatibility," she said, "more than just being suited to each other. It's as if you belong with each other, and always have, and know it from the instant you meet."

She gave me a helpless smile.

"I guess I'm not describing it well. But it's a feeling, mostly, that you two were meant for each other, and makes you both feel as if the Universe and everything in it is yours—and you are part of it."

She was a California beauty, long-legged, with sunny blue eyes, and honey blonde hair, somewhere in her late twenties, and surprisingly unmarried.

"Have you had a soulmate?" I asked.

She nodded, and her eyes sparkled for a moment and then dimmed.

"Yes, I have," she said, hesitating a moment. "I hope so."

The restaurant was beginning to fill and Nikki, who was doubling as waitress-manager, had to scurry off.

"Be sure," she cried over her shoulder, "that you look up my teacher, Muriel Isis. She can tell you all about your soulmate."

I considered what Nikki had said. When I thought of soulmates, I had a romantic picture of Romeo and Juliet, the Brownings, Heloise and Abelard, even Damon and Pythias, though the latter, like Ruth and Naomi, out of the Bible, were of the same sex. It had not occurred to me that the waitress fetching my breakfast or the young man who delivered my bottled water could be involved in anything as esoteric or erotic. Movie stars, perhaps, but not ordinary mortals like myself, and the others who stirred in and out of my life.

From what Nikki had said, Muriel Isis could tell me much more. But it was a while before I caught up to this unusual teacher, who, unknown to me, had also assumed the less exotic name of Tepper. Meanwhile, my curiosity piqued, I looked into the subject and soon discovered something novel and unprecedented was happening in the world of materiality. It was being attacked by love.

After the sexual revolution of the Sixties and early Seventies, in which promiscuity was a by-product of the Pill, a reaction was almost inevitable, as multitudes of young people discovered satiation did not necessarily bring satisfaction. They were ready for a more pristine monogamy, for a singleness of love, that would satisfy their yearning for something exclusively theirs, which they could reassuringly cling to in a world of swiftly shifting values.

I found an almost universal yearning for a soulmate, a perfect love, to banish the monotony of mundane living and bring the fulfillment and happiness we all desire. This sense of awareness, of anticipation almost, appeared to affect adults of all ages and persuasions. Where an average person was once content with the prospect of a secure and comfortable marriage, there was now a desire for something more. Psychics and counselors of every description were besieged, not with the usual questions about career, romance, and health, but with, "When shall I find my soulmate?" Some of this had to do with marital disillusionment and the high divorce rate, but, generally, it was a sign of a burgeoning belief in Eastern reincarnation which promised a continuity of life in a world on the brink. In the disenchantment of Vietnam there was new thirst for beauty and perfection, for new heroes, as the day of the antihero ended as abruptly as it had begun. The easy acceptance of reincarnation, particularly among the young, amounted almost to a revolution in Western thought.

I discovered children toddling up to perfect strangers and saying, "I like you, I knew you before."

And greeted with a laugh, they would often say where and when.

Whatever the old believed, the young were ready to reject.

One day I sat down with my friend Alberto Sarno in Sarno's Cafe Dell Opera in Hollywood, as he told a pretty girl that I was doing a book on soulmates.

Kirsten Schroeder, Minnesota-born and California-bred, lifted a golden eyebrow.

"Soulmates, what are they?"

"Do you believe in reincarnation?" I countered.

She shrugged a slim shoulder. "What else is there?" she said.

In learning about the mystic Edgar Cayce, many had read that love at first sight, the instant feeling of familiarity with strangers, was a lingering remembrance from the dim past, with the promise of a love that passeth earthly understanding.

But even without reincarnation, there were still many who related their search for a soulmate to that distant past, attributing that instant of electrifying recognition to genetic memory, which we shared with the animals, or the collective unconscious described by humanist Carl Gustav Jung, who felt the wellsprings of distant memory—déjà vu, if you like—were the product of an atavistic racial recall from the time the first man trod the earth. And just as the fledgling swallows flew to

Capistrano on the same date each year, and the salmon swam up the Columbia River to spawn and die, so, they said, did man subconsciously recall his past—in vision, dreams, or hypnotic trance.

There was a whole soulmate subculture, I discovered, with classes and seminars all over the country on finding soulmates. Students were taught how to pray, meditate, visualize, and dream for the desired soulmate, and as their hopes materialized they reported their successes in growing and enthusiastic numbers.

There were differences as to the nature and quality of one's eternal partners. Some, like soulmate authority and evangelist Elizabeth Clare Prophet, held there were not one but three kinds of soulmates: the twin or counterpart; the companion soulmate, who was more of a project-oriented love partner; and the karmic soulmate, whom we were often uneasily drawn to to learn some hard lessons from the past.

Some said there were many soulmates for each of us, and others held there was but that special one. And he or she might not necessarily appear in any one lifetime just because we wished them to. Soulmate counselor JZ Burnett, guided by her spirit channel, Ramtha the Wise, took the view that our soulmates existed on this plane, even if we weren't lucky or diligent enough to meet up with them. "What is the point," Ramtha asked, "if he or she is on some other planet?"

The actress Shirley MacLaine, one of Ramtha's—the Ram's—well-known students (along with actresses Joan Hackett, Linda Gray, and others), had not yet experienced a soulmate, though she had once married, and had still another redeeming relationship lasting for years. And she cheerfully acknowledged she had no expectation in this lifetime of a perfect union. But with her spiritual development, reflecting itself in her recent book *Out On A Limb,* that prospect took on a new immediacy. For as the individual becomes increasingly ready, so does the likelihood of his meeting his mate.

In the soulmate subculture there are no firm boundaries. Ramtha—in agreement with the dictionary—holds soulmates to be heterosexual in nature, while others, like MacLaine, see no reason why a beneficent Creator would deprive so many of his children of equality in the pursuit of happiness.

In the quest for a soulmate, there are many questions

one has to put to oneself. How does one distinguish love from infatuation, an obsessive attraction that might soon burn itself out? What about relationships that begin slowly and ripen into a deep and abiding love, if only both partners are patient and trusting enough? What about the antagonistic attractions that bedevil so many, bringing excitement without peace, consummation without contentment?

And karma, what about karma—the credit and debit ledger from the past—what part does it play in the present and future? What conditions does it carry over? What opportunities does it provide? These and other questions I asked myself, hoping the answers would come.

While I wasn't quite sure myself how reincarnation worked, I was quite aware by now that this belief in rebirth was an important facet of the whole soulmate concept. I was aware that many creative giants—Shakespeare, Tennyson, Kipling, Wordsworth, Thoreau, and others—believed firmly in the continuity of life. I was amused that Benjamin Franklin promised that he would one day return like a newly revised book, intrigued that Mark Twain recalled in his dreams the same sweetheart in a dozen different places and times, bemused by General Patton's recollections of a Roman camp in the South of France where he had never been before.

As for Emerson, so much of what he saw and did was crystallized by visions and upswellings from the hazy past. I was aware in the Bible of Jesus asking His Apostles who men thought He was before, and their answering Elias, Elijah, or one of the older prophets. And His reply that this was not He but John the Baptist. I was continually meeting people with baffling experiences pointing to some recent or ancient connection. Novelist Taylor Caldwell, with her constant recall of the past, encouraged our friendship, convinced we had known each other in Christ's time, a period she had shown an intriguing familiarity with in her *Dear and Glorious Physician* and *The Great Lion of God*. We were both scribes, she advised me, and knew both Christ and the Apostles. It was an exciting thought, but I still didn't know what to make of it, or how it fit into my life.

And yet most of the world, predominantly in the East, believed in the continuity of life, of one life that kept returning till it had learned all the lessons this planet had to offer. And even here in the pragmatic United States, polls showed that twenty-five percent of the adult population believe that the soul never dies, ever returning in a new body until it achieves perfection.

As they spoke of their soulmates I saw people's faces light up with a radiance they had never known before. How could one be anything but selfless and loving, when he or she was inspired by an overflowing love that knew only tenderness and compassion, not only for one's mate, but for all of humanity.

Others yearned for a soulmate, not even being sure what a soulmate was. But I soon found there were plenty to keep them informed, not only as to when and how they would meet their great desire, but how to identify the desired one with an assurance they had never felt before.

"It is a union that must be earned," said one teacher of soulmates. "The person is well-advised to elevate himself for this shining role. What good would it do for a Skid Row bum to have a soulmate, unless he can turn his life around?"

But there were those who disagreed, notably Richard Sutphen, a soulmate programmer and author of *You Were Born Again to Be Together.*

"The common denominator," said he, "is still affinity out of the past, for each soulmate finds the other on his own level. Who knows what lesson in humility the bum had to learn, and having learned it, what heights he can aspire to in this life with his soulmate out of the past?"

For Russ Michael, the author of *Finding Your Soulmate* and *Miracle Cures*, the individual has to rigidly program himself, physically, mentally, and visually.

"You can't get your soulmate just by wanting one. You have to do something about it. It's like looking for a friend out of your past. In line with the Judaic-Christian ethic, you have to work at it."

Michael was comfortable with the notion of multiple soulmates. When he ran out of one, undiscouraged, he programmed another. And each time, as I noted, during his sojourns to Virginia Beach and San Diego, he turned up a lovely soulmate for each coast.

"You visualize and you pray, and you write down your expectations, giving it a relation to reality," he counseled.

"Before I made my first physical contact with a soulmate I

took a few moments daily, visualizing her and musing with her on the mental plane."

What worked for him, he felt, would work for others. And I must say, as I surveyed his most recent soulmate—a youthful, vibrant adjunct to his venturesome life—he had invoked very well.

"Be regular," he wrote. "Pray (for the one) the same time each day.

"Use the same prayer each and every time. Reduce the invocation to bare simplicity in written form, so it is easy to memorize. Through meditation, getting into a higher level, tell your subconscious mind what you want. Say when and where, listing the exact time, year, month and day, and the exact location, country, state, city. And hold your faith intact. Your soulmate will appear."

In meditation, like prayer, the powerful subconscious mind, reaching out into the universe, would hopefully do the rest.

Searching their own souls, through subconscious self-regression, hypnosis, or deep alpha-thinking, many reached back into time for a dimly remembered mate who would one day exalt their present and future. And while others were regressed by experts, there were those who were reluctant to undergo such excursions into the past because of the fear they might reveal too much, particularly of themselves.

Some took other routes, as in the comparing of astrological charts, and others went to psychic artists who, presumably tapping the subconscious, sketched the likeness of the soulmate to be drawn into their futures.

But it was not all that simple. For nobody else could choose but you. How were you to really know the mate right for you? How much was the wish the father of the thought? What traits and qualities were you to look for?

Some have found a way.

"You have to pinpoint him first," said actress Robin Blake, after attending a class on visualization by programmer Terry McBride of San Clemente, California.

"Just write out your list," said McBride, "and start believing that everything you ask for will materialize."

Robin made a list of ten qualities she prized above others

in her soulmate, and meditated on each one in a daily affirmation of the subconscious.

She didn't visualize his face, only his mystique, what he would be like, how it would feel to be with him, making a joint project of this emotional experience.

She picked out the qualities she liked to think of herself as having, believing her soulmate should be in her own image, for compatibility's sake.

Not long after, the paragon appeared. "So far it's great," said a radiant Robin. "He's very warm and loving, very intelligent, well-bred, kind, sensitive, honest, with a sense of humor."

What more could one human being be? And she had written it all down on one page, and her alpha brainwaves, the offshoot of her subconscious mind, connecting with his, had made it happen.

But there were many pitfalls for aspiring soulmates.

"Too often," advised renowned Hollywood psychic Gladys Jones, the poet laureate of the soulmate movement, "people confuse sexmates with soulmates. And when that first flush of romance passes, find they have built their relationship on shifting sand."

Having just found a soulmate in a man forty years her junior, the octogenarian Jones philosophized in her *Mortal and Immortal Love*:

> We were so different,
> I wondered why we met
> And so we finally parted
> But it's a love I can't forget.

"The reason parting brings such pain, even when the relationship may be short-lived," Jones observed, "is because of a long remembrance of experiences in the past. Soulmates are not made of clay."

You proceed cautiously but surely, not passing up a relationship because you might get hurt, yet aware of this possibility.

"This man was so much younger," said Jones, "still there was an engagement of minds, rekindling the exciting days of long ago, when we had been lovers in every way."

But for everything there was a season, and each had its reward, for not only the young loved and were loved. And in keeping with the New Age, traditional barriers of age, race, religion, and station were constantly transcended in a universal manifestation of a new togetherness.

It was the individual, the microcosm of the macrocosm, I was concerned with. And his future lay in his past—of that I was convinced. But how to plumb the past? I remembered now how Taylor Caldwell, regressed to biblical times, had recoiled in horror at the stoning of her "daughter" Mary Magdalene, and on her knees appealed to Jesus to rescue her from the angry mob. Her terror was so real, so devastating, that we quickly returned her to the present, lest she expire before our eyes. Nothing that Taylor Caldwell had ever experienced was more vivid and real.

Once before, as a teenager, she had visualized the faces of two men, and later met and married each of them. It had also been a mind-boggling experience.

But why had she seen these faces?

She gave me a pitying look. "Because I knew them before. That's why."

As we had gotten into Caldwell's past, showing its influence on her writings, so I decided to delve into the subconscious memories of our soulmates. And to help me with this I wanted somebody who had a rapport not only with my subjects but with myself to develop a productive climate.

"Do you believe in reincarnation?" I asked Dr. Boris Bagdassaroff, a hypnotherapist and professor of psychology who had come to my Malibu home to discuss past life regressions.

"I'm not sure," he said, "but I remember what wise old Socrates said. 'What a man remembers he must have known at an earlier time, from a previous existence.' "

"And how about soulmates?"

His eyes brightened with a satirical smile.

"You mean people who loved for an eternity?"

"Something like that."

"Sometimes," he said, "six months seem an eternity."

I had wanted somebody objective, and found somebody iconoclastic. There would be no danger of his being anything but objective.

I knew little about him personally. He had a beard, and a foreign name, and yet he looked and sounded very American.

"My mother was Irish," he said.

"Was her name O'Neil?"

He looked at me closely, without surprise.

"Very good," he said.

He had mentioned he lived in Beverly Hills.

"On Doheny Drive?"

He nodded, laughing.

"We should be quite a team."

He paused at the door.

"Instead of picking out specific time periods, why not let the subconscious mind turn back to the time slot it considers meaningful?"

"Why not?" I shrugged. "After all, the event is the important thing."

He had his hand on the doorknob.

"Another thing," he said, "I like my people to keep remembering. While it may be traumatic in some instances, the subconscious mind keeps spinning until they finish the scenario they started on the couch."

I hesitated. "But wouldn't this dredge up more than they can handle?"

He smiled. "They will get rid of a lot of garbage and will take on their new soulmates with a clean slate."

Our subjects were to be chosen at random. There was no visible pattern. I had known actress Susan Strasberg for years and knew something of her personal life. I had admired actress Terry Moore, but knew little of her relationship with billionaire Howard Hughes, and less of her current romance with a much younger man she had met in a taxicab. I was familiar with the late singer Dick Haymes, who once rivaled Sinatra and Crosby, but had not previously met the lady psychologist who was his most recent partner.

It was obvious on meeting handsome actor John Ericson and his wife Karen that they should be soulmates if they weren't, not because they held hands or peered soulfully at each other, but because they dramatically reflected the oneness of kindred spirits.

I was careful not to make this a book of Hollywood stars, hoping to reflect a much broader cross-section of society. I went to classes and seminars, took myself around the country, mingling with the variety of people I wanted to reach.

I had lost sight of Nikki's teacher, the Reverend Muriel

Isis, after she changed her name and moved off. Nikki could not help. And so I meditated, concentrating on locating her.

Two or three days later, wandering into a shop in Santa Monica, I turned and saw a familiar face.

"I was looking for you," I told Reverend Muriel Isis.

"I know," she said, "I am here."

She was in Glendale, California, now, with *The Lighted Way*.

The Reverend Isis was no exotic Egyptian goddess, no ancient mother of the Universe and mistress of magic, but a friendly, attractive teacher of metaphysics, who had found her own soulmate. For the New Age she had gone back to the modern name Tepper. She was optimistic, not only for herself, but for others fortunate enough to live in this memorable Age, which had barely dawned, she said, in 1981. From the Uranian tide of events, and the astrological portents, Muriel concluded that the Age of Aquarius, with its message of universal love, was upon us.

"Like it or not," she said, "we are children of the Universe, affected by the nature of the planets, just as the ocean tides are affected by the moon, and plant life by the sun."

This new dawning seemed almost too good to be true, a perfect Utopia, with a groundswell of love resolving hate and hostility, and destroying those who would destroy the earth.

"Love is the greatest force," said Muriel. "Two people loving each other can, as Christ said, perform miracles. Multiply that by millions, and you have a vast army of lovers. Had the Age dawned a hundred years earlier, Hitler might have found his soulmate in Vienna, while a struggling young artist, and the world would have been spared fifty million lives."

I had noted few major changes in a troubled and troublesome world. The murder rate was still perilously high; it was unsafe to walk the streets at night. The killing was going on in Afghanistan, the Middle East, El Salvador, Northern Ireland, Africa, and other places too numerous to mention.

"Give it time. Love's revolution is just beginning," Muriel said with a cheerful grin. "We're only a couple years into the New Age and already we see signs of change. Where men traditionally sought younger mates, we now see older women in strong love relationships with younger men, without appearing ridiculous or self-conscious."

I had noted myself, without thinking too much about it, any number of middle-aged women being assiduously courted by men fifteen to twenty years younger. Oriental-Caucasian romances were common among the young, and black and white marriages were not unusual, as love became its own justification, making no apologies to the mores of the day. The longing and secret yearning for a love-mate was never more apparent.

"Yes," said Muriel, "they're searching, but first they must search within themselves. That's what I tell my classes. You can't just get your soulmate for the asking. My soulmate was a gift from God, in a vision. Once somebody has a vision, he should follow it and make it a reality."

"Visions?" I said. "How many people have visions?"

"You open your subconscious mind and the vision arrives."

Her vision had materialized in a dream, the ultimate of the subconscious state. She saw the face, each plane and lineament, of a man she had known as a friend, but had not thought of romantically.

"In the dream," she recalled, "he was wearing a crown of red roses—roses of course being the symbol of a spiritual love. He took my hand and walked with me to an altar that was surrounded by living water. He filled a chalice with the water and I drank from it. And then he drank from a second chalice."

She was then half-awake. In this twilight stage she saw him gazing deeply into her eyes and felt immeasurably drawn to him. It was as if she had become part of him. After she awakened the dream stayed with her, and its significance deepened in her consciousness. When she next saw him, she was vitally aware of his presence and was moved emotionally just as in her dream. He, too, seemed to regard her differently. She wondered for a moment whether her dream may have subconsciously affected him.

In the next few months, they became so close that they fancied themselves soulmates. For some reason, though, she had never told him the dream, perhaps not wanting to influence him. And then one day, at a spiritual service, apparently out of the blue, he reenacted in every detail the dream of the two chalices.

"He actualized the experience, exactly as I had dreamed it, and looking into his eyes as I drank from the chalice, I had the most wonderful feeling of having realized all this before."

I looked forward eagerly to meeting the students of such a teacher. I pictured the bright faces straining for her pearls of wisdom. Did they already have soulmates? Or were they shopping about, hoping and groping, anxious to satisfy the longing so many experienced almost from birth, often without knowing the source of that atavistic melancholy, which the Germans, with their gift for a phrase, called *Weltzchmerhzeit*?

"Some have, some haven't," said Muriel. "I tell them don't be negative, always expect and visualize the best. It's not so much a matter of thinking as feeling. When you feel something, it's closer to the soul."

And what was this soul we had been hearing so much about?

"I would say it was the immortal part of a person, which is not only his link to his past and future, but to the Universal Consciousness when the need for communion with the soul arises."

"But why all this preoccupation with the soul and soulmates?"

She frowned a moment. "With all this talk of nuclear warfare, we are faced for the first time with the realities of extinction. So in a worldwide atmosphere of pessimism and instability, there is a growing human need for a lasting love, as a reassuring link to a sense of continuing universal purpose. That's what the New Age is about."

I wondered how many of her students felt this way.

She smiled. "Why not find out for yourself?"

There were some fifty or sixty in her class—men and women, young and old, rich and poor—nearly all with one thing in common—a soulmate awareness. "Very few of these people have found their soulmates," said Muriel, looking around the room.

Actually, only a handful had been that fortunate. Nevertheless, it was a cheerful and optimistic group.

Young or old, most of the group seemed attractive, giving off an aura of radiant goodwill and happiness. Strangers spoke to one another, and when it came time for refreshments, there seemed to be more people serving than receiving. Everybody—nearly everybody—was on the upbeat. There was singing led by Muriel. First, "Getting to Know You," next, "On a Clear Day, You Can See Forever."

A smiling Muriel gave soulmate readings around the room.

"Your soulmate," she told a smiling Joanne, "is going to an island that is very green. He is a world traveler and very spiritual but also makes very good money. He will devote his life to helping others, both physically and spiritually. You will teach others with him."

From her expression, Joanne appeared to agree. She was one of the few who had found her soulmate. He was bound for the Emerald Isle Ireland.

Muriel, like other teachers, stressed self-improvement as a prelude to that wonderful moment of glorious union and to a vision or moment of truth which might bring it on.

"First, you must know yourself, the true inner being. Once understood, that being enables the immediate recognition of another inner self."

Her sweeping look took in the room.

"We are our own creators, learning from our mistakes and indiscretions, directing our future by the choices we make."

Bobby, a quite attractive blonde, was listening raptly. From the nodding of her head, I could see that she agreed. Indeed, the room seemed to think as one, except for a young man with scraggly hair, who rose noisily to his feet.

"How can you believe all that junk about reincarnation and soulmates?" he demanded. "Look at all the divorces and fooling around. You're all kidding yourselves. There's no ideal mate."

There were a few tolerant smiles and a mild shaking of heads.

"We've all been through that stage," an older man told me with a shrug, adding, "What's he got that's better? I don't know about you, but most of us are looking for somebody who wants the same thing out of life we do, somebody with the same value system. That's my idea of a soulmate."

Muriel could be quite accurate. "You have never found your soulmate," she said, coming to me. "Stop looking, and it will materialize. It will happen when you least expect it. Keep your mind clear. Your prayer will be answered." She smiled. "God hears you when you speak but once."

It was a pleasant meeting, and even as it ended, nobody

seemed disposed to leave, not even the youth who had scoffed at the others. In fact, he was speaking more volubly than ever.

Muriel didn't seem to mind.

"He'll come around. You know what Shakespeare said—he 'doth protest too much, methinks'!"

I had observed a good-looking man, no more than thirty or so, sitting by the door. The eyes of the younger women— and some of the older—had rested on him from time to time.

He was the first to get up, and I noticed the room's disappointment. "Sorry," he said, "but I have to get to the airport to meet my soulmate." He smiled. "She's so perfect, she always arrives on time, even when the planes don't."

CHAPTER 2

By Love Possessed

"Love possesses not, nor would it be possessed, for love is sufficient unto love."

As the minister spoke, the already radiant bride took on new radiance and the mature, wise-looking bridegroom new stature. I had been told they were soulmates, who made this discovery after recognizing one another as the lovers they knew forty years before.

But this was clearly impossible, for the bride was barely past thirty, and looked even younger.

Baffled, I turned to a neighbor who knew both well.

"How could this be," I said, "when she wasn't born until 1950 or so?"

"You don't understand," she replied in a whisper, "the other girl died or disappeared, I'm not sure what."

"And now that's she again?"

I was struck with wonder.

"Sssh," she put a finger to her lips, "there's a wedding going on."

They had been high school sweethearts, so I was told, when love's sweet dream had been disrupted by her moving away, and his going off to the wars. By the time he returned, she had apparently taken sick and died, and he never heard from her again.

And now he was a man in his sixties, and this same dead or long-lost girl, reborn, was the fulfillment of his boyhood dream. It boggled the mind.

As I looked about me there was no hint of unreality. The bride and bridegroom were very real, as were the minister and the guests. It was like any other wedding, only a little friendlier, with all the guests seeming to know and like one another.

Perhaps because she was so radiantly happy, the bride actually did appear reborn, and the renewed bridegroom looked none the worse for the festivities.

Despite the difference in years, I saw nothing incongruous as they stood before the minister, hands clasped, waiting for him to complete the ceremony that would signify their oneness. I looked around the lush California garden, asplash with color, and saw that others saw as I did—a couple happily united in a love that transcended time and tradition. And as the minister recited from *The Prophet*, "Love has no other desire but to fulfill itself," we all felt a pleasant warmth from the bright glow of their love.

Joining the well-wishers in the receiving line, I was struck not only by the bride's blonde loveliness and ardor, but by the contrasting reserve which manifested his regard for his golden years.

I found a reassuring strength in his handclasp, an even, quizzical look in the brownish-green eyes. He was obviously not one to be carried away by some starry-eyed fantasy, nor indulge in wishful thinking.

I had known the bride, Savilla Higgins Bryan, for some time, without knowing much about her. She was the widow of the brilliant Los Angeles hypnotherapist, Dr. William J. Bryan, and from a well-known Tucson, Arizona, family. Her new bridegroom, William Kenneth (Burl) Schilling, was also a hypnotherapist. Oddly enough, she had met each of them while enlisting their professional help.

I had heard often enough of people claiming a past life experience together, but this was the first time any one had professed a reunion with a lover reborn from the present life. It was certainly an intriguing state of affairs.

After the guests had left, I approached the bridegroom. He was quite relaxed, not so busy or involved that he couldn't chat for a while. He spoke a few moments about a book I had done on yoga, and seemed pleased I was interested in this extraordinary experience.

"We'll be happy to share our blessing with you," he said.

We got together a week or so later. They had no need for a honeymoon, just being together, it seemed, was honeymoon enough.

"You can understand my confusion," I said, as we sat down together.

Savilla nodded amiably, touching her husband's arm.

The light from his eye seemed to light up hers, a strong vibration establishing an almost physical connection between them. There was a charge of electricity in the room.

Her eyes turned reluctantly to me.

"It seemed such a coincidence," she said, "but I don't believe in coincidence. Things happen for a purpose, even if we don't know that purpose at the time."

She had gone to Burl to correct a smoking problem. "I had not known him before, nor even heard his name, until my sister mentioned he had helped her with a weight problem."

As she walked through the door, and he came forward, she was overwhelmed by the feeling she had known this apparent stranger before. "The thought struck me like a bombshell that we had always been close and loved one another. Nothing like this had ever hit me before. I was dumbfounded."

I was to hear this so often, with so many soulmates, that it was like a litany of love. And yet Savilla had been reasonably happy with her life, living alone, painting, meditating, trying not to think of her recent bereavement, not looking for a relationship.

She had overslept that day and was late for her appointment. But Burl put her at ease immediately. He was as much charged up as she. "He hugged me hello, and I hugged him back—he was a long-lost friend. We talked a long time, I had the strangest feeling we had so much to make up for. We discussed just about everything but the reason I'd come there—art, literature, the creative process, our connection to God. It was very inspiring, and all the time I had a sense of déjà vu, as if we had been like this many times before."

Grudgingly, finally, they got down to the business at hand—her smoking.

After the session, she was exhilarated in one sense, dismayed in another. Her rational, cold, detached mind resisted this outrageous assault on her sanity. It could be an emotional aberration, she told herself, produced by a subconscious void in her life that her consciousness hadn't been aware of. But why then wouldn't she react to somebody of her own age and station, not an older man in the latter stages of life, married and divorced with three adult children all older than herself? She could not hope for children, nor would he, she imagined, want any at his age.

She meditated and thought about it endlessly. She kept telling herself she was not some lovesick teenager, and that whatever her feelings they were sincere and honest and from the heart. But taking a good look at the situation, she canceled the next appointment with Burl, giving herself time to think about things.

As she mentioned her indecision, I looked up to see Burl smiling, and sensed he had gone through a similar process. Catching my eye, she slipped her hand into his as though emphasizing their oneness. She spoke with a freedom and openness natural to their relationship, and I could see Burl listening as intently as myself, for much of this was obviously new to him as well.

"I certainly didn't think I was ready to fall in love again," she said. "I was still recuperating from the most devastating loss, even believing as I do that death is an illusion. I remember writing in my journal how confusing it was to experience simultaneously such deep sadness from Bill's death, and such deep joy because of my amazing reaction to Burl."

Even as she spoke, I wondered if the full import of the situation had struck her. "This would not only mean," I said, "that while you were having a past life with Burl, he was having a past-present life with you."

"Oh, yes," she said, smiling, "I came back this time before he could get away."

Three weeks had elapsed since the wedding and I already saw great changes in them. Savilla was a natural beauty, with her Grecian profile, clear skin, and tranquil hazel eyes, but there was an animation now I hadn't noticed before. I had never seen Burl before the day of the wedding, but I sensed a new vigor and vitality in his eye and in his demeanor. Her youth and freshness seemed contagious.

They had no trouble with reincarnation. She accepted what seemed plausible and he had regressed too many people into past-life experiences not to consider that possibility. But he also saw the likelihood of a genetic memory in which the brain cells remembered the past, just as every other cell of the body did in knowing enough to heal and sustain itself. And with it all, there was an inexplicable emotional impact of such nostalgic force that nothing could explain it but a previous connection.

There was no questioning their attraction, and their love. Still, with the disparity in age, I wondered what they could find in common. I imagined that Savilla—an athletic type—rode horseback, skied, jogged, and played tennis, and I couldn't see a much older, sedentary Burl enjoying or participating in any of these activities.

"What do you do together?" I asked.

Savilla correctly read my thought.

"We have something more uncommon than common interests," she said. "We have not only a common love but a common remembrance of that love."

After the first electrifying meeting, she had decided to regress herself, having picked up the technique from her first husband. She had noted that patients' regressions invariably produced a past-life experience which appeared to correctly pinpoint their problems in this life.

At this stage, she had not fully analyzed or clarified her feelings for Burl. All she knew was that she had this overpowering and quite illogical feeling for a very unlikely mate.

"The feeling was so powerful, with such an obsessive familiarity that I just knew there must be some deep hidden tie somewhere."

She had not discussed Burl with a soul, not even the sister who had recommended him. And now without mentioning her plan, not even to Burl, for fear he might think her a silly little girl, she called on the memory bank of her subconscious mind.

"I put myself under by closing my eyes and relaxing, breathing deeply for a few minutes. I told myself I will count backwards from ten to zero, during which time I suggested to myself that my mind would be blank, and when I got to zero, I would see Burl's face as I saw him in a past life."

But she was in for a surprise. "If I'd tried to picture it beforehand, I would have thought I would tune into some romantic interlude. But what came through was quite a shock."

Looking back, she realized she had made the mistake of taking Burl back to a much earlier life, instead of the past-present.

"I had only got to five when a very vivid image filled my mind. The face was that of a dead man whose body was being dragged out of a river, his hands tied behind his back. All I could recognize was his eyes, they stared out at me so."

She had the unmistakable impression it was Burl, and she was horrified. He had been murdered. It was London, the Victorian era, before the automobile. She saw herself again as a young woman, twenty-five to thirty, dressed in black. The symbology was obvious. She was in mourning. The regression so depressed and affected her that she was dazed for hours after. But at least, she told herself, her subconscious mind hadn't tried to paint a wishfully rosy picture for her.

Not knowing what to make of it, I looked at Burl to see how he was taking it. He nodded solemnly, his eyes seeming to fill with pain. "I was startled myself," he said, "for all my life just the thought of somebody tying my hands behind my back was enough to send me through the roof. I would rather they hang or shoot me."

After this shocker, she was leary about another regression. And yet it had left her with the prevailing feeling that life was precious and fleeting, belonging to the living, for had not Christ said: "Let the dead bury the dead."

Since she lived in Los Angeles and Burl in Santa Barbara, she saw little of him that first month, while trying to work things out in her head. He was busy with his practice, and she with her artwork, painting all day and far into the night. Frequently, she would sprawl out on the rug and relax, letting her mind float over the day's events or visualize what she wished to put on canvas. She was musing in this fashion one day when she fell into a deep reverie. Her mind began spinning back, unbidden, into time. She was in a spontaneous regression.

Electrifyingly, she was back in the year 1940, years before her present birth, when she and Burl were joyously together, in love as only young people can be, living every beat next to the heart.

Savilla's eyes glowed at the recollection.

"I saw Ken clearly," she said, using the name he used as a youth. "He wasn't conventionally handsome, but he was eighteen and the best-looking thing I'd ever seen. I was about the same age, with brown hair and green eyes, just feeling how great it was to be alive. We were walking arm in arm down a dirt road outside of Chicago. There were white picket fences, tall trees whose shadows made subtle patterns on the road, and the sweet scent of flowers opening their buds. It all seemed so beautiful. I had never been so happy."

She clearly saw Burl in a brown military uniform, and had the feeling he would be leaving for the service. A feeling of sadness overcame her. She was leaving as well, but only moving with her family to another state.

She brooded so much over the parting that she became ill, and couldn't rally her spirits. Burl, or Ken, was off in the service by this time. They were completely out of touch.

"I had this terrible fever," she recalled, "constantly getting weaker until I slipped into a coma and died. I was no more than nineteen."

In one past life or regression, Burl had horribly died, and now she herself had tragically perished in Burl's own lifetime.

I had once questioned the validity of such regressions. But I had discovered that in virtually every instance—as with novelist Taylor Caldwell when she was regressed into many past lives—that whenever anything dredged up was subject to verification, it invariably was validated. And so I had no reason to scoff but let the story speak for itself.

The regression had triggered a dream Savilla had shortly after Bill Bryan's death, almost a foreshadowing of past and coming events. "In my dream I had gone to a high school reunion and fallen in love with someone I had known then but did not recognize in this life."

How then had she been so quick to recognize Burl, some forty years after the fact when his visage was altered by the roughage and wrinkles of time and partially obscured by a beard? She responded easily.

"I had no trouble with that. I could see in his eyes that he was one and the same person."

"And you," I asked, "who were you?"

"I did not look as I do now. I was younger, of course, and had brown hair and green eyes, as I said, and I wore my hair up."

"Did you have a name?"

"I've had a little problem with that, but I had a strong impression of a V."

Why hadn't the name come through?

"Probably," interposed the more knowledgeable Burl, "because people aren't meant to remember too much. Otherwise, they may be overwhelmed by a past too painful or traumatic for them to handle."

Nevertheless, the initial had been enough to startle him for there was a phonetic similarity. But there was one discrepancy he found puzzling. "She spoke of my wearing a brown military uniform, and the only uniform I wore in the service was Navy blue. But thinking about it I recalled that in high school I wore the brown uniform of the ROTC (Reserve Officers Training Corps)."

Meanwhile, as both kept probing their hearts, the therapy sessions went ahead, and Savilla was soon able to stop smoking. Burl was a very effective hypnotherapist, and very scrupulous, not believing in socializing with his subjects.

As he held back uncertainly, Savilla, increasingly committed, was baffled and hurt. The relationship wasn't moving nearly as fast as she felt it should. She was getting flak from her family because of the age difference, Burl being about as old as her mother. There was no support for the relationship anywhere, only what her heart and mind told her. She needed encouragement.

Burl had a lot to think about. At his age, he had about given up on marriage. "It had to be somebody who wanted for me what I wanted for myself, who could share my work, and my life, who was compatible in all respects."

And, aside from professional scruples, there was a strong sense of the absurd.

"I was some thirty years older than Savilla and had a horror of looking ridiculous. I felt as she did, very much in love, constantly recapturing the exciting feeling of long ago. I thought of her as that girl reborn. They were so much alike, in expressions, attitudes, gentleness, yet with a perception that missed nothing."

He was well aware that some people were saying that, like Svengali with Trilby, he had hypnotized Savilla into loving him, but both he and Savilla knew it was impossible to successfully suggest anything unacceptable or contrary to a person's will or character.

"If anything," said Savilla with a laugh, putting the accusations to rest, "I hypnotized poor Burl."

As if to punctuate her point, she now leaned over and fondly kissed the bald spot on his head.

It was quite touching, but what, I still wondered, had finally brought him around?

"The love was always there, and the remembrance," he said. "Just as Savilla, I remembered the strolls through the tree-shaded lanes and the secret trysts that were all our own. So the urge was there, and with it the dream that Savilla had fulfilled. For in my dreams I must have seen her a thousand times."

And so what had happened?

"In my quandary, I decided to test the reaction of several former students, all women younger or the same age as Savilla. I had realized for some time we were into a New Age, and I was frankly interested in what their thinking was."

He discussed the situation from the beginning, mentioned his feelings and those of Savilla's, and then asked each one of them what they thought he should do.

He smiled in reflection.

"Almost in unison they said, 'Go for it.' "

And so he did.

The two of them were learning something new—something old—about each other every day.

"I'll open or close a door," said Savilla, "and suddenly realize I had done this for him before. We're constantly sharing feelings of déjà vu from the distant and not-so-distant past."

Was there any growth, expansion, new understanding of the spiritual, all attributes which, I understood, were the hallmarks of true soulmates?

They tried to define their love, and how it differed from any love they had known before. "Previously," said Savilla, "my concept of love was framed around a giver and an object of that love. Now," she frowned, groping for the right expression, "we are united in love."

Burl had been listening intently.

"It's not so much experiencing love, as being love itself."

He looked at Savilla and smiled.

"That is how we think of ourselves. We are not two anymore, but one."

She nodded.

"Every day is a new revelation," she said, "for in rediscovering our love for each other, we find ourselves tuned into the Universe, and the Creator of that Universe, growing, expanding, in every respect, so that our lives together seem infinite in an infinite world."

As a reporter, I had long ago learned the value of examining people's motivations. There was absolutely no reason for either Burl or Savilla to embellish or embroider their love. She was not affected by what others thought, and, in the end, he had let his heart take precedence over his head.

Theirs was obviously a joining of equals. Even had there not been continuing lives interrupted by death, it would have still been fascinating to observe how they had come together.

I had a number of questions, but it was getting late. I asked if we could meet again, far enough into their marriage for a better idea of how they were getting on.

Weeks passed before we met again. They were busy with things they had left undone for a generation. At her urging, Burl had moved to Los Angeles, a smog-ridden habitat he had once forsaken, cutting down on his practice to confine himself to teaching. They needed to make up for all the time they had lost, because of Burl's feeling that his years with his soulmate were precious few.

We had lunch on a terrace nestled comfortably between the hills and the sea, a striking setting for a haunting romance. They were more assured, more in tune, more loving. Their hands touched as they spoke and their eyes melted on contact.

"It seems to be agreeing with you," I said.

Burl nodded silently, while Savilla, as before, became the spokeswoman.

"Loving," she said, "seems to develop one's capacity for love. I can look back objectively now and see that every love relationship"—she paused to intertwine her hand with Burl's—"those that continue and those that don't, have taught me to love more, to give, receive, and accept more. I'm learning from being with Burl, responding to his patience, understanding, and wisdom. We live with ideas, not places. We know where we were and why we are back together. We met when our hearts and souls were ready. Our minds followed inevitably."

She was convinced that even the negative had a redeeming hand in reuniting them. "Even the most destructive things have guided us in a positive direction." She had begun smoking after her first husband's death, a habit he had always detested. Yet, this negativity had led her directly to Burl. "I never would have met him if I hadn't developed a smoking problem—or would I? Perhaps, God would have found another way."

Curiously, they had the same dreams. In one, they saw themselves as children after the turn of the century, walking hand in hand. They were not yet lovers, but there was a tight bond, and romance was in the air. In these dreams, they were invariably husband and wife. Other times, while embracing or kissing, they would share a spontaneous regression. "There was a flowing of lives together," said Savilla. "One time we were cave people, and I could see Burl as clearly as day, in skins and a breechcloth, ready to protect me."

This would flow, kaleidoscopically, into a life on a tropical island, where living was made easy by a benevolent climate, and there was time for love.

It seemed at times as if they were a couple of love-struck kids again, back in high school.

She had brought a couple of pages from her journal to show the extent and intensity of her longing, her self-doubts and misgivings, before she and Burl were finally joined.

"When Ken was here today," she wrote, "time seems to have stood still and moved swiftly at the same time, like one big sweep of beauty and joy and love. And then suddenly he's gone and it's as if an angel had swept through my life for the briefest moment."

A week later, she lamented:

"I cry off and on for hours after he leaves. This is partly because I miss him so and partly because what we share opens the door to everything I feel. There is all this sadness and all this joy and I cannot contain it all within me. I feel a little lost because I want to talk to him, and hear from him how every emotion we have, every thought, however sad and grievous it may seem, helps to stimulate us and make us grow. Oh, how simple it seems from his lips."

Other times she wavered, fearful of being judged, wanting to be perfect, without the capacity for perfection.

"I was afraid of disappointing him by being who I am. I'd tell him of all these fears. I wanted him to know exactly what he was getting into, even to how much I hated to cook."

He always made her feel so much better. "He'd assure me he didn't want to change anything about me, but to love me exactly as I was. 'But you don't understand,' I'd say. 'Sometimes all I eat for dinner is Cheetos and Fig Newtons.' "

He would laugh.

"You forget I know all about you from all those times we have been together."

They had a sense of humor about themselves. While they did not make a joke of their age difference, they could still laugh with others who found it amusing.

Savilla's bridesmaid, her fourteen-year-old niece, Heather, had been speaking to a friend after the wedding. "My friend was asking about Heather's boyfriend who was sixteen.

" 'Oh,' " she teased, " 'so you like older men?'

" 'Yup,' said Heather, looking at me. 'The older, the better, right, Savilla?' "

After meeting Burl through her, Savilla had told her sister that she would like to speak to her privately. Once they were alone, she confided Burl's and her love for each other. Her sister heaved a vast sigh of relief.

"Is that all?" she said. "I can understand. He has all the qualities you like. He's kind and sensitive and spiritual." Suddenly, she paused, obviously thinking of the death of Savilla's first husband.

"Hold on," she cried, "I want a guarantee from Burl's doctor that he's going to live forever."

Savilla responded with a laugh. "Yes, we both are."

Burl had sat silently through most of this, appearing to be reflecting on what his young bride was saying.

His eyes lit up for a moment as he drank in her blonde loveliness, savoring her vibrant and eager lust for life.

"Savilla was almost too young, too beautiful. You've got

to be sure that when you ask the Lord for something that you are ready for what he gives you."

I looked at him in surprise.

"And you asked for Savilla specifically?"

"Not by name," he said. "I had been meditating with a group for the purpose of attaining our deepest desires and goals.

"As a rule, he opened the meetings with the prayer:

"What things soever ye desire when ye pray, believe that ye receive them, and ye shall have them.' "

And one day shortly thereafter Savilla appeared.

"When Savilla came into my life I knew she was God's gift to me from the past. The long search was over. My heart told me this."

His misgivings about what others might think had receded with their acceptance. The heavy burden of loneliness had been lifted magically from his shoulders. He hadn't felt this good for years. "I have never been happier," he said. "I'm getting younger every day, and I have high hopes our love will help others to raise the barriers of an aging society unaware of the New Age."

He took Savilla's hand and they looked into each other's eyes. In that moment I saw a similarity of expression, a look that seemed to know no time or space, and I knew then why the eyes were called the windows of the soul.

I had no validation of their having lived and loved before, but my search was only beginning, and there were many challenges. What did all these regressions mean, all these meditations? I knew what these two believed, and how they had reacted to this belief. I knew that a beautiful and talented young lady, endowed with all the qualities this world finds important, had chosen an unlikely mate from a misty past, and that as improbable as it seemed, they had recognized one another on sight, and fallen miraculously in love.

I knew I was with a man and a woman who had taken vows that would be unbroken until death, and perhaps after that.

"I do not know how long we will be together in this life," Burl said solemnly, "but I know that I will treasure every moment of it." He paused and his eyes shone. "And in the future, if love makes us worthy, may we again find each other as we have before."

CHAPTER 3

The Search

I didn't have to look very far to know what a soulmate was. What matter what Webster or any dictionary said? People everywhere were searching to end a loneliness, an emptiness that made them feel alone even in a crowd, or especially in a crowd. For then the realization of this contrasting inner need was made painfully clear.

I remember well what Eamon de Valera, the founding president of Free Ireland, said when some suggested he had grown too old to relate to all his people. "All I have to do," he said, "is search my own heart and I know what my people want."

So search your own heart, search it honestly and long, and you will know what it wants. Somebody kind, somebody gentle, my own heart told me, but not without spirit. Somebody who made light of adversity and misfortune, and shared the triumphs, however small. Not some infallible paragon, nor some gem of perfection. Better she have weaknesses so you can love and comfort her in her own need, bringing a smile to a misty eye. And best of all, somebody to be at one with, facing a cold, demanding world unafraid, because you are no longer alone.

No matter what others say, she need only be beautiful to

you. For beauty is in the eye of the beholder—and the beholden. She shall not be a statue of marble or stone, but of flesh and blood and soul, knowing you better than you know yourself, your beginnings and your ends, as they manifest in you and merge with her. Always the right word, or no word, the touch of a hand or a lip, a smile, saying more than a thousand words. In all things she will be what you would want of yourself, giving for the joy of giving, with no thought not your thought, no love not yours.

Two souls not like one, but one—soulmates.

Elizabeth Clare Prophet had gone over all this herself, knowing the pitfalls and the wonders of the quest for love's fulfillment. She was one to have recognized her soulmate and known a twin love that evoked a strength and vision she had not even known she had. And as she gained strength, so she had more to give. It was like living a dream come true. She knew what it was to look into somebody, and have her life change, knowing that other life would change as well. She knew what it was to love and cherish a relationship forged before she was born, to nourish it, build it into a force affecting the lives of multitudes, and then know sorrow as that special person, that ideal soulmate, that twin flame, died as he was ordained to die, knowing that he had left somebody to carry on his mission.

At his memorial she remembered the Emerson lines they had shared together. It was what they both believed, lived by, and—they told themselves—would die by. Her mood lightened as she thought back on it: "Nothing is dead. Men feign themselves dead, and endure mock funerals and mournful obituaries, and there they stand looking out the window, sound and well, in some new and strange disguise."

At twenty-two, Elizabeth had peered into a mirror, and the face peering back was not hers. She had looked at the mirror casually, and lo and behold, saw the face of the man she had just accepted as her spiritual teacher.

After her initial surprise, she examined the face, and found a likeness to herself she had not noticed before. Mark Prophet had the same high cheekbones, the same square set to his jaw, the same steady gaze that held humor and compassion.

It was shocking, yet reassuring. She had been debating whether she should join her fortunes to a man twenty years older who thought her his twin flame, while she, seeking only a teacher, was satisfied she had found him.

In that instant she knew she would follow him to the ends of the earth.

"Not only did I see his face, but myself as a reflection of his positive image. My whole being surged with a primal feeling that was a confirmation of my inner ties to this man who was practically a stranger."

This was all the message she needed to launch a remarkable career with her twin flame, which continued to grow and expand even after his death, as foreshadowed in his lifetime.

He still lived, as big as life, not only in the churches and teaching centers they had founded together, but in a continuing and fortifying presence. There wasn't a day she didn't ask herself what Mark would have done, and that an answer wasn't forthcoming. For, having merged their minds and souls, it was not difficult to foresee what Mark's thinking would have been. "I could look across a room and know what he was saying," she recalled. "And I feel his presence as keenly now. When one believes in infinity, the infinite is possible."

She was no starry-eyed dreamer. Indeed, I had never met anybody more practical, more pragmatic, so capable an organizer that her various centers ran like clockwork without her. But this was no deterrent to seeking metaphysical truths, as well as the physical, for in finding her twin flame, working together toward the same goals, having children, they not only divined each other's thoughts, but used this honing process to tune in similarly to the universal consciousness directing their energies.

Their life was out of a storybook.

She was a student at Boston University, when Mark Prophet came to lecture on Eastern religion. She didn't realize it at the time, but he had come to Boston primarily to meet her, having subconsciously picked up a message that reflected her yearning for somebody to lend purpose to her life. He did not even know her name, but he knew that she was there, and that he would recognize her when he saw her. It was no accident that she had attended that meeting in the upstairs room of an old office building she had passed by many times but never entered before.

His presence was electrifying. The next day they met

again. He looked into her eyes, and announced, "You and I are twin flames and we will work together until my death, and thereafter, the Lord willing."

She was overwhelmed, but she did not draw away. There was something about him that held her, a dawning belief that she had known him forever, a conviction that she had a mission like his—even as she was telling herself that it was all unbelievable.

"When I saw Mark Prophet for the first time, I recognized him as my teacher. He, seeing me for the first time, recognized me as his twin flame.

"I was so single-minded about finding my teacher, so elated to have found the One, that I felt burdened by the thought of having to deal with another type of relationship."

She asked God for a sign.

"Weeks later I had my very astounding experience. I happened to look into a mirror when I was dressing. And that's when I saw Mark's face.

"Imagine looking in a mirror and not seeing yourself! It's a very shocking experience."

I reminded myself that people see with their minds. We could close our eyes and see what we were meant to see. But there was no questioning Elizabeth Prophet's sincerity or her clarity. She was as clear-headed as anybody I had ever met.

"Do you find that strange?" she asked.

"Not as you tell it, nor as it fits into the pattern of your life."

She had drawn close to examine the mirror in greater detail. "It did not fade but lingered so I could take in every plane and line. It was ancient. It had always been. It was sculpted in marble, etched in crystal, yet 'flesh of my flesh.' I saw that I was the reflection in the negative (feminine) polarity of that positive (masculine) image."

They began as teacher and pupil, but soon she was shouldering many of the labors he had borne alone. They were not ready to get married and their relationship remained that of teacher and pupil for some time. But even so, they grew together in the common bond of their publishing the teachings of the ascended, or spiritual, masters. She seemed to go through a spiritual rebirth, discovering an unsuspected strength in their oneness. "The more we gave, the more we received from each other."

It was this strength that impressed me when I met her

ten years before, shortly after Mark's death. Although the loss was a grievous one, and there must have been many dark hours, she was in perfect command of herself, discussing the things Mark had wanted her to do, and the bringing up of their four children in the shade of their father's love. She was very attractive, still young, in her thirties, and while I could see her marrying again, I could not visualize anybody taking Mark's place. But she would see to it, I was sure, that whoever followed would have his own place. She was not a person to do things by halves. Her steady eye, and determined chin, told you that.

She was bursting with plans for her Church Universal and Triumphant and new teaching centers in Santa Barbara, Pasadena, Malibu, and elsewhere. It seemed like the work of a lifetime. And yet when I saw her next, years later, all these plans had materialized and more. She had built, as Mark had wanted, a unique teaching center at Summit University, spread over 200 acres in the fabulous ocean-going resort of Malibu. At her Montessori school (attended by two hundred students ranging from preschool through twelfth grade) there was a unique emphasis on the personal, on quality rather than quantity. There were specialized classes where there were but two students, sometimes one, but they were taught with a love and patience they absorbed and gave back.

Mark had visualized a retreat that might one day serve as a model community, in which people married for a love that endured because it was self-renewing and was nurtured by the bonds of the community—a circle of joyous fellowship shared by all of its members. Her energy, with the posthumous gift of his ever-present genius, had realized this, his fondest dream, a 12,000-acre retreat in the wilds of Montana, which was to become a spiritual center and proliferate a community of its own, drawing student settlers of every religious background from every part of the world.

As we talked about all this, touring the Malibu campus, she paused before a large graciously designed Spanish-type building. We wandered through it, emerging to see students tilling the fields in the shadow of Malibu's verdant hills, and others walking arm in arm in the shaded lanes.

It all seemed so solid, so permanent, so different from the transient airiness of ordinary human commerce.

Her eye caught mine, and she smiled.

"Sooner or later the emptiness and futility of all this chasing is going to hit people. The desire for permanence and perfection in love, as in other things, is fundamental to human nature."

Soulmates were special to her because she had known her own twin flame and what it could do for those directly involved and for those whose lives brushed theirs. As in her own life, she wanted others to experience the energy and inspiration that kind of love generated. While the twin flame was the ultimate, there were various kinds of soulmates, and they were rewarding in different ways.

She was fortunate enough to have both a twin flame and a companion soulmate in this life, having recently married Mark Prophet's close associate, Edward Francis. Together they were carrying on Mark's work. With Francis's foresight and business sense, the Montana ranch and their new community of Glastonbury (his brainchild as well) were rapidly becoming the mecca of her movement.

The two marriages confirmed what she already knew.

"Usually when people talk about twin flames," she said, "they use the term soulmate. A soulmate is exactly what it says. It is a mate of the soul. It refers to a dual service you are destined to perform with someone other than your twin flame. And that is how I feel about Ed. He is my soulmate, my dearest friend, exciting to be with, a pillar of strength, and the love in my life. The depth of our mutual devotion comes from lifetimes of service together. He is as devoted to Mark's memory as I am. Our cause is the fulcrum of our love.

"Twin flames have no barriers between them. They have no rules of love. Twin flames are one in spirit and in their spiritual origin. Soulmates are souls sharing a complementary calling in life. They are mates in the sense of being partners, very much alike and very compatible because their soul development is at the same level. They work well together, are project-oriented, well-mated, and often have similar facial features and physique. On the other hand the mind, heart, and consciousness of twin flames flow together from the same fount. Their inner ties run as deep as the sea, beyond companionship."

The twin flame was not only a mirror of mind and spirit, but of the soul, the secret longings and aspirations, the link not only with the love partner but with the God-mind, the Universal Intelligence.

"When people ask, 'Can you have more than one soulmate?' they are generally thinking in terms of a purely romantic liaison. When I am thinking soulmates, I am thinking of joint endeavors—to publish a book, produce a play, compose a song, build a community or college—in an atmosphere of love and amity."

But coming together, as companion soulmates, didn't necessarily signify permanence. In so many cases, once the project was fulfilled, the togetherness vanished.

"One shouldn't feel committed to marriage because one has found a soulmate."

I must have blinked a little, for I had felt the two were indivisible—soulmates and a binding marriage.

She saw my uncertainty.

"Every day you see admirable people who married with the best intentions in the world. One partner becomes famous. They get involved in other circles. They accelerate educationally, professionally. With an end to their activities, they discover they have little else in common. Their value systems, they find, may be entirely different. They have very little to say to one another. These relationships often last a few months, a year, or a little longer. Then all of a sudden they're over."

"You make it sound like a business deal," I said.

She laughed. "Perhaps that's what the arrangement should have been."

Marry on your own soul level—your own consciousness.

"You have to know who you are. You have to know your own needs. We're all familiar with the expression, 'The honeymoon is over.' That has to do with the impact of karma, a past and continuing condition, in a marriage. This is why some people don't get married— they resist bearing one another's burden.

"They simply don't want the responsibility. They say marriage would ruin everything, but what they mean is, taking on each other's karma would really mess things up. But that is precisely the inner meaning of the ritual of marriage—that we love so much that we eagerly share the karma of our spouse. If marriage were a mere physical union, divorce would not be so emotionally devastating. All the battles about who owns what and who gets what, even to the children, really center around the excruciating process of redefining one's 'self.' "

As we chatted, I was reminded of the recent breakup of two married friends in the academic world. He was a brilliant professor, and she a student who had surpassed him in many ways, going on to teach and write extensively. I was astonished when they called it quits for I had never observed a couple who seemed more in rapport, who prided themselves so much on being soulmates. Even their smallest conversations vibrated with wit and humor, and with the substance of what they were working on together—a book on the many facets of the unconscious mind.

"I don't understand it," I told the woman, "you seemed so perfect together, you were so alive you stimulated any company you were in."

She had smiled a little sadly.

"I agree," she said, "but then we had our baby."

"Baby, what baby?" I cried.

They had hardly been married long enough for a child.

"Our book," she exclaimed. "We finished it, and then discovered we had nothing to talk about. I had idealized our relationship, made a fantasy of our working together like Marie and Pierre Curie." She sighed. "But there was no magic. There had never been any, outside of what went into our project. And when that was over . . ." She threw up her hands. "Goodbye."

So often sex and love were confused, as psychic Gladys Jones had pointed out, but the sexual attraction was still often more than a biological urge that sustained the species. For down through the ages, erotic feelings of adoration and desire had inspired reams of tender music and poetry that lived on long after the inspiration had died.

"What is wrong," I asked, "with the act of making love, if people are in love, or think they are?"

"I think there should be more. So many today get their kicks from a succession of romantic involvements. They go from affair to affair, constantly making karma, not adding anything real to the fabric of their lives. The world and they, spiritually speaking, are no better for the relationship."

"Isn't it enough to be gloriously in love, and feel it's great to be alive?"

"If it's enough for you. I wouldn't deny anyone their

free will in matters of love. Who can speak for another? Love is as beautiful as two people choose to make it."

Then how is anybody to know?

"There is an enduring quality about a good relationship."

"And a bad one as well."

She nodded. "Oh, yes, so many of us are wearing our karma on our shirtsleeves today."

"But how does one know—how could you tell it would be right after you met Mark?"

"Sometimes you can't say until you look back. But I knew it then." She smiled. "There's often too much going on all at once. As I see it now, the only thing that enables us to tell whether a relationship is right or not is the vibration of the heart. The outer testimony of the senses cannot report the truth of the inner reality. It's almost better to be like a yogi, to stop the outer perceptions, and meditate upon the heart. It's amazing how we come to the right conclusion when we're not pushing ourselves in one direction or another by a sense of false obligation, intimidation, sympathy, sexual magnetism, or whatever is extraneous. Sex will not endure if the soul is not satisfied."

And if a soulmate doesn't work out, what then?

"What about those who found old resentments and animosities too much to handle?"

"We are in a New Age," she said, "the 2,000-year Piscean Age giving way to the Aquarian Age. And with it there is a new dispensation regarding divorce. No true spiritual leader ever approved divorcing for simply tiring of a plaything or desiring a better sexual partner. But in the Age of Aquarius, we're in the process of moving from the plane of physical and mental awareness to quickening spiritual awareness. We have many areas of karma, and some can only be balanced through marriage. When making a decision for or against divorce, one must search his soul to discover whether he has done all he can to make a marriage work, and whether it is more costly to remain together than to separate.

"We are in a place and time when all things are coming to roost. All the birds we've sent forth from our mental body, all the fishes from the emotional body, all are flying or swimming back into the mainstream of our lives. This is the age of resolution."

As we marched around the Malibu campus, known as Camelot, I was struck by the children, some no more than toddlers, whose eyes brightened as they tripped over their own feet to greet her. She knew all their names. They called her Mother, though their own mothers often stood but a few feet away, smiling.

"The children are happy," she said, "because the parents are happy. And the parents are happy because they have a sense of sharing, of giving without measuring. They are in a process of learning from experiences they have had long before."

Like many who marched to a different drum, she had more than her share of criticism. As she patted a child, who clung to her as for dear life, she smiled. "I have been accused of being mercenary, despotic and even Satanic, usually by people who have no idea what we are teaching and care nothing about finding out. But Mark always said if we built our church on love we would have that problem. What so many don't understand is that discipline is a form of love, and without discipline there can be no teaching or learning, and no institutions of benefit to man."

She spoke without resentment.

"Do you ever strike back?" I asked.

She smiled. "Once you've loved your twin flame, you have enough love to go around. You don't waste your energies."

Her eyes moved slowly over the lovely campus, resting for a moment on the students hurrying to class. "This is what we built of our union, Mark and myself, and it is still building. What we planned and conceived is ongoing and will never stop, because the energy that was released will continue to make things happen."

I followed her into the chapel where hundreds of her followers were expectantly awaiting her discussion on soulmates. While predominantly youthful, they were a cross-section of middle-class America, what one might ordinarily find on a Midwestern campus. There was an atmosphere of high spirits and humor.

Mark's picture was prominently displayed. He was clearly the inspiration for anything she had to say about twin flames. I was struck by the rapt attention of the students.

"There isn't a person in this assembly," a guide whispered in my ear, "who isn't interested in knowing his purpose, and how he or she can accomplish it, preferably with a helpmate."

She mentioned Mark first, as I felt she would. Not as a memorial but to show how two strong-minded people handled their affairs in such a way there was no danger of not having their own space.

"Mark and I had to work out our divisions. It's not enough being in love. You have to know what to do with that love. There's a rhythm in life, an interchange, in which people have a part, as do the elements around us." Her eyes swept the big room. "With twin flames, there is a good deal of energy flowing back and forth, but there are still differences of opinion, and decisions which can be made by only one person. Very few committees get things done. Sometimes Mark would make the decision, sometimes myself."

Cheerfully, they gave of their egos.

"Marriages don't work because each person wants to be important all the time. If two people want to become as one, one must sometimes yield. Mark would surrender in some things, and so would I. Only robots always agree. He pushed me forward, trained me, made me a messenger. But a lot of people didn't perceive any of this and would criticize me for not asserting myself. But there was great balance between us." She smiled. "And though I'm for a true Women's Lib, for equality of opportunity, God made us different for a reason. By nature woman is self-sacrificing, and needs to be in order to feel exalted and special to a man."

As had so many others, I wondered what had become of the sweet, gentle creature anxious to please a man, yet be a tower of strength when the burdens he carried became heavy and onerous.

Elizabeth may have read my mind across the room.

"A woman, soulmate or not," she was saying, "can certainly have a career while being a mother and bearing a child. She determines this with her mate. If there is a divine plan for two people to be together, then the Creator also has a plan whereby the partners' talents can be harmoniously fulfilled. People need to feel their own strength, the same strength they see in their mate. But then there is always the moment when one also needs to feel helpless in the arms of the beloved.

Inside of the most powerful people you know is the little child who needs to be loved."

Her face lit up the chapel. "The key is giving, wanting to give, taking pleasure in giving without asking for anything back. 'Cast thy bread upon the waters: for thou shalt find it after many days.' "

The mysticism of the East was no mystery to her. If it made sense and was helpful, why not make use of it? And so she spoke of the chakras, the seven invisible centers which controlled the body and mind, and which related to love and sex.

She called them the seven rays of life, influential in every human attitude and action. The first ray, the power to create by the spoken word, was in the throat; the second in the crown, the wisdom center. The third and pink ray was the love flame of the heart. The fourth, the white chakra, the seat of life itself, at the base of the spine. The fifth ray, the third eye, centered in the forehead and related to science and healing. The sixth, purple and gold, below the heart, in the solar plexus. It was the ray of peace and service. And the seventh, the violet ray of Aquarius, second from the base of the spine, the indicator of the soul itself—and the Aquarian Age.

"The more you balance karma with people of the opposite sex without the entangling alliance of a sexual encounter, the more swiftly you can rise on these chakras to the crown of life where you have a date to meet your twin flame. The overexpenditure of the life force in these encounters takes the energy, the Kundalini fire you need for the reunion with your twin flame." She smiled. "Don't get me wrong. I'm not against sex. I'm only saying you have to be careful: you don't have an unlimited expense account."

I kept looking around the room to see how this was going down. It was not an idea that would win anybody votes at a college rally. But as she quickly clarified, it was not a question of sin versus righteousness but of priorities.

We had now come to the question period. "If you want to present a hypothetical situation," she smiled, "I'm sure we'll all understand. Or you can make it a personal question which may be helpful to others."

Hands flew up, bodies half-rose, but a youthful Joyce got to the floor first. Her question reflected a wavering loyalty to twin flames, which so many looked on as an unattainable phantom.

"I have a fear about the reality that I really have a twin flame," she began. "I've meditated on it, and I finally had to believe, though there are times I don't feel his presence, now or for the future."

And what if the twin flame, yet unknown, should die? What then happened to the other half of the polarity?

The answer was reassuring. "Keep meditating, keep your own flame burning bright, involve yourself creatively in living, and don't worry about dying. There is no connection between the fear of death and the twin flame, not when you live in infinity."

Another young girl believed she had found her soulmate, but was afraid he was into black magic.

"There could be work we might perform together. But I was wondering about the wisdom of staying."

"In dealing with a soulmate," Elizabeth said, "someone you have a love tie with, get him to change his energy. Make it plain you are here to help and love, but there is a point beyond which you cannot go. Sometimes we get involved sympathetically, saying: 'I'll go down the ladder a bit and help him or her.' And then you no longer have the energy to climb back to where you were.

"You lose your integrity, which is your integration with your Maker. You cannot afford to lose that because then you won't have anything to give to anyone."

The student looked a little disappointed. "We have talked about exorcism," she said hopefully.

"Exorcism can be done only when the individual wants to do it for himself. Some people like to say, 'OK, exorcise me and I'll be fine.' Especially when they want a relationship."

The student's face fell. "So this should not be any kind of a romantic involvement."

Elizabeth: "People like to be helped, but they aren't always willing to pay the price to get it for themselves. You discover the only help you can really give anyone is your loving support when they decide to help themselves."

Almost as a corollary, pretty Julie from Atlanta stood up to ask:

"When one person is working out his karma beautifully,

and the other steps out of line, must it not necessarily affect both of them?"

The answer was not all she expected.

"The person attaining has a right to pull up the one who's faltering, to love until the last mile. Then if it becomes a losing battle, he has the obligation to himself to cut himself free from the one pulling him down."

Inevitably, a question about the telltale vibration of the heart, from young David from Germany.

"Could you explain how one goes about discerning that feeling of the heart, that vibration, that would let you know the person you are looking at is your twin flame?"

I could see the faces perking up, and sensed the audience hoping for something more personal, something of Elizabeth's experience with Mark Prophet. Elizabeth gave a little sigh, which none would notice had he not looked closely. She appeared to be lost in her own musings.

"You look into the mirror of your mind," she said at last. "Is your motive pure? Is your will sure? Is your desire pure? If so, you will receive the heart's sure message. No matter what clouds came across the sky, I thought back to that day when I had seen the face on the mirror and knew I had seen the inner man. And if you don't see this, if you don't look into yourself, you will be miserable, and you will be the loser."

There were endless questions.

Deborah had a relationship that wasn't working. "I have a desire," she said, "to clear up the resentment between myself and my twin flame."

I smiled at Elizabeth's answer.

"It's obvious you have karma with your twin flame. Twin flames do make karma with each other in various embodiments. So there can be a tremendous sense of injustice between twin flames. Through the ego, one allows the problem to become bigger than love. You can watch your love destroyed because there was no will to forgive. 'You did this to me, therefore I will not let this love bloom.'"

There were acknowledging smiles among the young.

"So if we're to renew a relationship with a twin flame we must practice forgiveness. As Jesus said, 'Forgive seventy times seven,' if necessary."

If you dream an amorous dream, does that mean your

subconscious has invoked your soulmate while you were peacefully slumbering? Was the unsleeping brain making an effort to tell us something? So wondered Peter of Spokane, Washington, as he stood up, and looked around a little nervously.

"I hadn't any feeling about soulmates," he said, "then I had a dream of being in a gigantic place with large hallways and rooms, people moving all over the place. A beautiful young woman came up to me. We held hands as we walked, and it was the most exhilarating feeling I've ever had. I woke up, crying."

The dream had occurred a year before, and again just recently. He would have thought no more about it, but two weeks later he saw this identical creature in a Spokane classroom. He spoke to her, not daring to mention his dream, and then as the conversation dwindled, she walked off. He had lost her.

"As my chakras begin to open," he said, "and I begin to feel things, this twin flame—if it was she—would she be going through the same sensation at the same time?"

"If your paths are meant to cross again, they will," Elizabeth said. "But if you run all over Spokane looking for this person, you can get on the wrong track. Meditate and visualize her as you did in your dream. Your inner light will lead you to her. Search within your heart first, you will find her if it is God's will."

Barbara, next, spoke with the candor of her generation.

"I've been having a relationship with a man for two years, and it's developing quite nicely. But how do you know when you are whole enough to make a commitment to marriage?"

For one who had made that decision the answer posed no great problem.

"That's not always the question. Your mate may be the perfect complement who makes you feel whole, but only you can make yourself whole. The lack of wholeness isn't the problem, so much as expecting the other person to fill in which only you can do."

Just as the planets had an orderly course, so, too, did our lives, even amid the seeming disorder. We were all affected by universal laws we were only now beginning to discover. So my thoughts ran, when a young man, ironically named Mark, hurtled me back to reality.

"Should one be looking for one's twin flame," he asked,

"or should it come naturally? A few months ago I didn't know anything about twin flames and my life was a lot easier."

He stopped, surprised by a burst of sympathetic applause.

"Don't waste energy looking for a soulmate," Elizabeth advised as before. "God loves to do things for us if we let Him. But we have to give God this opportunity"—she smiled—"by diligently developing ourselves and serving Him."

"What do you do," one youth asked, "when you're just bursting for an attractive young woman who will respond in the same way? What is wrong with doing something perfectly natural? And while you're not thinking soulmate, who knows but that you might find one?"

Elizabeth replied:

"This brings up free love and what to do when you know the other person isn't your soulmate. Sex today is in advertising, music, in everything people talk about. We are brainwashed to believe we are not normal unless we have sex constantly. In casual intercourse, the energy is misspent and is no longer available for other forms of creativity."

There were still other questions, at other sessions, reflecting the ever widening interest in soulmates.

One young man commented on the striking similarity of features in soulmates:

"People have told me that soulmates look alike and sometimes I've heard that twin flames look alike. Is this a way to tell if we are twin flames, soulmates, or karmic mates?"

Elizabeth: "Even people only having karma in common may look alike, perhaps from sharing so much in the past. However, I've seen karmic marriages where people can't see what they have in common or understand why they're together even when they look so different. Looking alike is incidental. You have to find the inner tie in your heart."

The next was a question many have asked, even without thinking of soulmates.

"Concerning past relationships that were karma-creating, is it best, once they're over, to leave them be?"

Elizabeth was marvelously practical.

"Relationships that are over are over for a reason. Everything that could be derived was derived. A certain nostalgia often takes over and we somehow imagine the person we knew as still having the same relationship to us as they did. But, of course, they couldn't unless they have grown as we have. It's best to let sleeping dogs lie. Often you get the other's wavelengths, and you think you want to reestablish a tie, when you may only be responding to the other person's thoughts."

The vagaries of love were explained for a girl who wondered how she had ever gotten into so many relationships that turned sour.

"I really thought I loved the person, but now I regret it all."

All was not lost. Otherwise, Elizabeth pointed out, she would not have come to the point of reexamining herself.

"Love, often, is something that happens to the heart without conscious will. Our rational mind may be saying it is an unwholesome relationship. But the heart loves on. We are, in effect, a prisoner of our karma—we owe someone something or they have done something to us. A balance must be struck. When enough love has flowed heart-to-heart and the karma balanced and old resentments are resolved, suddenly one day the faucet may turn off and you are no longer love's prisoner."

But only those who love know when love has run its course and has to be cranked up. "Then you know love has run the cycle of its destiny."

Of what purpose a book on soulmates, if it didn't help to find a soul partner—twin flame, soulmate, karmic mate.

Spiritually oriented, Elizabeth spoke of a God-consciousness heightening the love-consciousness.

"If you have this consciousness, you will attract someone with the same consciousness. Like attracts like."

First learning of a twin flame, she opened the Bible at random. Her eyes fell on the passage: "For thy Maker is thine husband."

When this thought reached a certain intensity, Mark Prophet appeared. There was no doubt in her mind that her readiness opened the door. "Because I was aware, I attracted my counterpart, who was aware of his counterpart even before, since he was more advanced."

So how did the average person not into daily worship arrive at this God-consciousness?

"Visualize a white flame and think of yourself as floating in a sea of infinite consciousness, with no beginning and no end, in which you merge with the Infinite. Imagine this as a sea of love. See the twin flames rising out of this sea. Out of one flame comes the lover and the beloved. See the flow continuing as love gives birth to love, and to a self-awareness which expands the boundaries of our reality.

"Visualize your energy rising from the lower chakras. See your spine as you would a thermometer. The base of the spine is the bulb part of the thermometer, where the energies of the Kundalini are locked in the white chakra.

"Visualize your energy as a pearly white fire rising up your spine, willing it to rise, with mind, heart, and desire.

"Standing, direct the energy to your heart, because in the vibration of the heart you will know your soulmate. With this energy, create any image your heart desires. Visualize this white energy on the forehead, and see it now as a star, the secret love star. Anchor the energies from your body to that star which becomes the focus for raising the energies of the lower chakras."

You exercised the body as well. "Reach for the heart star, reaching high with your right side, feeling everything pulling up from your right foot all the way up your side. All your muscles are pulling up to push that energy up to that star. Alternate the two sides, stretching one and then the other side, while visualizing the star and actually releasing energy from the chakras.

"Do physical yoga in moderation, not neglecting your spiritual growth. Exercise keeps up the flow of energy. Engage in a sport regularly—yoga or tennis, swimming or jogging, bike riding or bowling—to keep energy flowing between your chakras. Without this energy, there is no heightened consciousness and no soul fulfillment."

All in all, I thought the sessions had strikingly reflected the general yearning for a soulmate. Almost every facet of the relationship had been touched on but one.

And so I asked Elizabeth Prophet:

"What happens to one's freedom when he joins his soulmate to the center of his being?"

I thought at first she had not heard. Then I saw by her eyes that she was for the moment in another time and place.

"You don't give up freedom," she said, "but gain it, freedom to love as your soul wills, with all the depth and breadth your love now knows."

She smiled, and I knew of whom she was thinking.

"You are as free as a bird," she said, "and you can soar to heights no bird ever dreamed of reaching."

CHAPTER 4

Cayce on Soulmates

It was inconceivable to do a book on soulmates without Edgar Cayce. He was the first person I knew to have tied reincarnation and soulmates together. He had certainly found his own soulmate in his wife, Gertrude, who died three months after he did, passing over blissfully, feeling they would be rejoined one day soon.

"They were so close, so in tune," I recall the mystic's son, Hugh Lynn Cayce, telling me, "that it was almost inevitable my mother would follow Dad. He was her whole life, just as she was his never-ending support."

These twin souls died as they lived, believing unquestioningly they were to be together always. Each had a smile as they cheerfully faced, not the Unknown, but for them, the Known.

On New Year's Day, 1945, Edgar Cayce cheerfully told visitors, "It is all arranged. I am to be healed on Friday, the fifth of January." His friends understood what he meant when they arrived on Friday for his funeral service in the Cayce home. But, living, he had a more personal farewell on his mind. The night before his death, as his wife reached across the bed to kiss him goodnight, the dying man looked at her reflectively, and said, "You know I love you, don't you?"

A lump came to the throat of the woman who had made

him her whole world through forty years of marriage. She nodded, unable to trust her voice, sad only that he was leaving first.

He smiled gently. "How do you know?" he repeated.

"Oh, I just know," she said, for in loving she had never questioned his love, nor measured what each had given the other. She had not only been his domestic partner, but had shared his work, the unique gift of peering behind the veil which was to bring him fame long after his death. There had been nobody he had trusted more to ease him into trance and conduct the psychic readings that helped so many to deal with life and death.

As they looked into each other's eyes, his hand touched hers. "I don't see how you can tell," he said. "What have I ever done to make you know? You have spent your life doing for me—but I do love you and always have."

She hushed him as though he were a child, closed his eyes, and kissing him lightly, stole from the room. He died the next night, her name on his lips.

Gertrude faded rapidly. She told friends she felt as though one of her vital organs had been bodily removed. She had two sons at war to live for, but she felt her husband gently pulling her to his side. Three months after Cayce's death, on April 1, 1945, on a beautiful Easter Sunday morning, Gertrude Evans Cayce followed her husband hopefully beyond the divide. The Cayce family lived as it believed. On March 31, the day before his mother's death, Hugh Lynn had written from his Army post in Germany: "It makes me deeply happy to know how ready you are to pass through that other door. There is so much beauty in your living that I cannot be sad at the thought of your joining Dad. You held up his right hand—sometimes both hands—so it does not surprise me that he may need you now."

And the son designated by his father's reading to spread the Work showed his readiness for the task. "We have come, Mother," he saluted, "to an understanding of karma in a way that we have for a long time been explaining to others, and I find that your life represents so much that is fine and beautiful that I cannot allow my selfish desires to mar this period of waiting and wondering."

And so he released her with love, just as she had released her twin flame, the only soulmate she ever had.

In many ways Edgar and Gertrude Cayce epitomized the gay, bright side of soulmates, as well as the serious purpose which made a lifestyle of giving. They would speak frequently of their lives in the past, as they touched on present conditions, teasing one another about previous connections in such exotic places as Egypt and Persia.

There was much to be learned, much growing to do, and it was through adversity and trials with the outer world, and between themselves, that their love established itself. Misfortune, more than joy, made soulmates keenly aware of the depths of their emotions, sharpening the chord of understanding developing their love. In 1931, when he had been a psychic for some twenty-five years, Edgar Cayce reached the very nadir of his career. He had been ignominiously arrested in New York City for fortune telling and lost to the Depression the metaphysically oriented hospital that had been founded on his health readings. He was discouraged, despondent, ready to give up. Gertrude suffered with him, not only knowing what he was going through, but having experienced some of it herself. After Cayce's arrest in New York, the newspapers had photographed the mystic with Gertrude and his beautiful blonde secretary, Gladys Davis. One newspaper cropped off the picture of his wife, and showed him only with his secretary, insinuating they had been trapped in a hotel together by the police.

Cayce's belief in his own purpose was cruelly shaken. Before he had always been strengthened in adversity by the conviction he was doing God's work, and now he wondered:

"Why," he asked, as the Psalmists had before him, "would God allow my enemies to triumph if I were truly His servant?"

Gertrude pointed to the tragedies and misfortunes that had befallen other missionaries of the Lord, particularly one whose word was clearly more enduring now than two thousand years before. And she added:

"He is testing you, Edgar, as He did Job."

But Cayce was not convinced.

"If God wanted me to heal people," he said, "why didn't He let me become a doctor?"

She smiled patiently. "For then, don't you see, you would have been a doctor like anyone else."

He gave her a despairing look.

"If I am helping people, why should I be trampled on and my family left destitute? I must be doing something I shouldn't."

Suddenly, a smile replaced the tender concern in her eyes.

"You did, Edgar," she cried out almost jubilantly. "Don't you remember back in Egypt eons ago, when you were a high priest, and broke the law of the Pharaohs by making me your wife?"

His jaw dropped, and then, suddenly, he started laughing, and she joined him until the tears rolled down their cheeks.

"You see, Edgar," she finally managed, "you're still paying for me."

He was a unique man, living much in his own mind. There were times when he seemed involved only in the strange world of his subconscious, leaving her desperately alone. At these moments she needed all her patience and courage. And these innate qualities, forged out of their crises, were thereby sufficiently developed to preserve and enhance their relationship. They grew together at the same pace. All the facets of her intuition were honed and sharpened. She knew when to speak to him, and comfort him, when he was torn by some nameless vision, and when to let him be.

They had not been married long when he burst into the house one day and staggered into the bedroom, remaining there for hours. When he finally came out his face was calm and composed, and after a while, he spoke of the vision he had seen, of a great World War, and many of the young people he saw dead in that war. She was enough part of him to know what he had suffered and that he would come out of it on his own way with her silent support.

It had taken some adjusting before Gertrude fully understood the dimensions of the remarkable mystic she had married. "Imagine," said a friend, "being a housewife with two small children, the rent and the grocery bill unpaid, and then the elation when out of the blue somebody helped by a reading sent a check that would exactly meet these obligations—only to have the head of the household, on his way to pay the bills, blithely buy a fishing rod and tackle instead."

But Gertrude loved, not in spite of these idiosyncrasies,

but for them as well. She would throw up her arms, and then shrugging say, "Well, the Lord provided once, he will provide again."

Perhaps because he believed his father and was influenced by his psychic readings, Hugh Lynn also found a soulmate who gave him the support he needed when he made his father's life work his own. As the Bible observed, a prophet had little honor in his own land. Even as the fame of Edgar Cayce spread through the world, the work of the mystic was either unknown or regarded as something sinister, bordering on witchcraft, in his hometown of Virginia Beach. And when Hugh Lynn made it clear he was to involve himself wholly in furthering his father's message of reincarnation, soulmates, and psychic health readings, friends and relatives urged his bride-to-be Sally Taylor, the sister of a physician, not to marry him.

"It will never work," they told her. "He's living in the clouds." Gertrude Cayce was to tell the uneasy Sally, "I married Edgar thinking he was a successful photographer, and that was all. But people started coming to him for help. They wouldn't let him alone. He would go to sleep, diagnose their illness, and prescribe the remedies, and they would get well. It was hard to believe and hard to accept. But it happened. So, how could I tell him not to help all these people, when only he could help them?"

And soon she was drawn into it herself, the only person he trusted to put him in the trance which transformed this unlettered fifth-grade dropout into a veritable sleeping encyclopedia.

Sally's indoctrination was not quite as dramatic. She had met Hugh Lynn while keeping house in Virginia Beach one summer for her physician-brother. She was on vacation from her teaching job, at a time when Hugh Lynn was beginning to put forward his father's work. She admired his zeal but, with a doctor-brother, found it difficult to reconcile metaphysical diagnosis with the more orthodox treatment of recognized therapists.

As to reincarnation—at this point it was way over her head. When Hugh Lynn, on a date, would talk enthusiastically about rebirth, she would quickly change the conversation.

"The music is playing, Hugh Lynn," she would say. "Why don't we dance?"

Admiring Hugh Lynn as she did, drawn to him by a

magnetic bond, she had to look into what he believed in so implicitly. "While dating him for four years, I gradually became interested in reincarnation as it was explained in the Cayce readings and saw how much of what Edgar Cayce dredged out of the past influenced the present."

She was then ready to take the irrevocable step.

"When I married Hugh Lynn, I knew I would be marrying his life, and what he wanted to be, just as Gertrude had with his father. I was impressed by the way she loved him, comforting him in adversity, sharing his small triumphs. They were so much a part of each other, and that was what I wanted with Hugh Lynn."

She had been struck by Gertrude's self-effacement and Edgar's humility. He had no sense of personal grandeur.

"One day a crateload of the first book about him arrived. It was *There Is a River*, by Tom Sugrue. The rest of us excitedly took out the books and started leafing through them, but Edgar didn't even open the book. He just examined the crate, said it would make good kindling, and chopped it up with a hatchet. I don't know if he ever did read the book, though of course, he knew what was in it."

In his curious devotion to family affairs, he kept three bankers from New York waiting in the parlor, while he dressed a chicken for the evening meal.

"Let them wait," he said. "I'm needed in the kitchen."

Life with the son didn't figure to be easy. "I knew what it would be, and it took me four years to decide," Sally said. "I was drawn to him right away, but I saw other beaux, constantly comparing. It was important we have the same value systems, that I want the same things, regardless of how I felt emotionally. So many young people rush into things because they are infatuated, without realizing that people need the same values for a relationship to work. I couldn't have married Hugh Lynn, however much I loved him, had I not come to believe in the psychic things he believed in. For then I could not have given him the support he needed when he set out to let people know how his father's readings could reshape their lives.

"How could there be such philosophic differences—one of us believing in one continuous life, drawn out of the past and into the future, and another believing all life ends here.

Feeling differently about life itself, how could we join our lives?"

The light came to her eyes as she recalled how Hugh Lynn had struggled to prepare himself. "He knew he would have to become an accomplished speaker, so he would gather a captive audience of young people from his Sunday School class, or his Boy Scout troop, never more than five or six at a time, and he would talk about his father, just as if they were all in Carnegie Hall."

She was present at these rehearsals, and helped gauge the reaction of the young listeners. When Hugh Lynn finally thought he was ready, he began his tour of the cities talking about his father's readings, leaving the reassuring feeling that an uneducated Edgar Cayce had succeeded only because God's hand had been on him. "It was important," said Sally, "for people to know that God was not indifferent to man."

There were mountains to be climbed, and Sally climbed them with Hugh Lynn. She thought often of Milton's poetic line, "They also serve who only stand and wait." It was a waiting that developed her patience and fortitude, as it had Gertrude's before her. There was never enough money to go around. For Hugh Lynn, in the beginning, was not doing anything people thought worth spending money on. There was little to keep his new family going, except for the few dollars he gleaned from his talks and Sally's part-time teaching. And yet he had to carry on, directed as he was by his father's own psychic readings. And Sally understood, even though the work kept him away for long periods and seemed almost a fixation. "It became my obsession as well, an obsession that he succeed in whatever he was undertaking." Whenever somebody would listen, he would scrape together what few dollars he could with her help, and take to the road. There was nothing grand or glorious about it.

"He would start out, speaking in New York, with only enough money to get there. He couldn't have gotten home, not to mention going on from there, had he not received some money from a collection after his talk. And he never knew what that might be."

She stayed at home, raising their two boys just as Gertrude had hers, teaching whenever she could to help pay the bills.

"I had my reward in marking his progress, watching

overflowing crowds flocking to hear him speak, of seeing him fulfill his dream of an Edgar Cayce library to which thousands would come to study his father's readings." She rejoiced with him as doctors, once scornful, explored the Cayce health readings and successfully treated patients by them. Her heart swelled with pride as the very universities that had shunned the father opened their doors to the son. There was even a clinic dedicated to his treatments, launched in Arizona with remarkable success. These were the triumphs they shared, the fruits of his long ordeal, and of her faith.

"He had something to give the world, but he needed the strength to do it, and I like to think some of his strength came through me. We both lived for what he had to do.

"I never forget what his mother had said about her husband. 'How can he do anything else, when there are people to be helped?' "

As Hugh Lynn was to say later, not only of his father and mother, but of his wife, "The condition of soulmates was one of ideals. Had not Edgar Cayce said: 'Such as we have in an experience found an ideal may be said to be soulmates. And no marriages are in heaven nor by the Father save as each do His biddings.' "

Hugh Lynn and Sally visited me in California after I had written *The Sleeping Prophet*, a biography of his father, for which I had been overly credited with spreading Edgar Cayce's work.

"If not for you, Hugh Lynn," I said, as Sally nodded, "there would never have been a me. For you held your father's torch aloft during all those lonely years when few would listen."

He did not respond at the time, but later said, with a misty eye:

"And had it not been for Sally there would have been no me."

Hugh Lynn had zealously pursued the goal of seeing his father's life made into a motion picture, not so much for the aggrandizement of the Cayce name, but because of a feeling that the world needed to know more about this remarkable man and his rare insight into Universal Law.

When Hugh Lynn suggested a book as the basis for such a movie, I sadly recall his wife companion taking my hand, and saying, "You must help this wonderful man to realize his dream."

I say with sadness, for while the book was published, the movie had not yet been made at Hugh Lynn's passing on the Fourth of July in 1982.

But he was never daunted or dismayed, for Sally, his twin flame, never lost faith. She knew the movie would be made, as he wanted, when the time was right.

"Hugh Lynn can do anything he sets his heart and mind to," she often told me, with a faith almost sublime.

After his death, she was still very much aware of his presence. "He is saying you must go ahead," she said, "he is right there helping you."

So confident was she that some of this confidence rubbed off on me.

As a reporter, I had prided myself on not accepting anything I couldn't see, hear, smell, or touch, but after years of exploring the Unknown I had concluded there was much more to the Universe than most of us realized.

In his Work readings, Edgar Cayce had remarkably predicted my coming to Virginia Beach to assist the Foundation established in his name. He spelled out my name, phonetically, and mentioned the very man who would first tell me about Cayce. All this occurred twenty-five years later as foretold. And *The Sleeping Prophet*, catching the public fancy, did cause a certain revival of his work.

Marveling at one implausible phenomenon, I did not scoff at another. The Cayce readings said that Hugh Lynn and Sally had been together many times before—in China, Egypt, and elsewhere—and while they made no fuss about this ancient connection the two never doubted they belonged together into eternity.

He spoke to me often of reincarnation, of the purpose it put in a life that often seemed purposeless. It almost seemed too pat, too plausible, too orderly. "Yet," he would smile, "what could be more orderly than the movements of the planets, including the one of which we are a part?"

He had no doubt Sally and he had known each other through the ages. For theirs was a love beginning with the first look of recognition, and bringing the dawn of many ancient memories they shared together.

While not entirely disbelieving, I had not seen anything my journalistic pragmatism considered proof. But I was impressed by the past-life recollections of people universally acclaimed for their solid accomplishments. How could one lightly dismiss the hero of World War II, General George Patton, who had many remembrances of that distant past? Not only did he visualize himelf as the Roman general who beat back the Carthaginian invaders in ancient Sicily, but he recalled the battle more accurately than the historians who had studied it for a lifetime. "You must have been here before, General," commented his guide, the Signora Marconi.

"Oh, yes," smiled Patton, "a long time ago."

Where did all this come from? Even the most intellectual knew that something didn't come out of nothing. Where there was a cause, there must be an effect. And the reverse was true as well.

"I would like to believe in the continuity of life," I told Hugh Lynn, "and a soulmate who spelled out that continuity."

"You will one day," he said with a smile.

"What makes you so sure?"

"Haven't you ever felt you knew somebody before?"

"Yes. But that was a case of déjà vu."

"But what is thinking you have been someplace and known somebody before, but a remembering? Haven't you ever met anybody who made the hair on the back of your neck bristle and somebody else you wanted to immediately embrace?"

Of course, I had met people like that, as who hadn't. But how did I know that it didn't have something to do with the way they looked, spoke, behaved, or smelled?

Hugh Lynn shook his head. "With the rustling of a past-life memory there is usually an emotional response, as real and vivid as any real-life experience."

As I thought about it, I recalled a teenage girl finding her own grave from the past in a cemetery wilderness which officials had no record of. As she stood on that unmarked mound, the tears welling in her eyes, she mistily described her own funeral, and the husband lost long before. I was so struck by the reality of this emotion that I found tears coming to my own eyes. For that moment she had lived before, and I had shared that moment.

I had marveled that Mozart could compose symphonies at four and Josef Hofmann play them at three. But just because we didn't know where these gifts came from, did that necessarily mean these men of genius had lived before, subconsciously remembering these talents and aptitudes?

I constantly met people with experiences pointing to some old or ancient connection. A doctor friend, a distinguished surgeon, had nightmares as a child, seeing a ghastly gray line of wounded and dying in the agony of Gettysburg. At Anzio years later, as my friend bound the injured's wounds, an older doctor cried out in astonishment, "Where did you pick that up? You are ligaturing the wounded as my grandfather did in the Civil War."

In legendary Atlantis, or on Main Street, Edgar Cayce concerned himself with the need for love and companionship. Without a soulful feeling of being joined to another, of loving and being loved, there was a hollowness, an aridity in life that inevitably diminished the individual.

"At times," said Hugh Lynn, "my father understood this as a desire towards union with God; other times a union with another person."

The Cayce readings, as summarized by Hugh Lynn, helpfully guided the choice of a companion—particularly in marriage. "Associations with some individuals are more conducive to growth than others. This is easier to accept if we think back to the influences various friends and acquaintances have had on us in the past. A marriage should be founded on a shared purpose, the capacity to help each other grow.

"We as spiritual beings or souls experience our growth in consciousness through a series of lifetimes in physical form. We have likely been here before on the earth, and had close personal relationships with particular souls before. Attractions to another person and thoughts of marriage are related to memory patterns (even subconscious memories) of having been with that soul before. These memory patterns are released subconsciously in meditation, prayer, dreams, or under hypnosis, whenever the mind delves into that area of the brain which is the storehouse of the past."

While twin souls were the ideal, Edgar Cayce observed that we may have been married to many different souls in the course of other incarnations.

Two generations before Elizabeth Clare Prophet, people were asking him about their soulmates, nearly always with a wish to narrow the experience to one soulmate.

"Which of these partnerships is the best to build upon?"

"That, of course, bringing the best opportunity for growth."

"Does a soul have one other special soul it is meant to be with whenever possible?"

"This it shall learn for itself."

Some of the questions were personal, some abstract, but still casting light on man's age-long quest for a mate.

Q: I am interested in the theory of twin souls. Can it be seen whether my husband and I are twin souls?

A: It depends on the purpose. No two leaves of a tree, no two blades of grass are the same. They complement one another.

Q: Is there a spiritual affinity for every soul in the physical world?

A: If this is meant as in sex, no. If this is meant as in helpfulness, the spirit and will should be as one with the Creative Force.

Q: Were these two united for a certain purpose? Is that how they are drawn together?

A: United, for a purpose.

Q: Is there a soulmate for me, where shall I look for it?

A: As ye study to show thyself approved unto God, a workman not ashamed, rightly dividing the world, it will come in thy experience and ye shall know it.

As before, Hugh Lynn capsuled the Cayce readings:

"What then was a soulmate? Was it the soul one had married in the most incarnations? Apparently the soulmate condition is built by shared physical experience over a long period. But, more than just a physical attraction, there is a capacity to help each other at the physical, mental, and spiritual levels.

"While we may have more than one soulmate, we should be careful about leaving a marriage partner because of an attraction to someone who appears to be a soulmate. Edgar Cayce tells us that those already married can rest assured there is an opportunity for learning with the present partner. For those not yet married, who would like to find a soulmate, the readings suggest choosing someone who will bring a 'more helpful, more sustaining, well-rounded life, someone with the "right vibrations." '

"But even finding a soulmate does not guarantee a good marriage. They will have to *work* at it for the relationship to flower."

Somebody asked Cayce:

Q: Has this girl the type and quality of womanhood best suited to this man for a successful life?

Cayce could almost have been speaking for himself and his son.

A: May be made so in each. No one is suited exactly in the beginning unless foreordained through the ages of the mating of each, from the bonds built over many lifetimes of being married.

Cayce established reincarnation with soulmates, and soulmates with reincarnation. Hugh Lynn was intrigued that the Kabala, an esoteric Jewish doctrine known to Christ and the Apostles, linked reincarnation and soulmates. "Those abiding by the laws of the Lord would meet and marry their true soulmates. But those who defied God's law would be denied this union. Impurity kept soulmates apart, morality brought them together."

"In other words," said Hugh Lynn, "the proof of a soulmate marriage is how it works. My father felt that people had much to learn even in marriages where there was much friction. For these relationships were obviously a way of working off karma from the past."

I remember Hugh Lynn discussing a marriage that had gone sour. "It was all there, the love, the caring, the vibration Edgar Cayce spoke of. But too soon they forgot they were meant to collaborate in some useful endeavor, one complementing the other. They drew apart in separate enterprises, with separate thoughts, associations, and entangling alliances. There was an opportunity to go on, or kick it all away."

In some ways Edgar Cayce had anticipated the New Age by fifty years.

"Know that the soul is rather the soulmate of the Universal Consciousness than of an individual entity." And so it helped to be tuned in to the world around you, the mind reaching out like an antenna to pick up the vibrations helping us to connect with the person we needed.

There was no doubt in Sally Cayce's mind that Hugh Lynn was the only soulmate for her. But she could conceive of situations where more than one soulmate could enter a person's life, based on the history of their past.

Knowing of their love, I had crossed the continent to talk to her.

"There is nothing more important than love," she said, "and if it isn't worth a trip you aren't saying very much for it."

I soon saw that she had taken Hugh Lynn's passing very well.

"We were never out of each other's minds," she said. "But all life is a transition, and that transition can be painful or easy, depending not only on our faith in God, the Creator, but the God in ourselves."

She had traveled some with Hugh Lynn. They had been in China, Egypt, India, the Holy Land, and other special places together, but it had never been necessary to go anywhere with him to be with him.

"I could just think of him, and know where he was and what he was thinking and feeling. We blended together over the years, all we had to do was examine our hearts to know how the other was."

She seemed frail, and hobbled a little on a cane now, but she was full of inner vitality. And her voice was strong.

"Tell the young people love has to be nourished. It can't grow in a desert. People don't have to like the same things, but they must want for the other person what he wants for himself. Hugh Lynn and I were very different people. He was over-generous and I was thrifty. He thought on a grand scale, and I in terms of the home and the children. I admired him for what he wanted to do, for his quick perception of events, and his flexibility. He looked young past seventy, because he never got old. He lived every day as if it were the first day of his life and the last. And I lived it with him. There were no secrets between us. Thinking of each other so much, we became over the years like the other." She smiled. "Young people are disposed to think of themselves as always being young. They should ask themselves, before they leap, is this someone they can share growing older with—yet never old."

I stared out into the garden of the house she had shared for so many years with Hugh Lynn. It was a lovely spring day in Virginia. The azaleas were in bloom, and the buds shooting out of the trees. There was a fragrance in the air, and only the chatter of the birds broke the silence. Nature was renewing itself as it had from the beginning of time.

Whatever died in the winter came back in spring, I told myself. And as I looked across the table at Sally Cayce I had the sudden and exciting feeling that love, too, had its springtime.

"What do you think of mostly?" I asked.

The brown eyes twinkled in the still lovely face.

"Of Hugh Lynn, and how proud I am of what he accomplished, and which still lives on."

CHAPTER 5

Susan and Burton

It seemed like I had always known Susan, but nearly always as an observer. She was sixteen when I first met her, already a star, her name in lights on Broadway. She was in the title role of the *Diary of Anne Frank*.

I carried away an impression of an eager young beauty, with a nimble mind made doubly sensitive by her extreme youth and idealism. For our interview she had thrown off her role as a sacrificial victim in a Nazi concentration camp. She viewed her stardom with a childish delight I found equally delightful. I remember very little she said, but I do recall my surprise at her extreme perceptiveness, not only about newspapers, the theatre, and the people she knew, but about me as well. Was I there because it was an assignment for which I was being paid, or had I a special interest in her? As I looked into her beautifully sculptured face, noting the gleam of bright inquiry in the dark, luminous eyes, I shook my head with a rueful smile.

"I am afraid," I said, "that it is purely an assignment."

Her hand fluttered reassuringly. "I understand," she said. "We're all on assignments."

Over the years our paths crossed spasmodically, in New York and California. But it was not hard to keep up with her.

In those days, everything she did seemed to find the front pages. She was an alluring eighteen when she starred with Richard Burton and Helen Hayes in Broadway's *Time Remembered*. He was much older and married, enchanted by her youthful innocence. She was captivated by his animal magnetism. She counted the hours and minutes before they would meet again. It was pure ecstasy to be on the stage with him, to be caressed, spoken to with lavish endearment, to be the object of his affections. She did not know then what the elements of a soul relationship were. Nor would she have cared. All she knew was that she was deliriously in love with a man every woman seemed to be after. There were moments of anguish when she thought of the wife back in England, but the experienced lover was able to dismiss her misgivings with a word and a kiss. Her feet were planted firmly in midair. She was his "baby girl," his "angel," his "Luv." Every time a thought of the Lady Sybil back in England ruffled her brow he would passionately reassure her. "We will be together forever and a day. You belong to me." He taught her little phrases in Welsh, such as "Who do you love," and the corresponding, "I love you," which she parroted dutifully for the relatives from Wales who visited him backstage. He introduced her proudly as his pocket princess, a play on her diminutiveness. He seemed so carefree and easy, so available, that it became easy to forget he had a wife and child somewhere, and hordes of teenage groupies in the wings.

As the relationship wore on, there was more often pain than pleasure. Caught up elsewhere, he wouldn't visit or call for days, and she would sit alone, adolescently contemplating suicide to punish him. But then he would write passionately, eloquently, with the same fervor he dispensed on the stage. All was forgiven as she read: "I will stop drinking. Shall I tell you why? Because if I don't I shall die, and if I die, I shall not see you again, because, my sweet one, your loyalties could hardly be expected to follow me into the house of dust, the worm's pasture, the grave. So expect to be loved even more recklessly than before, even more singularly, even more intensely."

And then he wouldn't show up.

Burton's drinking was not the only distraction. The man to later marry Elizabeth Taylor twice had an almost hypnotic effect on young women, who pursued him until they were caught. "God," Susan found herself saying through her tears, "the man should have a harem."

The romance dawdled through the run of the play, then he departed for England and his wife, again amid fervid protestations of undying love. She saw him briefly in England, then years passed before she saw him again. He was standing on the steps of a Santa Monica hospital leaning on a bodyguard. He had just recovered from a serious infection. Even then, his hold on life seemed fragile. His hands were shaking, his face pale, with dark circles under the eyes. His hair was shot with gray. The years had reduced them to small talk.

"Little Susan," he said, touching the vein on her forehead, as he had once done so affectionately.

She smiled and they stared at each other awkwardly.

"It was lovely seeing you," was all she could say, and she turned away, not looking back.

She walked on sadly, wondering how something that had once meant so much could now mean so little. Was love always so transient, burning itself out in a hot flame of feverish infatuation? How was one to know what was real and rewarding in the way of love, what something we were meant primarily to learn by? But as she thought about it, wasn't her infatuation as real as the love she had borne young Christopher Jones, whom she married and had a child by? There seemed so much to endure in these relationships, as though a pound of pain was exacted for each grain of pleasure.

Mature now, divorced from Jones, who had moved painfully in and out of her life, she considered the fate that had brought them together. The things affecting her most were always externally imposed, it seemed. She was twenty-two and he two years younger. The setting was ripe, waiting for the actors on cue. And they responded. The scene was New York. She had walked into a Broadway restaurant frequented by the theatrical profession. Her eyes lighted on a friend, actress Shelley Winters, and a young man with burning eyes. He had brown hair streaked with gold, high cheekbones, and a sensual mouth. He was wearing a shirt unbuttoned to the waist, skin-tight pants, and—though it was freezing—only a light jacket.

As she entered, he turned to Shelley, and said urgently, "Introduce me, I want to meet her."

"She's not for you," Shelley replied. "You don't even know who she is."

"Oh, yes I do," he said. "That's Susan Strasberg. I'm going to marry her."

Shelley knew little about the tense young man, with the clean, clear profile, except what she knew from his appearing with her in the Broadway play, *The Night of the Iguana*.

Susan had stopped for a moment, then moved on without even catching his name. There had been no instant spark, no magic.

But Chris Jones couldn't forget that piquant face, the soft hazel eyes promising so much. As a talented newcomer, he was admitted as an observer into Lee Strasberg's Actors Studio. Susan's mother, Paula, rapturized over him. "He has that same animal magnetism Marlon and Jimmy Dean had." Her father was not as enthusiastic. He didn't like the way Broadway's newest discovery looked at his daughter. He had a disconcerting habit of sitting in the balcony of the studio and staring down at her. Susan found herself getting self-conscious and uncomfortable, even terrified as a feeling of foreboding came over her. She tried ignoring him, and thought he would tire of his little game. Then one day, some friends stopped by the Strasberg summer place and Chris was with them. He had engineered the visit. At the height of a summer storm with thunder and lightning for a setting, he did an erotic dance, appearing both ominous and superb. She felt his closeness, his urgency, and when he brushed against her, she was suddenly electrified. She had vowed there would be no more actors after Burton but she was irresistibly drawn. She was in love, wondering only why she hadn't known it before. She felt an ardor welling up from depths she had never plumbed before. He seemed to be everything she wasn't. He was poor, Southern, an orphan, defiant, torn from the roots of the country. She was protected, gentle, from a well-to-do conventional Jewish family. It shouldn't have happened but it did, and she had no wish to stop it, even though she knew there were stormy days ahead. But they would be exciting, this she knew from the powerful emotional upsurge out of an unknown past which drew her on, even while she was telling herself he wasn't right for her. He had the look of love, a face whose every nuance and mood shook her with excitement. She became romantically poetic as she thought about him, which was constantly. Only a woman desperately in love could have written as she did in the biographical *Bittersweet*:

"The setting sun filtering through the skyscrapers chiseled his high Indian cheekbones and outlined the straight line of his nose, the sensuous thrust of his lower lip. Lean and tightly coiled, skin glowing with energy, he seemed strong and masculine and self-assured, unlike me, who quivered at every unexplained shadow, including my own."

She knew nothing about reincarnation or soulmates at this time.

Actually, he was more into it than she. From the first moment he had seen her, he felt he had known her before. He had fallen in love watching her on television in the Chekov play, *The Cherry Orchard*, which she had done with Helen Hayes. He had marveled at a closeup which reminded him of his beloved mother who had died when he was three. As he looked on, spellbound, his mother's likeness superimposed itself over Susan's face. They were bound together. "You are like her," he told Susan almost shyly. "She was small and dark and beautiful like you."

She felt remarkably at one with him. If he was happy her heart sang. If he was sad, she wept. Sensing his insecurity and dependency, she subordinated herself, became subservient, to secure his love. But he remained jealous and insecure. If anybody looked twice at her, he was ready to jump at them. Her work was the only rival he had, and even that was secondary. She turned down a play, directed by her father, to drive across the country with him. She didn't see other people because he didn't feel comfortable with them. She got rid of friends, family, even the theatre she loved. They fought, made up, and slept like children, curled up together. Her parents were concerned by his violent flare-ups, but she argued they were only marks of his devotion. He made her feel something emotionally, sexually, where she had felt nothing before. Even pain was better than the numbness after Burton.

His career was going well. The critics acclaimed him as the brightest new star on the Hollywood horizon. He did *The Looking Glass War*, *Three in the Attic*, *Wild in the Streets*, *Ryan's Daughter*. But success didn't ease the simmering tensions. He seemed to be walking on the edge of a cliff. A seminude picture Playboy used to publicize Susan's role in *Camille* threw him into a jealous frenzy. He saw all of male America leering at her. After a stormy scene, he apologized abjectly, saying that she appeared so pure and innocent it drove him mad to see her sullied.

She thought marriage and a child would help, but after Jennie's birth it got no better. In Rome, where she was making a picture, the old jealousies flared up. This time she struck back, breaking her wrist. That night, having difficulty getting to sleep, tossing and turning, she had a strange dream, which foreshadowed the end of their bittersweet love.

"I was a young French girl, Marie, in the second Napoleonic Era," she recalled. "I was living in the country with my father. And there I fell in love with a young charming soldier. I clearly saw his blond hair and blue eyes, his soldier's cape worn dashingly across one shoulder. He took me from my father's home to Paris, and I began a life of debauchery that led to my death when still not twenty-one. I knew the soldier's name in my dream, and repeated it so I would remember. It was not a familiar name. As I looked at his face it began to disintegrate before me, the features changing until they became familiar. I said, in my dream, 'Why, it's Christopher. It was Christopher all the time.' Then still in the dream, I said to myself, 'You see, Susan, you still haven't learned. You must love the soul, not the flesh.' "

She had once felt numb, unloved, even in the bosom of her family. Marilyn Monroe had come to live with the Strasbergs, who were her mentors and more. She was like another daughter to Lee and Paula, who felt the same mysterious pull toward Marilyn as she felt for them.

Susan's feelings about Marilyn were ambivalent. She cared for her, understood that Marilyn's needs were greater than hers, and empathized with her as she had with someone else who had come dramatically into her life—the real Anne Frank, whose sorrow and fortitude she had made symbolic of a whole people's tragedy. While Susan was not into astrology, she was intrigued that the three of them—Marilyn, Anne, and herself— were of the zodiac sign of Gemini, with Leo (the Sun) rising, signifying positively, the bringing in of Light, and negatively, wanting to be in the Light. As the only daughter of illustrious parents, she expected the parental attention which, alas, she now had to share with Marilyn.

She wondered later whether she could have given her more. "From my own searching I knew what Marilyn must have suffered. She never knew what it was to have a child's early love. She came to my father and mother, crying, 'Shelter me, feed me, love me,' and they did because they loved her in a strange and special way, as if she had been a child out of some past experience."

She wept at her father's eulogy of Marilyn, for it not only described a dear friend, who was not quite a sister, but herself as well:

"We knew only Marilyn, a warm human being, impulsive and shy, sensitive, in fear of rejection, yet ever avid for life and reaching out for fulfillment."

They did not believe Marilyn had killed herself. She was at the peak of her fame, and was eagerly planning a number of projects, including a television special with Susan's father. She was still full of herself. Only a short time before her death, she had proudly lifted her blouse, and remarked to Susan, "I'm in better shape than I've ever been."

Marilyn's untimely death had a profound effect. It made Susan realize you could search too hard and too long for happiness. You had to be ready first, to know your inner needs, and how to fortify yourself, so you would not be one of two towers leaning on the other, but two strong upright columns building a firm foundation for a fulfilling love.

Sadly, she brought out the picture that Marilyn had sketched of herself. It was the only self-portrait Marilyn had ever done. It showed her impressionistically, as a little waif, with one stocking sliding forlornly down to her ankle.

"This is how I feel about myself," she told Susan with a smile. "The original glamor girl."

Though intrigued by astrology, Marilyn had never developed Susan's interest in the metaphysical, and never had quite the same awakening.

In Susan's own awakening she realized she would have to find something substantial within herself before she could find it elsewhere. Chris's psychic feelings about her, her own dream, might have been pure fantasy, she told herself, but they left a mark. She had been brought up to believe that everything happened for a reason. Perhaps she was being told there was more to life than the rational process, which had already failed her. Without knowing it then, she was being drawn inexorably to the mystic, the metaphysical, which even the great thinker Einstein had acknowledged as the source of the relativity theory that changed the face of the earth.

She had a strongly practical side, a sense of self-preservation Marilyn had never known. She took stock of herself, and wasn't quite sure she liked what she saw. She examined her ideals, hopes, fears, sense of purpose. None of it seemed to add up to anything. Where did she come from, and where was she going? It was the eternal question people asked and nobody offered an answer but the churches and the metaphysicians. She had tried conventional religion, and it had struck no responsive chord. The alternative was clear. She peeped into the metaphysical world of the transcendentalists, of Emerson and Thoreau, Hawthorne and Louisa May Alcott. But with this curiosity there was a keen sensitivity about appearing ridiculous, not only to herself but others. So she drew back a little.

In her frank inventory of herself, she had dwelt on an inexplicable fear that had come over her in Rome, whenever visitors suggested a tour of the Catacombs where the early Christians hid from persecution and huddled together for common comfort and prayer. Along with this she experienced a strange compulsion to worship in Roman Catholic churches, bringing about a conflict of loyalties with her rich Jewish heritage.

She had sought out a psychic, Pattie McLaine, of Los Angeles. McLaine, knowing nothing of Susan's fears, or her mixed loyalties, mentioned in passing, "You know, Susan, you had a previous life in Rome, some two thousand years ago. You were a Christian, an early follower of Christ, and you hid out with other Christians to escape the Roman persecution."

While it seemed to explain a few things, it was still only a psychic's impression. But not knowing anything about reincarnation, she was still affected by this prospect of an explanation of her otherwise inexplicable behavior. Her search for herself had begun.

We had kept in touch over the years. She had read one or two of my books on the psychic, and without becoming a slavish convert to metaphysical concepts, felt there must be some substance to what such idols of hers as Shakespeare and

Wordsworth, Emerson and Thoreau, not only accepted but wrote so assuredly about. They had minds that were universally revered, and Susan still worshipped the mind.

I did not offer her very much when she came to me. I felt everybody had to work out their own psychic experiences for it to have much meaning for themselves. But the Roman experience, which she mentioned, did seem suggestive of a meaningful remembrance.

"It could be some sort of genetic memory," I said, "or a species of reincarnation."

She looked at me in surprise.

"Do you believe in reincarnation?"

By this time, I had been impressed by the regressions of novelist Taylor Caldwell, which indicated a certain subconscious remembrance as the source of many of her novels. One regression into a life in ancient Greece actually gave this remarkable author the substance for a novel about the Athenian ruler Pericles and the courtesan Aspasia, which she called *The Glory and the Lightning*.

"I have seen some evidence of it," I recall saying.

By now a rabid searcher, Susan—between acting stints—began her exciting exploration. She had asked me to recommend a psychic, predominantly spiritual, and I gave her the name of a respected Los Angeles reader, the late Vera Winston, who had psychically read for a host of prominent people, including Los Angeles's Mayor Tom Bradley.

When I later asked Susan for a report, she was vague and somewhat apologetic. "She's a wonderful spiritual lady," she said, "and she made me feel so much better . . ."

"But . . . ?"

She laughed. "I am not putting her down, but she told me something quite impossible."

"And that was?"

"That I was going to be writing books, very successfully, and my writing in time would become equally important as my acting."

Sometime later she called, quite excited, to tell me she had, incredibly, signed a contract to do a book about her life. That book was *Bittersweet*. It was an instant success, indicating a flair for writing that Vera Winston had picked out, and which the actress had not realized she had. Soon there was another contract with the same publisher, Putnam, to do a novel.

She tried now to remember everything the psychic had told her. "I know she believed in reincarnation, but I can't recall exactly what she said."

"I don't know why," I said, "she should be right about everything else, and be wrong on reincarnation."

I was fond of Susan and valued our friendship. She was one of the few actresses I had met, along with Shirley MacLaine, who had any wish to look outside themselves. She not only had spiritual convictions about some higher purpose, but the courage of these convictions. It was difficult, consequently, for her to find somebody sufficiently like herself to relate to emotionally.

But one day, with a smile in her voice, she reported the ultimate—a soulmate, no less.

"And you know him," she said.

He was Patrick Flanagan, an electronic prodigy, younger than herself, who was known best as the father of Pyramid Power. His pyramid tents presumably heightened the energy field, and preserved food and other perishables long after they should have rotted. Flanagan had reported they also improved his sexual sensitivity, though he did not advertise it as a sexual stimulant.

He had written on Pyramid Power, and now on the Secrets of Revitalization, which dealt with retarding the aging process.

I had met Patrick years before, with his actress wife, Eve Bruce, but I didn't know much about him other than what I could see and read. He was short but muscular, and had been an expert gymnast. *Time* and *Life* magazines had carried stories about him when he was considered the boy wonder of popular science. One of his early inventions, the neurophone, would presumably permit the deaf to hear, through picking up radio signals in the brain. Dr. William O. Davis, who once ran the Air Force's basic research program, hailed his intuitive powers. "It's important to realize that young Flanagan had the necessary intuition to invent his neurophone. You make discoveries intuitively, in the same manner you would paint a picture or write a symphony." But apparently nothing much had been done with it commercially, as Flanagan concentrated on his Pyramid power and geriatrics programs. He was nothing if not versatile, and, I would have thought, volatile as well.

They looked good together, Susan still fresh and youthful-looking, and Patrick like an advertisement for his rejuvenation book. But he was only thirty-eight and ran every day, carrying weights to build up his power. They were sure they had known and loved before. They had an instant rapport and held hands all the while we talked together, like a couple of school children.

When I mentioned I was doing a book on soulmates they perked up at once.

"Do we qualify?" Susan asked with a smile.

"There's no doubt," said Patrick.

I was amused by his certainty, when love itself had so transitory a place in each of their lives.

"Do you feel there is more than one soulmate?" I asked. Flanagan gave Susan a tender smile, and they touched lips. Richard Burton could have done no better.

"Well," he said, "since I've been married three times, I should say yes, and that soulmates vary in degree and quality."

I could see Susan's head nodding and I saw no reason myself why that couldn't be true. But they seemed such an unlikely pair, the boy scientist and the glamorous actress, to have found one another in the Hollywood jungle, perhaps there was something in their past.

With her natural curiosity, Susan eagerly agreed to a regression that might offer some explanation of her closeness to Richard Burton, Chris Jones, and now Flanagan. And Patrick, as a true scientist, was always ready to explore the Unknown.

Dr. Boris Bagdassaroff, our regressionist extraordinary, had an idea. "Perhaps," he said, as we discussed the project, "we should get to Burton first."

"And what," I asked, "makes you so sure he will turn up?"

"He was her first love, and she still has some feeling about him. Her subconscious should be teeming."

Because of her actress's sensitivity, Susan was a good subject. She went under quickly, and responded well, pausing but once or twice, as though expectantly appraising her own answers.

"We'd like to ask the inner mind," began Boris, "if Susan knew a person called Richard Burton in another time."

Susan lay completely relaxed.

"Inner mind," he repeated, "was there a time when the souls of Richard Burton and Susan were together?"

He paused. "You may speak when I touch your forehead."

"In the Orient," said Susan, stirring a little. "Not the Middle East, not India, or China, but from the clothes I see them wearing, it looks like something out of *The King and I*."

I was amused by her theatrically related description, which Boris immediately pounced upon.

"Siamese?" he said, recalling the musical.

She nodded. "Oriental, but not yellow-skinned, brownish, a mixture." She now turned to the man himself. "He had a great deal of power, and he ruled those about him with a heavy hand."

"What was your relationship, if any?"

Suddenly, unexpectedly, she began to laugh. I thought she would never stop.

"I was part of a gift package," she said at last.

A sigh, and again a burst of laughter, as though one provocative thought was breaking fast on the other.

"You won't believe this. I hardly believe it myself. The man's incredible. He had a harem even then. And I was in it. Can you imagine that? I was sold like a piece of chattel."

Her eyes were closed, and her respiration normal. She was still very much into her subconscious mind, though aware, typical of lighter hypnosis, of what was going on around her.

I had remembered her once saying that Burton had enough women around him to constitute a harem. Could the conscious thought have overflowed into her subconscious mind?

Boris shook his head and whispered for my ear alone.

"Each division of the mind is a source unto itself."

Susan still seemed absorbed with the seraglio.

"I can't believe it. In a harem, with Richard Burton again."

I looked inquiringly at Boris, and he quietly explained. With this curious dichotomy under light hypnosis, Susan had moved in and out of her subconscious experience. "She's making a conscious observation of a subconscious recall."

As if still marveling, Susan kept shaking her head.

"You shared this experience with him, is that not true?" Boris asked.

"But I was the victim." She considered the present. "And he may have been a victim as well, for he was missing so much. It was a compulsion. His heavy drinking was a desperate effort to run away from that sexual aspect of himself. He had a lot of excessive indulgences, and I an unusual education."

Boris was curious about the harem, as was I. I had never heard one described before.

"Were there many in this harem?" Boris asked.

"Yes, but I was better educated than most."

She clung to the intellectual factor which set her apart.

"How many were there, fifteen, twenty?"

"More like a hundred."

"Where did you stay, in your own room, or thrown in with the others?"

"There was one large room, with rooms off that. It was like a beehive."

"And Richard was the King Bee?"

"He was a sultan (laughter)—even then."

He had married an aging wife—with vast estates. The harem was an old story to her. She was not jealous. She had her separate quarters, and supervised the schooling of their children. Theirs was a formal union, a convenient arrangement.

Susan had some interesting sidelights on the harem. The girls were monitored closely, lest they became pregnant or infected. If so, they were summarily expelled. Prophylactically, sponges steeped in drugs were carefully inserted so they covered the opening to the Fallopian tubes. It was all highly technical, yet consciously Susan knew nothing of all this.

As we considered one man's indulgences, it became obvious that Susan's relationship with Burton was of a karmic nature. If reincarnation was assumed, they had a lot to work off. And perhaps they had. For Susan had learned through Burton the futility of a connection that had no give or take, no spiritual value, only a mindless fascination with the self.

Yet they had exciting conversations together, marked by Burton's recitations, and Susan's quick grasp of the theatre. There was more than a sexual attraction, or her youth, for the matinee idol had his pick of the teenage crop. Perhaps it was her wide-eyed innocence, making him feel young again.

And that may have applied as well to an aging sultan, sated with sex and bored with an older wife he had never loved.

"What went on with you and the Sultan?" Boris asked, almost automatically. "Did he know who you were?"

"Oh, yes," she said quickly. "We conversed on many subjects. And he listened to me. I was considered interesting. I was good with figures, but I made everybody uncomfortable. I was always talking women's rights."

This education she was so proud of protected her from the enemies she made through her candor. She was so adept at mathematics the overseer used her to keep the palace books, for even a Sultan had to show a profit to keep a harem going.

It was not all easy going. Whatsoever we asked, no clear line on their relationship came back. The Sultan didn't appear to be emotionally involved. But Boris kept on doggedly.

"Were you the Sultan's favorite?"

"Not sexually. I amused him with my stories and observations."

He was sturdily built, some forty years old, looking older from constant dissipation. They drank of the grape and smoked opium in small water pipes. It would have seemed a debilitating life, but she didn't find it so.

"It wasn't so bad," she said, "because I used my mind to escape into my own fantasies."

At eighteen she was given her freedom. It was pretty much the age she had met Burton in this experience.

"Did you recall anything else with the Sultan?" I asked.

"Nothing really. It was like a compulsion that I didn't understand. But there was the same stimulation, the poetry, the tales, the anecdotes, with learning the happy by-product."

The Siamese experience ended with her marriage to the overseer. It was not an exciting denouement, but she had had enough excitement for one life.

We had discovered, to our own satisfaction, that under hypnosis, subjects not only sharpened their memories, but gained a vast new insight into their behavior patterns.

Susan had a good laugh, subconsciously, over the Sultan's maintaining separate quarters from his wife while enjoying his seraglio. "He still doesn't understand that isn't acceptable." She snickered. "But he's done his best to make it popular."

With all this sexual preoccupation, what could have been gained or lost, karmically or otherwise?

"What could that poor overworked Sultan have learned?" I asked.

Her reply was wholly unexpected, and I had to remind myself it was her more knowledgeable subconscious speaking.

"Sexual activity, no matter how it manifests itself, is an attempt to attain spiritual release. When people are indiscriminate sexually, even to using sexuality in religious rites, there is the feeling that sexuality can bring about a transformation of body energy into mental energy. While many of these people are perceived as degenerates, they usually are more open than those who are repressed, and can more readily make spiritual contact. On an unconscious level, as I see it now, Christopher and I were trying to make spiritual contact, the sexual attraction being the primer."

"Stronger than with Burton?"

"The magnetic energy was greater. I was drawn to Christopher like a magnet."

"But was there growth in this relationship?"

"Enormous. It was like walking over hot coals. Either you get burned or you learn to walk on the coals so that you won't get burned. It becomes too much only if both don't go through the same changes. But it was still a cleansing by fire, a catharsis of the spirit."

In her new interest in metaphysics, she looked beyond the realm of known reality. She examined her dreams, considering their reality as windows into the past, just as Mark Twain's mysterious stranger had floated in and out of his dream world all his life. She had a sketchy recall of the dream putting her with Christopher in the French experience. Now, under hypnosis, her subconscious mind filled in the details.

"Tell me more about the French connection?" said Boris, with perhaps unconscious humor.

"Ah," she sighed, "then the attempt was made on an unconscious level to open up the blocked consciousness by using sexuality to excess."

She had dreamed the soldier Christopher, then Robert Le Claret, had carried her off to a Paris in the decadent licentiousness of the second Napoleonic period, when every vice was assiduously pursued and a hectic nation lived as if every day was its last.

"I was eighteen, a farmer's daughter," she began, then broke off with a laugh. "Eighteen seems a critical age for me. I keep repeating my patterns, because, I must admit, the personality has been a little stubborn in accepting certain lessons. In Paris, there were drugs and I became part of some kind of a sexual situation. There was a group of people involved, mostly of the wealthy, upper classes. I contracted an illness there. It was like tuberculosis, a respiratory disorder. And I carried this damage into this lifetime, with some vulnerability in the throat area."

In the time of the upstart Louis Napoleon, French sensuality reached its peak, as if a frantic people knew it must take its pleasure before Bismarck and his Prussians moved in. It was a simple matter for a pretty girl, lowly born, to be lured by the false glitter and glamor, seduced more by her own weakness and lack of resources than by any rake or rogue.

"My name was Marie," she said somewhat hesitantly, groping for a last name.

"Antoinette?" I said facetiously, thinking of the glamorous pasts people assign themselves in reincarnation.

She frowned at the levity.

"I came from a poor family. We didn't have very much, and the Revolution was already long over."

She had lived in the rugged area of Brittany in the northwest of France. When the soldier Le Claret came along with his army supply wagon, her father released her, and she went unquestioningly. Some money had been exchanged, how much she didn't know. But Le Claret was twenty-five and rakishly handsome, and she looked forward to a high adventure. And wound up in a house of prostitution.

Why was there so little progress? She had gone from a harem to a position of respectability, and later from a poor but honest peasant girl to a slatternly life which brought illness and disenchantment.

"I seldom seemed to live long enough for spiritual growth, except for occasions where I developed some psychic ability, once with Patrick, who was some sort of inventive genius. With Christopher I kept trying to break through with sexuality. But never with enough spiritual preparation. It was very slow, one step a lifetime, which is a hard way to go about it. In this life I've chosen to do it all, but in a progressive manner, by becoming attuned to the psychic. In this way, I'm awakening my memory to a full spectrum of emotional, physical, and spiritual experiences."

Being a child actor, Susan was self-educated in the present, as in the Siamese experience, and with her mind opened, she seemed to transcend any scattered learning she may have gleaned in this period.

"My father was self-educated as well, and so saw no need for a classroom education. This lack of conventional teaching patterns made me see a world free of strictures and limitations." And so she was free to turn for knowledge in any direction.

Marilyn Monroe had been a larger growing experience in Susan's life than she would have thought. They had never been intimate, even though Marilyn, with an instant conviction, regarded Lee and Paula Strasberg as the parents she had never had in this time. And with Paula and Lee's help, Marilyn had achieved an identity of her own, after being cruelly buffeted about as an unwanted orphan. It had been a struggle.

Susan had remembered Marilyn saying: "I was always afraid I was crazy like my mother, but when I visited a psycho ward I realized that *they* were really insane." She had seen Marilyn crawling on hands and knees to Susan's parents' door, having mixed too many sleeping pills and champagne, scratching on the door, because she wanted to live. She would not have taken her own life. At worst, it was an accident, a less than fortunate combination of wine and pills. Susan knew this just as she knew they had all been together before. Knowing Marilyn had been enough to teach her humility, for how much more had she than this tormented girl-woman who had reached the pinnacle of fame, without being able to fully enjoy it in her hunger for approval.

As she thought about Marilyn, Susan knew there was a reason for their all coming together. It was no accident Marilyn had chosen Susan's family, for there had been a bond of the spirit between her parents and Marilyn, as strong as that with their own flesh and blood. They had wept over Marilyn as though she was theirs, and so she was.

As she spoke about Marilyn, obviously moved, Susan expressed the view that a soulmate relationship could involve anybody of the opposite or same sex with a soul memory which induced them to share each other's lives on a loving level.

"You have touched on various lives," Boris said to the half-conscious Susan. "Were there other times when you and Marilyn might have crossed paths in some meaningful way?"

Susan paused a moment, her eyes still closed. She spoke slowly, as though trying to capture every detail of what she was visualizing.

"Yes," she said, "many times, we were related in France, before I was with Christopher, before the Revolution."

There was no precise sense of time, only visual impressions, in turning the mind back to the distant past. She saw not a clock or a calendar, but a person and place, not a year or a season, but a face and a form crystallized by an emotion. She saw Marilyn as big as life. Only the time and setting were different.

"She was quite plump, but lush, and blonde, not so different than Marilyn in this lifetime. I could have been her little brother. I'm masculine in comparison to her." She frowned for a moment. "She was actually Marilyn. I can feel it. I was younger, yes, a boy. And there was a parental connection. Our family was brought to prominence through her. She was a famous courtesan, and she ruled France through the King, and she lost her head for it.

"It was a time," she added, "when they wore very full skirts and the hair was piled up in a full sweep."

We smiled, as if we were on to something, for Madame de Pompadour, the first mistress of Louis XV, who had ruled France from behind the throne, had influenced the upswept hair style to which she gave her name.

But it was her successor, Madame duBarry, who fit the part. If Hollywood had to cast for the role, they would undoubtedly have picked Marilyn. As Susan said: "She would have probably done a better duBarry than duBarry."

Aside from being naturally pleasingly plump, she actually resembled Marilyn in mien and deportment, and had a similar background. After she became Louis XV's favorite, she remembered her beginnings, and like Marilyn, was overgenerous and friendly to a fault. She had come off the seamy side, born illegitimately Jeanne Becu, to a lower-class mother, Anne Becu, and a father, Vaubernier, a provincial clerk.

DuBarry's mother, despised for having borne not one, but two children out of wedlock, had been driven from her home, and then through her daughter's intercession, became a cook in a wealthy home, and found a roof over her head. As her daughter climbed the social ladder, the family's lot improved.

And when duBarry became the King's mistress, Anne Becu, now Rancon, became a Marquise, with a retinue of servants, and a chateau of her own. Curiously, her younger child, also born out of wedlock, was a boy. And Susan, without knowing any of this, had seen herself as an unlikely younger brother.

As a lady of easy virtue in the corrupt sink of Paris, Jeanne Becu first took the name Mademoiselle Lange. Introduced to the court by the adventurer Jean duBarry whose brother she married, she ruled over the last of the French monarchs to have absolute control of France. But like Marilyn she took little interest in politics. After Louis's death she formed a friendship with the new queen, Marie Antoinette. Her personal loyalty led to her following the unpopular queen to the guillotine. She had an admirable elan, and died bravely, turning to the executioner to say, *"Encore un moment, Monsieur le Bourreau."*

Susan felt no rivalry with a king's courtesan, nor with a Hollywood queen for that matter.

"Can't you just see Marilyn doing that scene? She always wanted to do tragedy."

Boris had the usual male curiosity about Marilyn.

"When Marilyn joined your household, what was your reaction?" he asked.

"I was a little wary. After all, we'd all lost out because of her way back then. And my subconscious remembered."

"Was she competitive?"

Susan replied slowly, still in that curious twilight zone of being under and yet aware of her surroundings.

"Not really. I felt no rivalry, no jealousy, though people tended to project that. She was in a class by herself, so insecure, so malleable, and yet, again, close to the seat of power, just as before."

"How was that?" asked a puzzled Boris.

"She had President Kennedy's ear, and could have given him information that might have helped people." She sighed. "There are opportunities in life, lost or taken, that influence the lives of others. Marilyn never seized these opportunities."

This was presumably a reference to the unpopular war in Vietnam, which Kennedy took the country into in 1961, and which might have dimmed his popularity had he lived. And which Susan appeared to perceive clearly under hypnosis.

We had heard stories of Marilyn and John Kennedy and Robert Kennedy, too, without knowing how true they were. But it was hard to conceive that this orphan girl, with no background, no education to speak of, an almost narcissistic preoccupation with face and body, could influence national policy.

"You forget," said Susan, "that this girl became a world figure in her own right, as famous as the President of the United States. If you consider her background, her French existence, you won't find it surprising. She knew intuitively how to tantalize the great."

And yet what could she have done? She had no knowledge of politics, international relations, or domestic problems.

Susan shook her head, still into her subconscious.

"She made mistakes in this life because she had that same power and yet continued to act as if there wasn't someone in power so much in love with her that anything she said would be listened to. When she tended to be frivolous or fickle, it boomeranged."

"You mean, so far as movie-making went?"

"No, personally, as well as professionally. Not only with the Kennedys, but with others as well."

But Paula and Lee Strasberg kept loving her as though they knew who she was from another time. They had tutored many great stars so it was something else that held them, and caused them to overlook behavior that offended others.

Before she married playwright Arthur Miller, Marilyn had embraced the Jewish faith of her husband—and the Strasbergs.

"Was it a feeling of wanting to rejoin her family, or was it another whim of the moment?" Boris asked.

Susan nodded.

"It was a combination of things, but mostly the need to belong."

In a way they were soulmates, though the same sex. They kept turning up together, influencing one another. Ages ago they had traveled in the same troupe, gypsy performers, moving across the face of Europe.

"Were you related then?" Boris asked.

"We were all related in the troupe, there was a lot of

intermarriage. It was great schooling, for the audiences were critical, and they would shout and throw things."

And was Burton in this troupe as well?

"No, this was a pre-Renaissance period."

"You had no other experience with him?"

"Oh, yes, we were in a Shakespearean troupe together. Burton was the star. He always had to be the star. We traveled through England, and it was fun. I was young and the audiences were exciting.

"Burton was as handsome and compelling as he was today.

"I loved him then," she said with a smile, "and though for never and a day, it was great while it lasted. Had I known at eighteen what I know now, I would probably have been spared the agony and the ecstasy. But just think of what I'd have missed."

CHAPTER 6

A Pyramid Soulmate

F ive minutes after Pat Flanagan met Susan, he asked her
to fly to Egypt with him.

"Why Egypt?" she said.

"We were there once before, and there is more for us to
do now."

"And why not Rome?" she said. "That may be another
unfinished story."

Susan, of course, was anxious to learn more about Rome;
Patrick, to go back to the Great Pyramid of Giza, which he felt
had been the inspiration for his own Pyramid Power, and his
instant feeling for Susan.

We had regressed Susan separately, and now were to do
them together. Susan had some trepidation.

"Just thinking of the Catacombs makes me break into a
sweat."

Patrick smiled.

"It doesn't exactly calm my nerves," he said.

Later, as Susan thought about it, she remembered, as a
child, her father taking her Sunday afternoons to the Egyptian
room of the Metropolitan Museum in New York City. She had
been fascinated by the artifacts, the tapestries, and curios of the
ancient Egyptian dynasties. She could see even then that her

father was struck by her inexplicable interest. As she grew older, she developed her interest in Egyptology, and felt, without knowing why, a link between the Lost Continent of Atlantis and the land of the Pharaohs.

She had been introduced to the exotic at an early age. Lee Strasberg had not been one to consider the esoteric, except for that compelling family attachment to Marilyn Monroe, but Susan recalled his once saying with his little smile, "If I had been anything before, it would have been a Buddhist."

As she looked back, it somewhat explained his visit to the holy temples of Japan in Kyoto, and his warm reception by the High Priests who had extended a rare invitation to join in the sacred Tea Ceremony of the Buddhists.

I had to smile at her recollection, for this quiet, thoughtful man had almost the look of a Buddhist and I was sure the Holy Men had no trouble accepting him as one of their own.

I had been baffled, as others, by an unexplained preoccupation with certain cultures and remember reading everything I could as a child about the budding Christianity of Rome—*Caesar and Christ, Quo Vadis, The Robe*. All held me strangely spellbound. And yet I had no idea of the significance, if any, at the time. In much the same way, I had an instant rapport with Susan, and later Patrick, and though this didn't mean knowing them before, it did simplify working together. There was a desire on their part to cooperate thoroughly, on mine a wish the regressions would be of a level to explain their relationship and perhaps more.

Susan had wanted to be regressed by the sea, and so they were hypnotized simultaneously in my beach home, lying comfortably next to one another. Boris took some time to get them relaxed and deeply under, using a special recording of soft music to ease them into the unconscious. Almost immediately we knew this session would be special. As he asked her to think of their most memorable experience, Susan's body trembled and she sobbed softly.

"We have crash landed from another planet," she said, "and there are only eleven survivors. We will never see anybody from our planet again."

"We lost contact with Arcturus," Patrick put in, speaking of a distant star, "before we crashed."

The tiny band was all that was left of an earthbound exploring party sent out many thousands of years ago.

Boris and I exchanged glances. What was there to be amazed at when it was all amazing?

They had landed on Atlantis.

"Now that you are here, what have you found?" Boris continued matter-of-factly.

"A low form of life," said Susan.

Then Patrick put in, as I reminded myself they were both under hypnosis:

"We're building shelters, and learning to communicate with the different life forms. And we are planning settlements, while establishing an energy source to communicate with Arcturus."

"And how do you plan to do this?"

"By internal cloning of organs inside our bodies. As the organs reproduce themselves, we stay as young as our organs, and continue to develop civilizations in Atlantis and elsewhere with the energy-producing thought forms we become capable of." From Arcturus they had brought the knowledge of the amplification of thought waves, by which they could instantly create needed energy without machines or fuels of any kind.

"And the destruction of Atlantis? How did it come about?"

"Through the misuse of power. The cloning techniques were misused for personal aggrandizement. We cloned one mind in the thought amplification process, rather than the group mind, and this brought about noticeable distortions of energy, with serious consequences. The rule of one leads to the abuse of the ego."

Moving on to Egypt with their thought form, they altered the field of gravity so that it became a simple matter to build the pyramids by raising these ponderous stones—a mystery which has defied explanation for thousands of years.

They seemed to have the virtually boundless power Jesus spoke of when he said any miracle could be wrought when two or more were gathered in God's name.

"Our god," said Patrick, "was the God of Creation. Once you understand the laws of Creation, it is possible to do anything."

He paused a moment, and I had an eerie feeling of being torn between two worlds, one fanciful and a little frightening, the other shaded by the reality of Susan's soft sobbing over the sound of the ocean.

"I want to go home," she cried.

Boris quickly asked:

"And where is home?"

"Near the ocean . . . the white sand. I didn't want to come here. I had to leave my family. But they need me here. That is what they tell me."

"Is this your home?"

"No, it is on the other side of the greater world."

"Why did you come?"

"The people here need help, and the ones who came before us got lost."

"Are you traveling with a friend, a love?"

"A friend who may be more."

This friend was Patrick.

His voice faltered, and it was clear he was experiencing great anguish as he spoke.

"The being we know as Susan was dying and I tried to save her. It was a genetic problem. Some of those cloned contracted serious ailments, having lost their immunity in a different atmosphere—an eventuality I had stupidly unforeseen." His voice became a murmur. "I couldn't bear it. I wanted to die. So I arranged to have myself destroyed. I drank a poison I had prepared and it destroyed my body."

Susan's sobbing had ceased, and her left hand began to twitch.

Boris became alarmed.

"Susan," he said, "something's happening with your left hand. Did this have to do with your death?"

The hand twitched almost convulsively now.

"Yes," she shuddered, "total disintegration of the body."

They had come to benefit the Earth, chosen because their minds were in tune over many lifetimes. But, as Patrick said, they had encountered the unexpected. "We found this area of the Universe had a much lower vibration, unlike the Arcturian vibration. And you tended to be debilitated."

"And Susan developed this genetic flaw?"

"She was exposed to an unfamiliar virus during the vulnerable cloning process."

Susan was very old by Earth standards when she died,

but she would have been like new had Patrick been able to deal with the unexpected. "I can only blame myself," wailed Patrick, clenching and unclenching his hands. "My magic wasn't powerful enough."

Boris now moved them out of a disturbing phase which Patrick was obviously reliving to his own discomfiture.

"Where," asked Boris, "did you two meet again?"

Patrick: "In Egypt, the Fifth Dynasty. I was a priest and Susan a priestess. I was a magician. I could cure disease, alter weather, move objects. I knew the secret of controlling gravity through antigravity. We built temples, in the pyramid form. And we fell in love."

Susan: "I did not recognize him at first."

Patrick: "It was a beautiful life, but she became ill and began fading. I tried all my magic and I could not save her. When she died this time I decided I would be with her again. We had a ritual to destroy the soul, which involved splitting the body and scattering it to the winds. I had my body cast throughout Egypt. I didn't feel worthy of existence, for having allowed her to die again. What kind of a magician was I? Of what use all this power?"

With all this tragedy, which should have stimulated the learning process, we still had no clear idea why they had come together now. In another relationship Patrick had experienced sex for three and a half years deliberately without an orgasm to ostensibly activate higher centers of the brain, thinking it essential to his spiritually joining forces with Susan at this time.

I could see in Boris a desire to get back to a more recognizable experience.

"When after Egypt," he asked Patrick, "did you find yourself in the flesh again?"

"In the Roman time."

"Do you remember your name?"

"John."

"Are you a Christian?"

"Yes, John is my baptismal name. Before that it was Patricus. I had been a soldier of Rome."

Again they seemed destined to die together without having known why they were brought together.

"I see a vast dark cave," Patrick said, "known as the Catacombs. We are clad in robes and sandals. In the torchlight

I can see Susan. She has long, dark hair. Her name is Maria. I keep looking at her, marveling at her beauty. I feel as if I had always known her, without knowing how or where."

Susan had roused herself, and appeared to be listening.

"I was only fifteen," she interjected in a small voice. "And I had come a long way from Judea. We had heard Jesus, and we knew He was the Promised One." She sighed. "But my father was still waiting for the Messiah, like so many in Judea, thinking only of liberation from Rome."

"And you were able to leave home so young?"

"I announced I was leaving. At fifteen, I was an adult."

"Did they try to stop you?"

"My father turned his back on me. I was dead for him. I ceased to exist. That I, a student of the ancient scrolls, should do this terrible thing, to betray a Messiah who would one day drive the pagans out of our holy places."

Some time before, she had begged permission to follow the Man of Galilee as He bore His heavy Cross to Calvary. They had refused to let her go.

"So I was forced to stay at home, knowing what He was enduring for us all. All of Jerusalem knew."

She had found it hard to forgive her father.

"But," I asked, "didn't Jesus say we should forgive?"

She nodded. "Yes, I didn't know that then."

Leaving finally, she turned her back on her old world.

"I took a new name because the old me had died. My father's daughter was no more."

She had taken the name Maria, not only because it was His mother's, but because it meant: Exalted of the Lord. It was a compound of the Hebrew Mara, to lift oneself up, and of Yah, for Yahveh or Jehovah.

The journey to Rome was ordained by Peter. They were more than a year in transit. They stopped along the route, working for their food and shelter, conversing in kitchens or in some stable about salvation and life eternal. The poor were enthralled by the promised Kingdom of Heaven for they were the disinherited, and the forgotten, without hope.

Some were Jews, others Greeks and Romans and Armenians, but all wanted to hear about the Jew who had forgiven His enemies as He died on the Cross, symbolizing life everlasting.

I had listened fascinated, trying to perceive some pattern, and only when Susan paused did I ask:

"And did you tell people how they could find this eternal life?"

"Through faith, through believing, through Christ."

"And God, what of Him?"

"They needed somebody to dramatize God for them, to bring Him closer into their hearts. That was why He came. No man took His life. He died to fulfill the will of the Father, to show mankind that life was continuous."

So where was He now?

"He will reappear when least expected, a wraith in the clouds, a face in the window, a hand on the door. He will be there when we stand heedless on the brink of disaster. He will be there, never fear."

Her face had become radiant, as though illuminated by a shining white light.

This was a Susan I had not known. All this, I felt, was not coming from her, but through her, as she would have been the first to acknowledge.

She had learned much from her Master, the disciple instructed by Peter, who had taken the tiny band on the long, arduous road to Rome.

And why Rome?

For a moment an exciting thought held me. Could the far-flung Roman Empire have been established for the single dominant purpose of providing a vast network for pilgrims like these to bring Christianity to the world?

In Rome, they soon found they were a proscribed sect, subject to arrest on sight. And so, they joined other hunted Christians in the vast, dank underground vaults of the Catacombs.

At first she could not bring herself to describe the tortures she and the others had endured. She would cry, making little animal noises, then turn her head, as if to avoid inquisitors.

Patrick had been silent through her narration. But now, his eyes still hypnotically closed, he spoke of his empathy for her even then.

"I felt a tremendous pain in my fingers, as if they were cut and bleeding, from trying together to claw ourselves out of that stifling hole."

As if remembering, Patrick seemed to have trouble

breathing. His breath was coming in gasps, his body heaving as he relived those last days in the thinning air of the cave.

The portrayal was so real, so graphic, that we found ourselves drawn along as if by reality.

It had not been difficult to visualize Susan as the gentle Judean, with starlit eyes and delicate features, Patrick as a sturdy, Christianized Roman soldier, who wanted nothing more than to die with her. But there was still a curious dichotomy with the present.

As we studied them, Patrick's hand slid down his body and he moaned. "I have this pain in my right leg and hip, it keeps coming back. It was almost as if I was born with it."

In trying to escape, he had been hacked across the leg by a Roman soldier.

He was still having trouble breathing.

"It's like asthma," he explained, "though not quite the same. Nobody has really ever been able to properly diagnose it."

"Now they can," said Boris with mordant humor. "Catacomb fever."

Another, besides Patricus, was devoted to the beautiful Maria. This was the freedman Marius, who had been lurking on the fringes, professing an interest in the new faith. Some had feared he might be a spy, but Maria scoffed. Hadn't he been baptized?

Though Marius had embraced Christianity, he still had not won over the tiny band of Jewish Christians.

Before the Romans closed in, he had helped the Christians with food and other essentials, but they still mistrusted his motives. "He did this for love of you?"

"Lust, love—lust yes, love maybe."

"Did you have a relationship with him?"

Her answer was grudging.

"Forced."

"Did you resist?"

"I wanted to kill him."

She sighed, ready to blame herself. "I knew better. I was very arrogant, like my father. I thought that I was different."

"Was there more than just that once?"

"Just that once. He knew I didn't love him. I shouldn't have used him that way. I had no right to think I could help him."

"How could you help him?"

"He had a difficult time. His mother had been a slave and he was never accepted, even after he became a freedman. He was shunned by the slaves, and by the aristocrats who employed him as a household overseer. So my sympathies went out to him, but he betrayed me. And then he betrayed the rest."

"But why the betrayal if he loved you?"

"He was afraid his masters would think he was one of us."

Marius had given her a chance. He had warned her that she would be buried alive unless she fled the Catacombs with him at once.

"But the others," she cried. "What of them?"

"I don't care about the others," he cried.

She had no thought of abandoning her comrades. The Catacombs, with its secret vaults, had developed a mystique of its own, out of the mystical love they all shared in Christ.

They knew every step of its intricate corridors, spread in tiers over hundreds of acres. But the genius that had conquered the civilized world was not to be frustrated by a tiny band of religious fanatics.

She sighed wearily.

"They sealed off all the surface entrances to the subterranean vaults and passageways. As the last light was shut off, we huddled together in the darkness and cold. We scratched frantically against the walls, hoping desperately to dig ourselves out. But reason should have told us that if it were possible we would only find Romans laughing at the other end. They had hauled so many of us off to the lions."

As the days wore on, their candles and torches flickered in the murky atmosphere.

"It had gotten very dark," she said in a faltering voice. "We gasped for air, having no energy left to even scratch the walls. But we still clung to life, hoping for a sign, such as He must have been given on His day of truth."

And then suddenly, as their eyes strained against the darkness, there was a murmur of voices and a white light gleaming off at a distance.

And then, wonder of wonders, the voices drew nearer, and she could distinguish faces and forms.

Her voice now rose in her excitement.

"There were my friends," she cried, "my other friends not of the flesh. I had seen them before, but I was never sure they really existed. But now I was frightened no longer. I knew I was not alone. Christ was there, and the others who had died loving Him."

"And so, what did He say?" asked Boris, who had been listening intently.

"He smiled and said that we would be with Him soon."

"And that heartened you?"

"Yes, for we knew then we would soon be companions of the Lord."

There was only one thing left for her now. And that was to forgive the man who had led the Romans to them in his jealous rage.

"I could not find salvation with hatred the last thought on my mind," she said.

"I could have given him more had I loved him more. It was like showing somebody the sun, then passing a dark cloud over it."

It all seemed so real, I found myself protesting:

"Don't blame yourself. You did what you could."

The ghost of a smile touched her lips.

"I have tried to make it up to him."

It took me a moment.

"You mean . . ." I began, incredulously.

"Yes," she sighed, not mentioning his name. "I had to die to get away from him. And yet he loved me." She paused. "And I loved him as well."

"And Patrick, what of him?"

She smiled wistfully.

"We have never been long together, nor shall we be, until we learn one day that on this Earth there is no greater magic than love."

CHAPTER 7

Terry Moore

I had been an ardent admirer of actress Terry Moore for some time. She was amusing with the lovelorn gorilla in Mighty Joe Young, enticing as the Colonel's daughter in *King of the Khyber Rifles* with Tyrone Power, and adorable with Fred Astaire in *Daddy Long Legs*. I read of her frequently, her long-time liaison with billionaire Howard Hughes, which ended in a disputed marriage, and subsequent marriages with football great Glenn Davis, oil magnate Gene McGrath, industrialist Stuart Cramer. She knew the greats of the world—Ronald Reagan, Paul Getty, Clark Gable—and she had a quality more priceless than money and fame. She stayed wonderfully young.

We talked about a book on Howard Hughes, and I was astounded that this woman in her fifties looked even better than she had on the screen twenty-five and thirty years before. She had been pretty and vivacious, and now she was beautiful and tranquil.

I didn't do the book, but I did go over it with her. It served to refresh my memory of her stormy relationship with that lean, legendary figure who controlled airlines, movie studios, aircraft companies, and yet was almost universally acclaimed as the nation's most eligible bachelor—until he fell in love with an ingenue young enough to be his daughter.

He pursued her, drawn perhaps by the youth and innocence he had long lost. She was flattered that a man with lady
loves like Jane Russell and Lana Turner should have chosen
her. She enjoyed seeing doors open that would have ordinarily
been closed, nightclubs and restaurants serving past their hour
just for them. His public image was confused with the real
Howard, until she suddenly realized, with an acuteness beyond
her years, that he was his image.

She had been a Mormon, a virgin, an old-fashioned girl,
but Howard's touch was enough to make the walls of Jericho
tumble.

Wildly jealous, he would investigate the young men she
dated, even if they were only escorts intended to publicize a
picture.

"He was so amusing," she recalled, "he would tell me
what a wolf a certain singer was, warning me to stay away from
him, and yet everybody in Hollywood knew the singer was a
screaming homosexual."

He was jealous even of her career. He didn't want her to
enjoy anything he was not part of. Everything was prearranged
and methodical. When he wanted to meet her, he had somebody call, as if for himself, and then just *happened* to drop by, as
they were having lunch. "He didn't plan a date," Terry said,
"he plotted one."

Even when Howard wasn't around, she felt she was
being watched by the people he paid to snoop on the women in
his ménage. Meanwhile, she suspected that his many business
trips were combined with pleasure—and for Howard that was
beautiful women.

Though she eventually married four times, she didn't
recapture the excitement of Howard until she met a brash
young cabdriver twenty years younger than she. He was Jewish,
the first Jew she had ever dated, though she had never thought
herself prejudiced.

Their meeting was extraordinary. A doorman waved as
she came out of her hotel in New York, the cab stopped, and
she stepped into it. There were thousands of cabbies in New
York, and out of that multitude Jerry Rivers pulled up with a
friendly smile.

He kept up a steady patter, looking back at her so much
she was afraid he would run into somebody.

"You don't sound like a cabdriver to me," she decided.

"I'm not," he said, "I'm a gynecologist."

She laughed so much that by the time she got to her destination it no longer seemed relevant. Actually, he was a businessman on leave, who, like the Grand Caliph of Baghdad, ventured forth in disguise to learn what people were saying.

"I had never met anybody like Jerry before," she recalled. "Can you imagine looking at a cab driver and thinking, as you looked at the back of his head, that you had always known him?"

They spent two days in New York together. With Howard she had to be careful what she said and did, but Jerry only shrugged, "You're entitled." He put on the off-duty sign, and she rode around Manhattan in the front seat of the cab. He didn't associate her with Hollywood, saying, "The only Terry Moore I knew played centerfield for the Cardinals."

Howard had billions and Jerry only prospects. And yet Jerry was more generous. "Howard was always afraid somebody liked him for his money. But Jerry could make a tuna sandwich, and you'd think it was a Roman banquet."

Both appeared to have profited from their relationship. In her teen years in suburban Glendale, few Christian parents would have let their daughters date a Jewish boy. "It was a taboo," Terry said, "and I can remember thinking how unchristian it was. And yet I went along, reluctantly, because that was the way things were. Knowing Jerry made me realize that Judaism was the root of Christianity. While I had always known that Jesus and the Apostles were Jewish, I hadn't stopped to think that without the Jews there would have been no Christianity. 'My God,' I thought, 'Jerry is of the same faith as Peter and Paul, Mark and Matthew, John, James, and Jude.'

"I remembered Jesus saying, 'My people shall be persecuted in My name.' It made me realize that any blow against a Jew, because he was a Jew, was a blow against Jesus."

Jerry, too, was going through a transformation. Listening to the Mormon doctrine, impressed by its links to the Old Testament, he found himself strangely drawn, as if over a familiar pathway.

"They were great people, those old Mormons," he enthused, "like the prophets Isaiah and Jeremiah of the Old Testament." He felt a kinship to the Mormon prophets, the fiery Joseph Smith who founded his Church in upstate New York, and his successor Brigham Young, who led the latter-day Chosen People into the new Promised Land of Utah.

Still, I must confess I was surprised by their coming together.

"I couldn't help myself," said Terry. "There was a magnet pulling at us."

Having watched their relationship flower, I had looked forward to regressing them to see if the subconscious mind, manifesting some form of remembrance, could explain what so many of Terry's friends considered an obvious mismatch.

Jerry, apprehensive of the Unknown, didn't want to be regressed, and I didn't push him.

Terry was ready to be hypnotized, but only by somebody she knew and trusted.

"I don't know anybody like that," I said.

"Oh yes, you do," she smiled. "You."

She looked at me entreatingly.

"Do you mind if Jerry sits in? We do everything together."

I didn't anticipate any difficulties, for it was easy to hypnotize anybody who wanted to be hypnotized. Actually, all the hypnotist did was induce a self-hypnotic state opening up the unconscious, or subconscious mind. He was merely a catalyst.

With some subjects, Boris created a receptive mood by darkening a room, occluding outside noises, playing soft, dreamy music from a series of tapes, all to induce an alpha-like state involving the memory bank of the subconscious mind.

Terry needed no inducements. She was an ideal subject. I used the meditative process from my book, *The Power of Alpha Thinking*. As I counted down slowly from ten to one, I had her visualize a succession of steps, then various colors, the pounding of the surf, a pleasant meadowland, and any exalting human figure she could think of—Christ, Moses, Gandhi, Lincoln. As the conscious process receded, I was hopeful the subconscious would take over and turn up the secrets of the veiled and distant past.

Terry responded quickly to the sleep suggestion, and was under almost before I could say Howard Hughes. I was careful, as Boris invariably was, to let her pick her own time and place, her friends and family, and tell her own story.

"Who are you?" I asked, tapping her to make sure she was under.

"Sally Bennett," she replied, spelling out her name.

Born on a North Carolina farm, she had grown up dreaming of going to New York City and becoming a dancer. For that day and age—the 1830s—this was like being a lady of the streets. But Sally persisted, and at twenty, she made her break and went to New York.

Pretty, with a dancer's shapely figure, Sally Bennett had many admirers, but was carefully determined not to let her father's irate predictions come true.

But then Roger Elliott came along. He was tall, dashing, rich, English-born, and he lived a life of indolence, with his horses, boats, and stables. He fascinated her. She had never known anybody like him before, and she was flattered that he had fastened on her after an ostensibly chance meeting, which she later discovered he had arranged to look like an accident.

Just as I was noting a parallel to Howard Hughes, with that curious dichotomy of time under hypnosis, Terry declared, in a taut voice:

"He was like Howard . . . he was Howard."

I leaned forward.

"How do you know it was Howard?"

"I saw Howard's face superimposed on his. It was like listening to Howard, the same gestures, expressions, the same remoteness. It was as if you were an object, some curio or jewel they had to possess, to enjoy when it suited their pleasure."

There was a heaviness in her voice.

"The moment I married Roger I knew it was a mistake. He gave me orders as he would a servant. He told me how many there would be for dinner, and he expected me to entertain at his pleasure."

He had thoroughbred horses, and expected her to become an adept rider. "He was proud of his horses and raced them, but he had no feeling for them, other than how many races they had won. He bet for huge stakes, five and ten thousand dollars a race."

I recalled now how much Terry enjoyed the track, but how upset she had become when Jerry made more than a token bet.

Roger would go away for extended periods on business, yet he never told her what that business was.

"I suspected it might be other women, from conversation I overheard, but I didn't dare ask. He would have flown into a fury. I was a prisoner in my own home, spied upon, every movement noted by servants loyal only to him." She had one unlikely friend, a young groom from Ireland. Her face lighted up as she mentioned his name.

"His name was John, but I called him Jonna. He was spirited, and would ride the best horses when he wasn't supposed to. He loved testing them."

He would sometimes ride with her when Roger Elliott was away. His hand would slip caressingly over hers as he helped her onto the saddle, or linger around her waist as he helped her off the horse.

"I did not want to meet his eyes, for he would be looking at me with an expression that mirrored my own.

"I told myself that I should insist on riding alone. But I would show up at the stables, my heart beating a little faster in the expectation of seeing him."

They went for long rides, around the lake by what is now Central Park. One day, she lost control of her stallion, and Jonna swooped down, grabbing the halter and bringing the runaway to a stop. He gently helped her off the horse. His arms were around her and he could feel her heart beating.

Her eyes took in the lean, handsome face, the mop of blonde hair that fell over his eyes, the expectant, half-open mouth, and she drew back.

"No, no, you must leave here," she cried.

She looked apprehensively over her shoulder. And as they neared the stables, she dismounted and walked the rest of the way alone.

One of the servants was waiting.

"Where is that Irishman?" he demanded.

"I had a fall," she explained, "he's bringing up the horses."

The servant gave her a sullen look. "The Master will fix him."

Terry's eyes were closed, her face tense, and her eyelids twitched, as though reliving the scene. It was a melodrama that could have been the plot for a movie, but it was also true of real life on which movies are based. Knowing something of the social barriers in early New York, I wondered how she could be conversant with an immigrant stablehand.

"Weren't you conscious of the difference in station?"

She laughed mockingly.

"What was my station? I was a farmer's daughter. I was no more than Jonna. My husband made me realize that, taunting me when I didn't perform in society as he expected."

"But wasn't it wrong to encourage him?"

"My marriage was wrong."

Her husband arrived the next day. He barely spoke at the dinner table. Then with a cold smile he announced that he would be giving a birthday party in her honor.

Her heart sank.

"I don't feel very well," she said.

"Then a party is just what you need. It shall be a masquerade. You shall come as a vestal virgin, dressed immaculately in white. You shall be the belle of the evening, my sweet."

There were twelve guests, her husband's usual drinking companions.

She was startled at his costume. He was dressed as the Devil, totally in black, snapping a whip, with obvious glee.

"It's as you see me, my dear," he said.

As she looked around the room, her heart almost stopped. For there was Jonna, held tightly by two servants.

"We have an honored guest," announced the host, "a stable boy."

Jonna faced Elliott unflinchingly.

"You disobeyed my orders," Elliott said grimly. "Nobody was to ride that horse. And you knew it."

As Jonna started to speak, Elliott furiously slashed him with the whip, raining blows on his defenseless head and face. There was a stunned silence, and then the cronies began to applaud. As Jonna slumped to the floor, Sally angrily stepped between them and snatched the whip away.

She kneeled and helped Jonna to his feet. He was bleeding and staggering a little. She helped him to the door, then summoned help to get him to bed.

Her story had left Terry emotionally spent, tears streaming down her cheeks. I took her out of it, but her subconscious continued active.

"Why," I asked, "did you marry Elliott?"

"He was so overpowering, it was a compulsion almost. But like Howard, he quickly tired of things he owned."

She frowned a moment, closing her eyes.

"They needed new excitement, new faces. They were jaded, life had given them too much and they lived in fear somebody was going to take it away."

"Why did you repeat the experience?"

"I didn't know, not then. I learned a lot, I learned I needed a Jonna, somebody sentimental, somebody to have fun with, somebody who enjoyed loving for love's sake."

I laughed.

"And where do you find somebody like that?"

She turned to Jerry, who had been listening quietly.

"Jerry," she said, "he was Jonna."

I groaned. "Oh, no, not that."

"As I was under, I saw Jerry's and Jonna's face at the same time, their eyes held the same gentle light and concern."

Jerry seemed to be mulling it over.

"What do you think?" I asked, turning to him.

He surprised me.

"I had the feeling, even in the beginning, that I was at one with Terry. None of the differences that hold people back—age, religion, social—had any effect on me."

He smiled, and for a moment, I could see how she thought he was the sentimental Irish youth with the tender smile. His face held a quizzical look.

"I don't know why it should make any difference, since I gather you don't have the same body, but Jonna's being Irish struck me a little, since I'm part Irish myself, though predominantly Jewish."

Terry laughed. "Maybe," she said, "I remembered the Irish in you."

In Terry's subconscious mind, Roger Elliott and Jonna had become as real and vivid as Howard Hughes and Jerry Rivers. And, if anything, more intriguing, for their lives were cloaked with the exciting mistiness of time.

Terry was anxious to discover what had happened to Sally Bennett, and even more, Jonna.

Again, under hypnosis, she picked out the same time and the same place, Manhattan Island. She was separated now from Roger Elliott, living alone in the big house pining for the departed Jonna.

As closely as I had followed her dramatic tale, I was not prepared for what was to come.

"There were people at the door, rattling the clapper with such urgency I knew something must be wrong. Roger had left me, but I was afraid he would return in a drunken rage. I hadn't left the house, for that was the only way Jonna could contact me."

The callers were from the police. There were three officials, so she knew it must be important. Her first thought was for Jonna, but then she realized that a stable boy would hardly be that important.

The senior officer assumed an expression of regret. "We are sorry to bring this news. It is your husband. He was found dead in his boat last night."

She sensed the officer searching her face.

"How did it happen?" she asked weakly.

"He was killed with a blunt instrument."

Again she had the feeling he was testing her. What would he have thought had he known that her first concern was for Jonna?

There had been a fierce struggle, from the look of the overturned desks and tables. The boat had been ransacked in its slip, and some silverware and money taken.

"Your husband had dinner on the boat with a guest," the officer said, with a shrug of embarrassment.

"You needn't spare my feelings," she said. "My husband had many friends."

"We wondered if you would know the lady."

"I have no idea."

Again he gave her a searching look.

"We are hunting for three men. They worked with your husband's stables. They were seen on the slip earlier in the evening."

"I know nothing about it," she said.

They believed Elliott had been killed when he put up a fight. The woman had fled.

She was asked to identify the body, a horrible experience, and learned later to her vast relief that the police felt Roger's death had been an accident. Some blood was found on the sharp edge of a metal fitting, and it was now thought he had fallen and struck his head. At least Jonna was not a murderer.

Shortly thereafter a letter arrived. As she looked at the labored scrawl she knew immediately who it was from.

"He didn't want me to know where he was, so he wouldn't involve me. The stable help had gone to the boat to air their grievances. There had been a scuffle and then Roger had fallen and hurt himself. They had taken the silver and the money to make it look like a robbery.

"Jonna had become interested in a new faith, of honest, God-fearing people. He could say no more. He was planning to move on, but would write again before he left the city."

She read and reread the letter, putting it under her pillow.

After Roger's death, the house went to a brother. She received nothing.

"I just wanted to forget those terrible years. They had left scars which I knew only Jonna could heal."

She went back to North Carolina, leaving a forwarding address. She saw the reproach in her mother's eyes. She had married rich, and had nothing to show for it. A young farmer, who had wanted her before, still wanted her. But she still felt Jonna would write, and she would join him, anywhere.

The weeks and months dragged on.

A forlorn voice spoke now from the couch.

"I could only believe Jonna was dead. He would not have forgotten, any more than I could forget him."

After two years, she married the young farmer. "He was kind and gentle, a wonderful man, but I had no heart for him. It was very wrong to marry him."

One day, visiting her parents, she put on an old sweater of her mother's. Her hand poked into a pocket and drew out an envelope. With a thrill she recognized that familiar scrawl. Her hands trembled as she tore open the envelope.

"I love you and always will," the letter began.

She read on eagerly. Jonna was in a place in upstate New York that she had not heard of before, Palmyra. He was with a group called the Mormons. He had been studying the new faith with a man named Martin Harris, who had been an inspiration to him. They would be leaving soon, heading by wagon train for the West to form their own community.

Her voice took on a new pathos.

"He wanted me to join him. They would be leaving in two weeks."

She looked at the postmark. The letter had been written almost two years before.

"There was nothing left for me. He was gone. I knew I would never see him again."

And she never did.

She died two years later, brokenhearted.

Weeping as she came to, Terry looked over to Jerry for reassurance. She held out her hand and he took it.

"I was afraid for a moment I had lost you," she said.

I had found myself thinking how wonderful it was if their search had ended at long last.

"Well," I said, keeping it light, "you lost a groom and found a cabdriver."

They both laughed.

"I don't care what he does," said Terry, "as long as he's mine."

I checked things over. There wasn't much. Jonna had studied Mormonism, and now Jerry was doing the same. Terry, of course, was born a Mormon, her creed a vital part of her life.

"She tithes the Church, even before she gets paid herself," Jerry observed wryly.

So Jonna had been in Palmyra, where Joseph Smith founded the Church, and from there the Mormons had taken off for western New York, Ohio, Illinois, and finally Utah. But, of course, Terry could have known all this, being a life-long Mormon.

"Now really," she said. "I've never thought much about that part of it."

"Does the name Martin Harris mean anything to you?"

She frowned a moment. "It means nothing."

"He was Jonna's instructor."

Looking back, I learned that the golden tablets which became the basis for Mormon teachings had been transcribed by Church elder Oliver Cowdery, and a colleague, Martin Harris.

But what did that prove? Coming from a family of Mormons, these things may have been mentioned many times in Terry's presence, her subconscious remembering, even when there was no conscious recall.

None of this had any effect on a smiling Terry.

"Long before I was regressed, I knew I had known Jerry before. We even pick up each other's thoughts."

The smile quickly turned to a frown.

"Even though Roger was hateful, I had always felt he loved me in his fashion. It hurt that he would cut me out of his will."

"Just like Howard?" I said.

She shook her head. "I know somehow Howard will take care of me. He always said he would, and he was a man who kept his word."

But Howard was long dead, so how could that be?

CHAPTER 8

Enter Mrs. Howard Hughes

I was an interested observer at the announcement of Terry's marriage. Not to Jerry Rivers, nor his Jonna self, but lo and behold, to Howard Hughes.

The announcement, may it be recorded in Heaven, took place some thirty years after the event with Hughes's blood heirs finally acknowledging Terry's claim as Howard's legitimate wife and widow.

While Howard wasn't present, having been called by his Maker some seven years earlier, Jerry was there to greet the press, and to confirm Howard being present in spirit.

Only two nights before, Terry had a startling dream in which she saw a former beau, Nicky Hilton—of the hotel clan— and Howard in very amiable accord. This surprised her no end, for the last time she had seen them together they were swinging wildly at each other as Nicky forcefully protested Howard's infidelities to Terry.

Terry, interpreting the dream, thought this rapprochement with Hilton was Howard's way of apologizing for slighting her in his will.

She had a distinct impression of Howard's support, that he would be with her in spirit as he already was in substance, Terry having now received a few million as a belated wedding gift. All in all, it was quite a dream. For there was also an overture to Jerry, the dead billionaire giving his blessing to the young upstart from New York who had presumably usurped him in two lifetimes, once as a lowly groom, again as a philosophical cabdriver.

Jerry, too, had his dreams about Howard. One dream had occurred at a time when Jerry had been trying to sell Terry's book *The Beauty and the Billionaire*. There had been no substantial offers, and Terry was discouraged. Her career had dwindled, she had lost her million-dollar home, had been wiped out in the stock market, and then—the crowning blow—nobody had appeared to be interested in her story. Or almost nobody. There were a few offers, which Jerry considered trifling.

"Perhaps," said an anxious Terry, "we should consider one of these offers."

"I'll sleep on it," said Jerry.

That night he had his dream in which Howard gave him an encouraging word.

"Hold on," he said, "you will get your price."

Jerry awoke that morning, half-expecting to see Howard, the dream had been so vivid.

Terry wasn't impressed.

"It doesn't sound like Howard. He was jealous of everybody. Why would he help you?"

Jerry looked at her uncertainly.

"Maybe he reformed."

Shortly thereafter, Jerry appeared to be babbling in his sleep.

"Yes, Jesus," he was saying. "Thank you, Jesus."

Terry listened for a while, mystified, then shook him vigorously.

"Wake up, Jerry," she cried, "you must be going through a conversion."

He woke up with a start.

"What happened?" he cried.

"That's what I'd like to know," replied Terry. "You were talking to Jesus Christ."

"No," he said, "he was talking to me. He told me to be brave and have faith."

I had noted certain singular changes in Jerry.

"You must be getting religion," I said.

He shrugged good-naturedly.

"Maybe it's the Mormons."

"It's something else," I decided.

Terry gave him a look of affection. There was a twinkle in her eye.

"The boy finally found somebody who loves him for himself, it's mellowing him out."

Jerry snorted.

"You make me sound like an orphan."

His mood changed. "You know what burns me up? People think I am taking advantage of Terry, using her connections. When I met Terry, I knew that was it. This was why I had been driving that cab all over New York. I was waiting for one passenger, and when she jumped into my cab the search was over."

Now that I knew about Jerry and Jonna, I looked more deeply into their initial reactions. In their excursion around New York, she had not cared particularly about the high spots, her interest centering in lower Manhattan and Central Park where she kept staring out the window with a sense of nostalgia as they drove around the lake.

"I have never been here before," she said, "and yet it all seems so familiar."

They had turned strangely silent, finally emerging on Fifth Avenue. And then the conversation resumed, Terry baring her problems unaccountably to a rough-hewn stranger who seemed like an old friend, though of a mold she had never dated before.

"I was very depressed," Terry recalled, "and Jerry looked at me in mock wonder, saying, 'You're the girl with everything, and if you don't have money, you still look like it, which is the next best thing.' "

He got her laughing, but the problem didn't go away. She missed terribly not working in film. The studios had stopped calling long ago.

"They must be crazy," said Jerry, "to pass up somebody like you. You're going to make a comeback."

She found herself laughing so much at the absurdity of this brash young cabdriver engineering her comeback that her spirits were enormously lifted, and she found herself thinking that she still had a chance in an absurd art form feeding on the young.

"I'll be your manager," he said.

She stopped laughing and her eyebrows tilted sharply.

"Why not," she cried. "I've been doing so little, you could manage me from the cab."

He stood up to his full height and waved an imperious finger.

"Don't talk like that. That's the manager's first order. Terry Moore is a great star. So act like a great star." He grinned. "You never know who's listening."

And so he had packed his bag, with his few floatable assets, and came to Los Angeles to be with the woman who had ended his search.

With a compassion she did not quite understand herself, she watched Jerry's struggle to relaunch her career. Friends said he was doing everything wrong, but she only smiled. "At least he is doing something." She was totally charmed by his efforts, even when they ran contrary to everything that had always worked in Hollywood. He hung up angrily on producers, agents, and impresarios.

"I won't stand for anybody telling me Terry is a back number," he shouted.

Terry had looked great for her age, but affected now by Jerry's confidence, the years melted away. People who had not seen her for years thought she must be her own daughter. Even the studios marveled, and she began to get parts.

"I thought she was dead," one Hollywood mogul remarked.

Jerry waved an admonishing finger.

"Terry is just beginning," he cried. "In a year you won't be able to afford her."

Terry's friends were horrified, protesting that he was holding her up to ridicule.

"Oh, let Jerry have his fun," she responded. "It's really very nice to be a star in the eyes of the man you love."

He seemed fascinated by everything she had done.

"Do you know," he said when I first met him, "that Terry won prizes for *Peyton Place* and *Come Back, Little Sheba*, and was nominated for an Academy Award?"

Terry gave him an indulgent smile.

Not many observers thought they would last. But a year

after Jerry's arrival, her pictures were appearing in the magazines again, she was doing specials on television, and getting calls for TV series and feature films. She even sold her book to the movies.

It came to me with a jolt that it was Jerry who made her young and vibrant again. We had been sitting around after dinner, just a few of us, chatting, and I was somewhat surprised that one of the guests, Shirley MacLaine, had little to say to Terry. I could see that Terry was a little hurt. Toward the end of the evening as Terry rose to leave, somebody said admiringly, "Terry Moore, you haven't changed a bit. How do you do it?"

Shirley looked up with a startled expression. "Terry Moore," she exclaimed, "I would never have recognized you. You look like a twenty-year-old girl."

Terry came back with a gratified smile. "But I recognized you, Shirley. You're always working."

I had not thought the thirty-eight-year-old Jerry particularly attractive or appealing to women. He was slightly more than average height, with a shock of dark, wavy hair and a pale, sallow countenance. His eyes, belying a brash aggressiveness, were a soft dovelike brown. So I was consequently surprised to see the prettiest girl at a party flirt with him outrageously.

Terry turned to me later, saying, "Jerry seems Irish to me at times, he has so much of the devil-may-care about him."

Whenever at home in Los Angeles, they attended services at the Mormon Center. Like others, I thought he was only trying to please Terry, but I soon learned otherwise.

"At first," he acknowledged, "I went because of Terry. But I found myself more and more interested."

Terry was bringing out something in him that had lain dormant for a lifetime. They were inseparable, in church, at business meetings, rehearsals, the theatre, benefits, suppers, dinners, even the racetrack.

She plainly relied more on Jerry than on her agents and managers. "I've been there before and it's all rather shallow unless you're in it with somebody you care about."

Like others who had seen her move through the upper crust of society, I had not understood this passionate and incongruous attachment.

And then came the regressions, and it seemed to fill the voids.

"I can see it all clearly," said Terry. "Sometimes when Jerry gets a little strong with other people, I want to say 'Down, Jonna.' But he had so little of me the last time that it is understandable he should push this time."

I had noticed that in the presence of the captains of industry and intellectual giants who were flowing back into Terry's life, that he had little to say.

"What's the trouble?" I asked.

"No trouble," he said. "You don't learn nothing talking."

I had my own ideas about how deeply Jerry accepted Terry's past-life experiences, and baited him a little one day.

"You have mentioned," I said, "that you were waiting for Terry."

He nodded. "What does that have to do with being Jonna, and the Mormons?"

"Well, why were you waiting?"

He gave me a puzzled look.

"What do you mean?"

"You must have had some reason for waiting."

He looked at Terry and a smile softened his face.

"There's the reason."

"But how did you know she was coming?"

"I just knew, I felt it in my bones."

I had to laugh, and Terry joined in with me.

He frowned, obviously not knowing what we were laughing about.

"You had a psychic feeling, that's what you're telling us, some sort of remembrance. It was in your genes, your subconscious, your bones, whatever you want to call it."

His eyes narrowed now, and he looked thoughtful. And then a triumphant look crossed his face.

"So why don't I remember more?"

"You remembered enough to know it was Terry you were searching for."

Terry had jumped up with the spring of a teenager.

"Oh, don't try to convert Jerry. He doesn't understand why I came back a Mormon."

Jerry laughed out loud.

"What did you have to do with it? Your parents were Mormon. What kind of *schmegeggy* is this?"

"I had a choice. That's what kind of *schmegeggy* it is," Terry came back. "And I chose what you had been, because I knew I would see you again one day, and I wanted to be what you were."

His eyes widened in wonderment.

"So that's why," he said, "you keep *schlepping* me off to church."

I had no idea whether Jerry would eventually become a Mormon as Jonna had, but I surmised that, even so, he would still keep his Jewish identity. Did not St. Paul say, "I am a man which am a Jew of Tarsus"?

While having no sense of a past life, Jerry's feeling of recognition on meeting Terry admittedly could only have come from remembering her.

So what kind of soulmates were they? Twin flames, karmic soulmates, or companion soulmates? They could be just as special, just as helpful, varying not so much in the intensity of their love as their impact on the world in which they moved.

I decided they were companion soulmates. While Terry was motivated spiritually, ever ready to help a needy friend or stranger, the relationship owed its specialness to Jerry's obsession that Terry get her due in all respects.

Companion soulmates, while not as ethereal as twin flames, were still a positive force by the very love they manifested, which overflowed quite naturally into the world around them.

I saw none of the resentments of karmic soulmates.

Having read through the transcripts of her transgressions, Terry was quick to point out that her subconscious mind had picked out but one life in the past.

"Perhaps," she said, "that was our beginning."

Her consciousness of Jonna grew as she let her mind float back, and new emotions were constantly invoked.

"Looking at Jerry now, I catch myself seeing Jonna as he looked then. They're so similar that it's almost painful at times."

"And why painful?" I asked.

Tears came to her eyes.

"I loved Jonna so. When he was frustrated and unhappy, I felt equally frustrated and unhappy."

This had not been apparent in the regressions.

"That's right. But then I was Sally Bennett, married and loyal to my vows. Now I'm looking back as Terry Moore."

I found it odd that her love for Jerry transcended that for Hughes, particularly since her marriage to the billionaire had been so dramatically affirmed.

"Roger Elliott and Howard were so much alike," she said. "Neither could be faithful very long, though Howard's work came first, even over our marriage. And he could be vindictive. After I left him, he became so angry that he told me he would fix it so that I never made another picture. He owned RKO studios then, and he threw his weight around.

"I always was a little afraid of Howard, just as I was of Roger, never being sure, never feeling an enduring warmth."

Then why had she married Howard? For money, power, prestige?

She reflected a moment.

"I loved him as much as he would permit. He prided himself on his sexual prowess, but even as an immature teenager I knew there was more to love than that."

She was with Howard from 1949 to 1956. As the years dwindled by, she saw him less and less, though he kept insisting he would always take care of her. After they parted, she had a feeling he needed her, and she tried to contact him. By that time, he was a recluse, in hiding, weakened by illness and drugs, barely knowing what was going on.

"I have loved you all my life," she wrote. "If you want me, I will be there."

The letter came back, unopened.

I could understand why Terry did not want to relinquish her ties to Hughes. Until Jerry, it had been the most important event of her life, an experience with a remarkable man such as few women ever had. She cherished his love and the memories that went with it.

"He was my whole life for so long," she said, "that I had to hold on to him. He was my security blanket."

I thought polygamy might have been the Mormon influence, but she shook her head. "No," she laughed, "Mormons don't do that anymore. Howard just had me mesmerized, and sentimentally I couldn't give him up."

Did she still think of Howard as her soulmate now that she had Jerry?

"They are different. Howard was a karmic soulmate, somebody I had to learn with. It made me ready for a more joyful love. Jonna was the love that had eluded me. And with Jerry, finally, there was fulfillment."

I had found it odd that Sally Bennett had come to New York from North Carolina at a time when respectable young girls didn't travel about unescorted.

"What surprises me," said Terry, "was that I went back to North Carolina."

Suddenly her eyes widened.

"But, of course," she exclaimed. "Years ago, when I was married to Stuart Cramer, he took me to his family's home in the North Carolina mountains. As I looked at the surrounding hills, I was overcome by the strongest feeling I had known all this beauty long before."

In her emotion, she had jotted down a few lines:

In memory of this wondrous day
A part of me will always stay
In the Blue Ridge Mountains of Carolina.

Jerry, too, had his memories.

"We all come from what we have been," he said with a smile. "How else would we be what we are?"

CHAPTER 9

The Ram Speaks

I didn't know what to make of JZ. She spoke of her spirit entity, Ramtha the Ram, as I would a brother or dear friend I admired. She played the piano marvelously, though she had never had a lesson, giving the Ram all the credit. The stirring music, played exclusively on the white keys, was all her own, though she couldn't write a note of music. She could paint, and paint beautifully, without instruction, because the Ram had said she could. As Ramtha, she not only predicted the future, but apparently made it happen.

She and the Ram were separate entities, merging only when she went into trance, and the Ram's personality took over. Often finding it hard to distinguish between the two, I used the names interchangeably when speaking of their work. The Ram was always positive, sure of Himself, while JZ claimed infallibility only when making claims for the Ram.

"I have never known him to be wrong," she smiled, "not even when he discusses the very sensitive subject of soulmates."

JZ and the Ram forged far afield, in guiding the lives of those who came to them for counsel. She advised actress Shirley MacLaine to turn down two bids for movies to await a third movie, *Terms of Endearment,* which the brilliant actress, costarring with Jack Nicholson and Debra Winger, thought her finest role.

"You will not only win the highest award for this coming picture," she told MacLaine, "but you will bring great enlightenment to the world with your writing."

He—the Ram—encouraged the actress to go on with her book, *Out on a Limb,* even as friends, including a number of intellectually oriented writers, argued that a book on way-out subjects such as reincarnation would endanger her standing wih her public.

The Ram assured her that the book would open new doors and add to her development, and indeed it had, personally and professionally. She knew no limitations now, having crossed a threshold of metaphysical understanding into the Unknown. And as her friend and admirer, I saw in the enhancement of her self a new opportunity for a soulmate who would be a worthy counterpart.

The Ram agreed.

"Her life, in a sense, is only beginning. She will draw to her that which she requires, and in doing so will achieve such fame as few actors have known, and great happiness as well."

Ironically, the most moving acknowledgment of the Ram, I thought, came from another fine actress, whose last days were made tranquil by the Ram's assurance of the peace she would find on the other side.

The late Joan Hackett, believing as much in the infinity of a personal Universe, left this unique testimonial of her own:

"I have been to psychics all over the world," said she, "and many have told me things that happened. But Ramtha was the only one who made it happen."

A smalltown housewife turned psychic, JZ Burnett looked more like a movie star herself, with her sky blue eyes and upturned nose. She had an appealing, often helpless manner of not quite knowing what strange and mystical transformation had overtaken her. But as Ramtha, the omniscient one, she featured a gruff, masculine voice (for Ramtha was all man), authoritative, incisive, often bitingly witty, and never at a loss, however pesky the question.

As if by chance, not knowing the Ram had said I would one day write about him, I met not only JZ but her husband, Mark Burnett, a dentist of Tacoma, Washington. I could have found no two more prosaic people, I thought, that is, until the discussion got around to the Ram. Both were enraptured with the Ram—Burnett, surprisingly, even more so than JZ.

Their initial experience with the Ram was a remarkable one. Burnett and JZ had come across a description of Patrick Flanagan's Pyramid Power, and constructed several cardboard pyramids on the order of the Great Pyramid of Giza, scattering them around the house to see if they would really preserve food and flowers as advertised. JZ then placed one of the pyramids over her head, and laughed, "Maybe it will do something for my brain."

Then Burnett stuck one on his head. Thinking how funny they looked, they laughed till the tears came to their eyes. At this unlikely moment, JZ happened to look down the hall and was blinded by a dazzling white light streaming from the ceiling. She blinked, then opened her eyes to see a towering male figure filling the doorway. He had a bland face with gleaming olive skin, a twinkling smile out of luminous dark eyes, and a shining white headdress that fell loosely over his shoulders. JZ sat stunned, her mouth agape. Mark gave her a startled look, wondering at the change in her.

JZ finally blurted out:

"Who are you?"

The baffled Burnett couldn't see any figure.

"I looked at the doorway," he recalled, "to see what JZ was staring at, then turned back, to see that her eyes were closed. There was an electric feeling in the room, as if our vibrations were rising, and JZ was saying in a strange masculine voice:

" 'I am Ramtha, the Enlightened One. I have come to help you over the ditch.' "

Not for a moment, watching JZ, did Burnett question the reality of the Ram, be it a superior guide who had walked into their lives or a dramatization of JZ's subconscious—which neither of them even thought about the time, because they were unfamiliar with the metaphysical.

"The intense feeling that accompanied the Ram's opening words was a remarkable part of this experience," Burnett later said. Because of this emotional impact Burnett never doubted the reality of this strange and singular experience.

"At that moment I had two conflicting emotions, one of awe at this strange happening, and at the same time a feeling of recognition or familiarity, as if Ramtha was somebody I had always known."

The Ram was very much aware of their antics with the toy pyramids. "He said we were like children, trying to become adults, spiritually, and he went on to explain that the little pyramids, which he referred to as fiery forms, were a symbol of the fire within us."

He discussed many things, including healing the self through a positive attitude.

"Greatness does not come from heroic deeds, but from a knowingness within, which is the key to the Universe."

As the strange voice came to a stop, JZ slowly opened her eyes, looked at Burnett, and said in her natural voice, "What happened?"

"I'm not sure," he said, suppressing his excitement, "but can you do it again?"

She closed her eyes, and again the Ram appeared as he was to appear many times in the future.

"There was nothing about our business and home life, however intimate, he wasn't aware of," JZ recalled, as we sat around my home. "He told Burnett he should advertise his office hours, though this was contrary to the rules of the American Dental Association at that time."

"Don't worry about it," the Ram announced, "there are forces at work that you don't know about."

Not long afterwards the rules were incredibly changed.

The Ram was concerned about something that was to greatly concern them. They were in grave danger in their present home, he said, and gave her the name of a Tacoma realty agent—Roy Burnside—whom she had never heard of before. Burnside, he told her, would provide a new safe home for them.

"In two days," he said, "your children will have a dream, and when they tell you of the dream, you will know you have to be out of the place you are now in."

Two nights later, JZ's two children dreamed of murderous robbers breaking into the house. Frightened, JZ went looking for a new house. She stopped at a realty office on the highway, and asked for a Mr. Burnside, and a secretary said, "I'll ask him to come out." JZ didn't bat an eye.

A businesslike Burnside found them a white house, as Ramtha had said, and they moved in the same weekend that their old house was broken into and pillaged.

An uneasy JZ kept asking Ramtha who he was and why he had come to her. She was told she would know in due time. Meanwhile, she was to listen and heed what he said, to grow so she could help others to grow, to think of herself as a master, a great teacher, because he, a great master, spoke through her.

Months passed while she got to know Ramtha, without her once thinking of going public. He spoke to her of holding Dialogues with people, and how she could help them. Almost persuaded, she asked: "Do we put an ad in the paper? How do we do it?"

"Just invite the people and the word will spread. You will abdicate the body entirely, and I will come into the body, but you will have no memory of this. When you speak, people will listen."

There was no doubting Burnett's devotion to the Ram. The Ram seemed to offer a pathway to the mysteries of life that Burnett had not gotten elsewhere. "The greatest quest," the Ram had said, "is the quest for self."

"I had always felt there must be more to God and religion than what I found in church," said Burnett. "The Ram seemed to be that 'more.' The intensity of feeling that occurred during a Dialogue was the result, the Ram told us, of his raising the soul vibrations of the people he was communicating with.

"It was not unusual for people attending a Dialogue for the first time to be uneasy or apprehensive, as there was a nervous feeling that the Ram had established contact with them even before they got there.

"Many of the people were sure someone had come beforehand and told the Ram about their private lives; the Ram was so bewilderingly accurate."

After a slow start, people had flocked to JZ's Dialogues. Her lifestyle changed dramatically. Money poured in and she was able to indulge a lifelong interest in Arabian horses, which she now felt she had ridden long ago with the great Ramtha and with some as yet unnamed person for whom she felt an unexpressed longing, someone not yet on the scene. It was a hungry yearning, a burning that would not be extinguished, but which she knew was to be satisfied even though she seemed happily married at that time.

I had listened to the story intently, not interrupting, for fear of distracting them, but it seemed to me that it could all be put down to an impressionable mind hungry for recognition.

"You must know," I said, "that you see with the brain. You can close your eyes and see whatever you like."

"Whatever I saw with," she said, "I saw the Ram."

In the beginning there were moments when she thought she was stark, raving mad. "I thought I must be possessed. I turned to the churches for help, thinking they would have some knowledge of satanic influences and rid me of whatever it was that was plaguing me."

She called a Presbyterian church, having been raised in that denomination. She told her story over the phone, and was told she had a devil in her and they didn't want any devils around.

"Call the Catholic church," they said.

She called a Catholic church and was told they didn't deal with demons either. "I asked if I could come to their church, and they said, 'No, Ma'am, we don't want you bringing anything like that into our church.'

"We called the Methodist church, the Baptist, the Assembly of God, and they would hang up."

Finally, she flipped through the telephone book and the heading—Churches-Spiritualist—leaped out.

Phoning one of these churches at random, they were finally received. One of the spiritualists offered to hold a seance to see whether this great Ramtha would come through.

"What would you say," asked JZ of the medium, "if I told you I had a Great One with me?"

"What would you say," said the medium, reaching out with her own antenna, "if I told you I believed you?"

There was a silence, and then Ramtha, as if responding to what had just been said, began to come through JZ in a most powerful way.

A look of awe came into the medium's eyes.

"I feel someone in robes around me," she said. "As if, I touched these robes, I would be touched by greatness."

The Ram now told them things that had not even been hinted at before. For the first time he explained why he had picked an obscure Tacoma housewife for his channel. She, JZ, stated the Ram, had been his beloved daughter in some distant time, his companion in peace and war, his sweet reminder of a time when his word was law. Burnett, too, had lived at that time as one of her father's warriors. It had been arranged for them to marry, but he was killed off in battle. She was just as well pleased, for when her father's young robesman looked at her, her knees quaked. He made her feel a woman though she was only fourteen.

They hadn't married because of her single-minded devotion to her father. It was a regret she had plainly brought into this life. There was a wistful note in JZ's voice as she spoke of this soulmate, even though Burnett was sitting next to her.

Obviously, this soulmate had not yet arrived, or we three would not be together as we were, watching the waves lap peacefully at the steps of my beach house. I looked at Burnett, but he did not seem to attach any importance to JZ's soulmate fantasy. He seemed very sure of himself.

The Ram's message for JZ, that day with the medium, was a memorable one:

"Oh, beautiful wise one, we hail your new knowledge and the great deeds you will perform. We salute you with lights from heaven."

Staring into the sky, they saw a huge ball of light sail low over the house, envelop them in its brilliance, and illuminate the heavens. The light was so dazzling that JZ hid her eyes.

What they saw was seen by thousands of others. The radio blared with frantic reports of UFOs and falling comets. If it was a hallucination, it was not theirs alone.

JZ had many things to think out. Not only of Dialogues, but of soulmates and life continuous. Having had trouble myself with reincarnation, I wondered how she had accepted it so readily. The Bible, she said, had predisposed her to this belief, though contemporary Christianity itself did not accept rebirth in new and different bodies. She had been only fourteen, in Bible class in Artesia, New Mexico, little Judy (the Zebra) Hampton, when her young mind was moved by Jesus telling the Jewish leader Nicodemus, "Marvel not that I said unto thee, Ye must be born again. That which is born of the flesh is flesh; and that which is born of the spirit is spirit."

She had asked her mother about it and her mother turned away. She questioned the minister and he only shook his head. She never went back to Bible class, but all these years the words kept turning in her head.

The advent of the Ram had made JZ restless, acutely sensitive to this unnamed yearning stirring inside her. She kept thinking of the young robesman, and conjured glowing pictures of him in her mind. There was a sense of tenderness and understanding associated with this fantasy. For what else could it be but fantasy, she told herself.

Privately, though not with calculated secrecy, she had asked the Ram one day how a person would know his soulmate, as distinguished from ordinary love or infatuation. As he often did the Ram answered with a question.

"Would you be happy to meet *you*? So prepare yourself, so you will be happy with yourself. Start dealing with aspects of thine self that you do not like. What you create in yourself you shall find. The soulmate is a mirror, and the mirror reflects itself perfectly. The neurotic reaches out for the neurotic, the negative for the negative, and so forth. That is why marriages fail. They have not prepared themselves. Looking for their counterpart, they find it."

The Ram was not one to deal in generalities. "What you need you will find without searching, in the most unexpected way."

She was unhappy, feeling that Burnett had become more interested in the Ram than in her. But she had no thought of separation. For one thing, she wasn't sure if the Ram would approve.

Constantly, the Ram put thoughts in her mind. She kept dreaming about playing the piano, and felt impelled to buy a baby grand, much to Burnett's chagrin, for it was expensive and she couldn't play a note. One night, unable to sleep, strange music surging inside her, she marched downstairs and sat down at the piano. She felt electric sparks flying through her hands. The music flowed from her heart out through her fingers. As she played she saw the Ram watching her, giving her a little encouraging smile. Roused by the music, Burnett and her two children slipped down to listen. A young neighbor, a pianist, listening over the phone, said incredulously, "That's the greatest piano I ever heard."

By this time, JZ's Dialogues were getting recognition in Washington State and elsewhere. But she found as time went on, her new life was not always fulfilling. She was still depressed at times, even with the success and adulation that came from channeling Ramtha the Ram.

"Sometimes," she said, "I feel so empty, as if my very heart ached."

Still, she and Burnett appeared as happy and harmonious as most couples I knew. I saw no clouds on the horizon.

I was anxious to witness a Dialogue with the Ram, and

to listen to JZ at the piano as well. If she could play the piano like a virtuoso, without a single lesson, then maybe there was something to our friend the Ram. The piano seemed a connecting link between her and this all-powerful one.

"Why was it so important to the Ram that you play the piano?" I asked.

"It wasn't for Ramtha," she said, "but for me. It showed me God as an unlimited creative force. For Ramtha only spoke for Him. I knew then that the God within us has no limitations if we but know how to invoke Him."

The Ram had also told her to paint. She painted without a lesson, painting the likenesses of people she had never seen, depicting jewelry and attire they habitually wore, even though she had been given no clue as to their appearance.

As we got to know each other better, she turned her conversation increasingly to soulmates, perhaps because she knew I was doing a book on the subject.

"Is there a soulmate for everybody?" she asked.

"Why not ask the Ram?" I said.

"I'm afraid," she replied, "that he might be judgmental."

Noting JZ's frequent allusion to soulmates, I wondered what would happen if one should actually turn up. Edgar Cayce had said a married partner should do the best he could with what he had, where he was, working through adversity to improve his karma. On the other hand, was it unreasonable to hope for some small smidgen of joy that would let us know the good Lord forgave us the frailties with which He had endowed us?

Out of curiosity, finally, I attended a Dialogue in Los Angeles, at Anne-Marie Bennstrom's ashram for the stars. I was not disappointed. For as Joan Hackett had intimated, it was quite a show. In trance, JZ was an entirely new personality. She sat erect in a chair, her jaw set, her eyes agleam with a penetrating presence. Her voice was sharp and staccato, with a positiveness richly ribbed with humor.

Even the glamorous stars in attendance had their questions about soulmates, and the Ram made it clear that ideally it was a condition to be earned. "Love thyself," the Ram said, "for in so loving you find that which you love as well."

After a while, still in trance, JZ, or the Ram, stood up and began pacing the aisles. Her eyes finally fixed on me. There was no hint of recognition. She came close to me, peerng into my eyes, and then her face broke into a knowing smile. "You shall find your soulmate," she said, in her harsh voice, "because of your book. It shall be a great success. Ramtha will see to that." He poked at me with JZ's finger. "And you shall write on Ramtha also, and it will become a movie."

I didn't know what to make of it. I had noticed Joan Hackett, and other stars as well, all raptly attentive. But for the most part it was a nondescript audience, what one would find in the average adult education class.

As I looked about, the Dialogue ended, and I could see Anne-Marie Bennstrom eyeing me with a sympathetic smile. She understood my confusion thoroughly.

A celebrated conditioner of people's minds and bodies, she was more knowledgeable than most. The metaphysical held few secrets for her.

"You are looking at a remarkable talent," she said, "but unfortunately she feels incomplete, through her belief in her need for a soulmate."

"And how would that help?" I asked.

We were standing a little to a side, watching as Burnett guided JZ away from the throng.

"You don't really know yourself," Anne-Marie smiled, "until you see the recognition of what you are in the eyes of the person who loves you."

"How do you know you have chosen correctly?"

"In the ideal relationship, twin souls, two souls merge into one, and there is no longer a divided energy. With this completion comes a sense of the totality of self."

Her eyes followed JZ out of the room. "We are only that which we want to become. JZ is still searching. Once we become something we cease to reflect it. We are it, and need search no more."

Her eyes turned to Caterina, her beautiful blonde assistant, like herself from Sweden. "The most perfect state," she said, with a nod for Caterina, "is a merging of two Higher Selves in a Cosmic Consciousness. Fundamentally, we are searching for the God within ourselves, our immortality, and this takes a knowingness that only a polarity of soulmates can assure."

She nodded again toward Caterina, who was looking especially radiant. "She owes much to the Ram. You might say he located her soulmate for her. Not that Caterina was looking.

She was happy, living each day as she found it, so busy she didn't know what she might be missing."

The Ram had picked her out in a crowded room, pointing to her in a very dramatic fashion.

"I am going to make a woman of you," Ramtha told the carefree Caterina, who was known around Anne-Marie's ashram as the "court jester," the Laughing Saint of Calabasas.

Caterina gulped a bit, but smiled good-naturedly.

"As you will," she said with a laugh.

"In two weeks," the Ram continued, "you will receive a red box in the mail with a reminder of yourself in it. This will foreshadow the arrival of your soulmate."

At the appointed time a gift box arrived as described, a figure of a clown inside. Caterina saw the connection immediately, for she was happily given to playing the clown.

She waited with some amusement for the appearance of her soulmate.

Golf promoter Ken Young was an unlikely candidate. He was considerably older, twice married and divorced. But when he showed up for Anne-Marie's conditioning program, Caterina and he realized almost at once that they belonged together. Three months later they were married on a hilltop near Anne-Marie's ashram. The Ram performed the ceremony.

Joan Hackett's thumbnail description of the Ram had intrigued me, for I knew her to be a highly sensitive and perceptive individual who had seen the Ram as a positive force in her life. But as I spoke to her later over dinner, Joan still couldn't decide whether Ramtha was really an entity of his own, or a dramatization of JZ's subconscious mind in some altered state of consciousness.

At this time, though I was not aware of it, Joan was fighting a losing battle with cancer, and would only live another three months. But aside from faint fatigue lines on her face, one would have never known she was ill. She was her usual witty self, mimicking the Ram's distinctive delivery until we found ourselves laughing uncontrollably.

She had been introduced to JZ—and the Ram—by an actor friend, Richard Chamberlain. They had gone to a meeting room, near Ventura, California, which looked to Joan like a large stable or barn. About thirty people were present, a typical cross section, young and old, rich and poor, skeptic and believer. Joan was intrigued by the Ram's performance.

"I thought it the worst piece of acting I ever saw but the best act."

The Ram had only good news for her professionally, presented with a positiveness that brooked no argument.

"You will make more movies," the Ram told her, "and you will win high honors in your profession. I will send you three offers in three days, and in one you will play a woman who is very much like you."

He may have read the actress's expression, for he quickly added:

"Have no fear, I will manifest it, so all will happen as I say."

The Ram had said help would come through "a man of humor." Joan had thought this purely a figure of speech. She didn't see how this particular "man of humor" could help in any case. He was constantly referring to her as a kook and crazy, good-naturedly perhaps, but still in a way that would cause studios to hesitate about signing a star that could be troublesome. But when asked about Joan for a lead in Neil Simon's *Only When I Laugh,* he said simply that she would be perfect. And so she got the part, which not only won her the Oscar nomination, but also the Golden Globe Award of the international body of film critics. She made two other pictures, quickly, including *The Escape Artist,* produced by Francis Ford Coppola, the producer of *The Godfather.* They were not quite as successful but still won her the plaudits of the critics.

As a keen observer, Joan had been struck by the apparent attachment between JZ and Burnett. She had particularly noted Burnett's intense interest in everything the Ram said, and his quick concern after she completed a long and grueling Dialogue.

"As she sat limply, completely drained, he would massage the tension from her neck and shoulders, until the color returned to her face and she seemed at one with herself. He appeared completely devoted, and if you had told me they were soulmates, I would not have been surprised."

There was a curious, almost sad smile on Joan's lips as she bid me goodbye.

"My next question to the Ram," she said, "shall concern my soulmate."

"Oh, do you have one?" I asked.

"Oh, no," she smiled, "I want one. I'm sure the Ram can do it if anybody can. But," she sighed, "we have so little time."

CHAPTER 10

The Eternal Triangle

As others, I had been impressed by the solidarity of J and Burnett. Even the name JZ Burnett seemed to su her. I had no intimation that anything was seriousl wrong. Then one day, I received a long distance call from he out of the blue. We chatted for a while, and then she said rather abruptly:

"You know, I have found my soulmate."

"I know," I said.

And then, of course, I learned it was not Burnett.

"I don't know what to do," she said, "I'm very happ about it in one way, unhappy in another."

It came as no great surprise, for there was no huma relationship, I had found, that was not subject to alteration But I wondered about the children. They were by a previou marriage but Burnett had considered them as his own, an there was noticeable affection on both sides.

"That is a problem," she sighed. "They love Burnett, h has been wonderful with them."

I knew nothing of the other man, his name or pedigree

"How can you be sure," I asked, "when you were sur about Burnett?"

"I didn't have to think about this one," she said. "I didn

even have to see him. I picked up a magazine, and there he was on a horse. Oddly, the picture was so shaded I could hardly make out his face, but it had an overwhelming assault on my senses. Don't ask how I knew, but I knew I had known him before, and knew as well that our relationship was inevitable. That could have accounted for my interest in horses, it was designed to bring us together."

And what did Ramtha think of all this? Wasn't he the great authority on human problems?

"He told me to thine own self be true."

I laughed. "In other words you have to figure it out for yourself."

I had nothing to add, for what could one person tell another about love, except that it, too, would pass unless cherished and renewed?

I mentioned how much I liked Burnett.

She sighed.

"Mark's a fine man, but I do wish he wasn't so preoccupied with the Ram. You would almost think it came through him."

She had no idea what she was going to do.

"Sometimes," I said, "if you do nothing, the situation takes care of itself."

When she rang off there was disappointment in her voice. But there were no easy solutions for affairs of the heart, not even for soulmates.

We stayed in touch, through friends, like Anne-Marie Bennstrom and Shirley MacLaine. But they were strangely mum about this new diversion, perhaps feeling it would break up like so many romances against the hard rock of reality.

Some time passed before I next saw JZ and Burnett. She had called from Tacoma to invite me for a weekend. I detected a new ring in her voice, a gaiety and laughter I had not noticed before. She seemed happy, radiant, awash with good spirits.

"Anything new?" I said.

She laughed gaily. "That's for you to find out."

Shirley MacLaine and her daughter Sachi were to be there as well. It looked like a very special weekend. And it was. On this occasion I met Jeffrey Knight, a young horse trainer from the rural outskirts of Los Angeles, who had been engaged by JZ to handle the Arabian horses she was eagerly acquiring.

I didn't know who he was, or how he fit in. He was no more than twenty-five, some ten years younger than JZ, with brown hair and dark complexion. He was pleasant-looking, without being handsome, unobtrusive, usually speaking only when spoken to. I wondered for a time if he was an Indian, he seemed so expressionless, and so much inside himself. Not until we all went out to dinner did I realize he was part of the household. I began to notice little things that had not previously caught my attention. There was a studied politeness between Burnett and the newcomer, and a tension in Burnett I hadn't seen before. Also there was a tendency on JZ's part to deliberately include Jeffrey in the conversation.

"And what do you think of reincarnation?" she would ask.

The question appeared to embarrass him. He would have liked nothing better than to keep in the shadows. At this point, he mumbled something, quite unintelligible to me, and it was months before I discovered that from boyhood he had memories of past-life experiences that still haunted him.

I wasn't quite sure what the equation was. For all I knew he was merely an adviser. He certainly didn't look the part of a Romeo, nor was JZ a Juliet. She had been a business executive in the television cable field, twice married, a mother, and she was of a spiritual, if not religious, bent. And I could tell from the way she spoke to him that she still cared for Burnett.

But as the evening wore on, I gained the impression that young Jeffrey was around to stay. There was no familiarity at the table, no token of endearment or affection. But there was a curious vibration, an electric polarity reflected in the simplest gesture, even to the routine passing of a plate.

Burnett himself acknowledged that he wasn't quite sure what was going on. "I'm hanging on," he said, "hoping it will all work out."

It was obviously a delicate situation. I looked to Shirley to see how she was taking it, and could glean nothing from her face. She was a consummate actress.

I studied JZ without seeming to. She was obviously more relaxed. She laughed frequently and there was a joyful tone in her voice. She was a happier person. So I decided.

JZ seemed amused by my attention, and drew me aside.

"I know," she said, "you're busting to know how it all happened."

I smiled. "And you're busting to tell me."

Her eyes danced. "I was leafing through this breeder's book, looking for some blooded stock. Suddenly, my eye was struck by this horse and then moved to the trainer. I couldn't see his face completely, he was wearing a cowboy hat. But as I looked at the picture, my heart told me he was my soulmate. In that split second I knew we belonged together. The feeling was so strong it almost zapped me out."

I thought of Mark holding on, trying to save the marriage. "What of Burnett?"

She shook her head. "We haven't been on the same wavelength since the Ram came. It was as though the Ram's coming marked a new cycle in our lives. Mark became enamored of the Ram, and would ask whether it was me or the Ram saying something. If I said it was me, he would twiddle his thumbs or turn to a book. He got so wrapped up in whatever the Ram said that I started doing the Dialogues by myself."

Without stopping to think about it, she had picked up the phone and dialed the horse ranch asking for the trainer.

"How much," she asked, "is the horse you have for sale?"

His voice was just what she would have expected, soft yet firm. But the answer took the wind out of her.

"Three hundred thousand dollars. A quarter share for seventy-five thousand."

"I'll have to meditate on it," said JZ.

"Oh, so you meditate. So do I," he said in that caressing voice that sent a thrill through her.

As she was on the phone, Burnett loudly observed that the last thing they needed was another horse. But JZ wanted a look at the horse, and its trainer. She planned to be in Los Angeles in a few days for a Dialogue and invited him to attend. It was to be at the Beverly Hills home of Richard Chamberlain.

Although there were many people in the room, they recognized each other instantly. No words had to be spoken. The understanding was implicit. She asked him to help her with her horses. He didn't hesitate, agreeing to move to Tacoma.

He had a strict upbringing, with strong Catholic roots. But as he dissected his feelings, he felt no lust, or carnal desire, only a feeling of having his loneliness assuaged. Unlike other youths his age he had not run around, staying so much by himself his family thought something was wrong with him. It was almost as if he had been holding himself back, waiting.

There was a tie, a yearning between them, but they loved Burnett and felt a confusion of loyalties. Meanwhile, the weeks passed, without the relationship getting any closer. JZ was saddled with guilt, and Jeff had no intention of declaring himself.

"I don't even know if he loves me," she said despondently. "He tells me he has nothing to offer but what's in his suitcase. He doesn't know if he will ever have anything. He tells me how much he admires Burnett and what a perfect husband he seems."

How could she tell him she couldn't sleep nights, as she lay next to Burnett, seeing not Burnett but Jeffrey, and that slow intriguing smile she had come to love.

"I don't know how it will all end," she cried, "but I'm only happy when Jeffrey is near me. I know it isn't fair to Burnett, but there is nothing more I can give him."

We seemed to have gotten away from Ramtha, and what this great wise master felt about them as soulmates.

She smiled with a flash of her earlier radiance.

"On the day I first saw that picture of Jeffrey, the Ram said: 'Prepare yourself. You are about to become a woman.' "

"Can he make it happen for you?" I said, recalling what Joan Hackett had said.

"Yes, but I still have to work for it."

"Suppose this is only infatuation, and you throw your marriage away?"

"That is already gone, or Jeffrey would not be in my life." She paused a moment. "As he was once before."

My head popped up.

"You mean, you actually recall Jeffrey?"

"Not in this life," she said, "but we were all together before. Burnett was the warrior I was to have married, the one killed in battle. We were to complete that chapter, which we have."

"And Jeffrey?"

She had a twinkle in her eye. "You don't know?"

She gave a gay little laugh.

"He was my father's robesman, the youth for whom I had been waiting for thousands of years."

I knew then it was only a matter of time.

By the time I saw JZ again, there were many changes in her life. She had now become a worldwide figure, known abroad as well as at home, her Dialogues popularized in tape and print. And wherever she went she was accompanied by her new soulmate. Burnett was no longer in the picture.

I had flown again to Tacoma to see them. They had vacated the house she had shared with Burnett, and were living outside the city on a ranch stocked with purebred Arabians. It was a scene of domestic bliss. The house was small but they were planning to enlarge it. The barn was large and modern. The investment was already bearing fruit. JZ had already sold one horse for a sizable sum, and had other offers. They seemed happy and relaxed together, and the children, Brandy and Chris, appeared to relate to Jeff as they had to Mark.

Mark was behind her, and she and Jeff were planning to marry after the divorce. This was their first Thanksgiving together, and they were a bit tired, having just flown in from a Boston Dialogue. But they were optimistic and upbeat, full of plans for the ranch and the Work.

At mealtime, I looked closely, if a little covertly, to determine the magic that had brought them together. It did not strike me immediately, the conversation was casual, what you would find in almost any home with couples fond of each other. I noted the easy warmth between Jeffrey and the children, thinking this essential to a lasting relationship, but still not insuring it.

Jeff didn't say much, but what he did say was to the point. Despite the ten-year difference in their ages, there was little question he was the head of the household, and that she encouraged this role.

After the children left the table, they felt free to discuss their situation frankly. The transition had not been easy. Here she was telling other people how to live their lives, and she didn't know what was right or wrong herself.

As her confusion grew, she didn't know which way to turn. And so, one day, she slipped into a light meditation and invoked the Ram's presence.

The Ram immediately appeared. He wore a sad smile, and there was an unaccustomed gentleness in his voice.

"You have lost sight of your purpose," he said.

She looked up, stunned, not understanding.

"Is it wrong," she asked, "to desire happiness? If God loves us, as you say, why do we have so much unhappiness?"

"You are incomplete in yourself," the voice came back. "You can have all the kingdoms in the world. But it won't make you happy because you are not happy with yourself."

"But my purpose, was that not to bring happiness to others?"

"No, first and foremost, to love thyself. For unless you have peace within yourself you can help nobody. Think not so much of what others think of you, but of what you think of yourself. That is where happiness lies."

Obviously, unless she was making it all up, this information was silently channeling through her own subconscious. And as one thought about it, it didn't matter much whether she was dramatizing this subconscious, or there was actually a Ramtha in the doorway, grinding out messages and scattering out lights all over the globe—if it worked.

So later, when Mark had asked what would make her happy, she said, "Moving in with Jeff."

"And," said Jeff, joining in for the first time, "when I asked what would make her happy, she said moving in with me. I realized then that it didn't matter that Mark could provide for her better. If you loved one another, and completed one another, if your feelings for each other eased your nakedness and aloneness, then it didn't matter that you didn't have a dime."

"Especially," I said, looking at the field of grazing horses, "when you have far more than that."

It had not all been roses, but their conduct together was a model for soulmates. They traded off their insecurities, airing them openly. Jeff didn't feel he was educated enough, substantial enough. She didn't feel young enough, beautiful enough.

"I would watch *Dynasty* on television, and she would get upset, thinking I was watching because of the beautiful women on the show. She had this complex on being older, which was all through her eyes, not mine. But we would get it out, examine it, and resolve this insecurity. And she would offset my insecurities by letting me know how much she relied on my judgment in buying horses, and how the ranch would have been nowhere without that."

They considered something else the Ram had said:

"Deal with the aspects of your being that cause unhappiness, then create in self that ideal which you want in your soulmate, thrust out anger, fear, and insecurity. By knowing yourselves, translate unhappiness into happiness, as reflected in the eyes of your soulmate."

As Jeff smiled, I caught a glint of hard resolve in the dark eyes.

"It's important," he said, "that people know that being soulmates doesn't make everything automatically perfect. Otherwise, there would be nothing to overcome and you wouldn't learn anything."

The former stable hand was growing. And so were the Dialogues. A happier JZ had brought out a more expansive Ramtha. The teachings had branched out into the counseling of the Lord God Jehovah, the number of people attending the Dialogues had tripled, and they were now taking place, ironically, in churches, as well as friendly homes and halls.

"We are booked solid for the next two years," JZ said, with an inclusive smile for Jeff.

I could see positive changes in them. He was still quiet, but with the quiet of assurance, not uncertainty. When he spoke there was a reason. His words added to the conversation. She deferred to him, even with the children. She respected the discipline he had brought into the home, a discipline to which the children responded grudgingly at first, then eagerly, as they realized it came from caring. In a way, it was easier for him. Not too many years out of their generation, he clearly understood their problems, having only recently left them himself.

Sure of each other, their empathy for each other grew. Jeff gave her a horse, for horses were his first love. And with only a couple of lessons from him, she could ride like a professional. This was something they could do now as equals. Both accepted equality in all things, mutual support in all endeavors. They were on the same wavelength.

"He doesn't interpret the Ram for me," said JZ, "but permits me to share the Ram with him, just as he shares his knowledge of horses with me. We each have our place, and defer to each other's strengths."

They had continuing help from the Ram. "Think about living and being happy," he counseled. "Once you are in a state of happiness you do not contemplate the end of anything—but the ongoing."

Through meditation they invoked memories of other lives together. In one of these lives, they had argued, and he had gone off in a rage. He returned to find her chatting with another man. He had been so jealous, so insecure, he turned and stalked off. "We never saw each other again in that lifetime," he recalled. "I didn't want this happening again. So now, when we have arguments and upsets, I make sure everything is settled on the spot. I don't want to lose her through some ego trip."

Meanwhile, the rumors were flying in Dialogue-land. Burnett had become a sympathetic figure, and many questions were put to JZ along the road, questions of loyalties and love. The Ram had been a rock his followers could lean on, and now that rock appeared none too secure itself. They realized some explanation was due the people she had given the Ram. She had brought them a ray of hope, some sense of stability, some feeling of a more enduring quality in their own relationships. And now many were confused by the turn of events.

The same thought ran through her. "How could I tell people to be faithful and loyal when I didn't appear that way myself? How could I teach what I didn't live by?"

She decided to take her case to her public.

And so she poured her heart out to the very people who had poured out their hearts to her. "In their response I got a perspective of my relationship with Jeff. We had been honest and forthright, not shabby or shoddy, loving, not indifferent, for we had not once stopped caring for Burnett."

They made their stand in New York City. Jeff had hung back at first, not wanting to intrude. "We are together in this and all things," JZ told him. "What you or I say and think comes from the oneness of us."

They faced a tractable audience. A few were challenging, but by and large the group wanted to be convinced.

"Does this now mean," a girl asked, "that you two are

ready for something new and wonderful, not just making money?"

JZ fielded this one.

"As you expand your life, your values change and hope-fully improve."

Having been told JZ and Jeff were joined inexorably as soulmates, some wanted to know how many find their soulmates as they had.

"Not that many," said JZ, "since so many marry because of social advantages. New doors open for soulmates because they demand the best in one another. The Ram says the call is not heard by the ears but by the soul. They could be on the moon and they would meet. Because you are aware, knowing the other exists for you, you attract your soulmate. That was how it was with Jeff and myself, we reached out and made the situation happen."

How did they meet, and when did they begin to know? These were the questions put to Jeffrey, these and how it was finally resolved. Jeff answered easily, a far cry from the stolid horseman I had first met as he retold their story.

"I was ready," he said. "I was never much for dating. I concentrated on my horses and that brought me together with JZ. When we spoke on the phone, I felt a strange yearning for her even then. So when she said she was giving a lecture at Richard Chamberlain's, I jumped at the invitation. I saw many famous people walking in and wasn't too impressed with any-body until she came in. I knew it was she right off. My heart skipped a beat. She came right over to me, and said that from the picture she couldn't tell what I looked like, but she would know me anywhere."

He was fascinated as she became the Ram. Her voice and features changed. She spoke like a man. For a while, he forgot she was JZ, even as the Ram came through with a message for him. Now he was hearing that in all his various lives, he had been afraid to go over the mountain, make a decision, and take the future in his hands.

"But now in this lifetime, I would achieve what I had never accomplished before, a spiritual union with my true soulmate."

Later, but before they got together, he had pointedly

asked the Ram if they were soulmates. And the Ram had answered typically with a question. "Do you love her greatly?"

And he said, "Indeed, I do," and then asked, "Will I meet my soulmate in this life?"

The Ram answered:

"Indeed you will."

But a sense of morality held him back.

"He asked how I felt about JZ, if I loved her like a lover loves a lover. I stopped for a minute, thinking of Burnett, and this beautiful family, and I said no, I feel close to her . . . but I didn't feel I could make her happy. I was not enough of a man for her, not enough to make her happy. So I wound up saying I loved her more as a friend than a lover."

There were rough days for the two of them after that. Listening to the tape, JZ felt rejected and told Jeff that friends it would be then. At this time of crisis the Ram, speaking through JZ, of course, took a hand again.

"He said it was time that I became a man and faced up to my responsibilities. If she was my soulmate, then we belonged with each other. Mark wasn't the problem anymore, I saw that now. I was. Mark could do whatever he wanted, control his own life. Whereas I saw now that I was not in control of my life. I was letting others influence my decisions."

What JZ wanted was what the Ram wanted, and on this happy note the affair was resolved.

Jeff had a pointer for the group. "The Ram said you reach heights of ecstasy and the depths of depression, and that made us know each other. Knowing each other, we knew how to bring our lives together, and how to help others. Without being together, we could help nobody, including ourselves."

As JZ stood radiantly at his side, he saluted her as his one and only soulmate.

"She made me a man, for which I am undyingly grateful to her. For had I not been this man, knowing what it was to come to grips with a tough situation, I would not be with this woman. For with the Ram she made me the man I've become, confident to be with a lady loved by so many people for what she has done for them."

The meeting was a great success. The people stamped and cheered, and hugged them both. For the world will always cherish lovers, as long as love lives on.

It was an ongoing story, reaching a new phase with their marriage in July of 1983, a ceremony, they felt, that only documented the love revived in this lifetime with a glance at a man on a horse.

But before any of this happened, I had one request of JZ. It had been on my mind since I met her.

She looked at me inquiringly, a smile on her lips.

"Would you like a Dialogue with the Ram?" she asked.

I shook my head. "No," I said. "I would like to hear you play the piano."

She moved with alacrity to her music bench.

Her fingers tripped lightly over the keys, the white keys. I had listened in my youth to recitals by Rachmaninoff and Paderewski. But I had never heard anything like this. The music stirred me as I had not been stirred for years. It invaded the senses, capturing mind, heart, and soul. I sat enthralled, unable to think, completely possessed by the fury of the keys.

"Who wrote it?" I cried as her fingers finally slid off the keyboard—"Beethoven, Tchaikowsky, Chopin?"

She moved her head slightly.

"Ramtha the Ram," she said. "His symphonic tribute to soulmates."

There was music at their wedding, though she did not play.

The ceremony was attended by friends from all over the world. I cheerfully noted a sharp break from tradition, so typical of soulmates. Instead of being given away by relatives, the pair marched down the aisle, arm in arm, and gave themselves away. There was not a dry eye in the assembly, as they were joined together in an individualized rite performed by Anne-Marie Bennstrom. Even the background music revealed the special character of the union. From the popular song, "I Needed You," the phrase rang out, "You gave me strength to stand alone." Every lover in the room touched his or her partner, as their eyes misted over in tribute to this greatest of all gifts from one soul to another.

Anne-Marie spoke of twin columns that stood apart, not leaning one on another, but giving love a firm foundation of freedom and trust. She handed them two candles, and as they merged the two flames with that of a larger candle, she said softly:

"Behold the twin flames joined into one. May this still and steady flame bring the bright light of knowingness to guide your steps into the realm of Foreverness."

It was a message not only for the radiant couple but for lovers everywhere:

"Know that this union is but a grander union with God, through which you become aware of your own wholeness and special place in the Universe.'"

She handed Jeffrey the wedding ring, and he repeated after her:

"Beloved woman, mate of my soul, body of my body, heart of my heart, I take you into my being, to merge and blend with the totality of that which I am. I will walk beside you through the Seasons of time when our love blooms and flowers, and into the winter of our years when we pause to reflect on the grandeur of our love. I will be by your side forever, with no armor save that of love. And with that love I will shield and protect you for as long as we know time."

And with this, Jeffrey put the ring on his bride's finger. They were one.

I had not expected Mark Burnett to be there, as the day belonged to the radiantly happy couple. But I had wondered how he was faring, and called him before leaving Seattle.

While I had not known what to expect, I was not quite prepared for a smiling, happy Burnett, looking some ten years younger. He greeted me with a hearty handshake, then turned to an attractive young lady, who was looking at him with a love-light in her eye.

"This is Trish," he said, "Trish Eubanks."

Over breakfast they soon brought me up to date. They had met at a Ram Dialogue three years before, when Burnett was still with JZ, and Trish, too, was heavily involved with someone. Once both were free, their friendship flourished at various Arabian horse shows each attended.

"I felt as if I had always known him," said Trish, "as if there had never been anybody else."

He agreed pleasantly. It had taken some time, but he was more than ready for her now.

After the separation Burnett had gone through the soul-searching process common to soulmates who have been painfully parted.

"The breakup was devastating," he said. "My commitment to JZ and the boys had been total. When it became clear that JZ did intend to go with Jeff, I spent months trying to get my life reoriented. I had no interest in dating. I had considered ours a true soulmate relationship. I was thoroughly disillusioned, but I had learned from life that good could be gleaned from any experience. I now remembered many of the things the Ram had said in his wisdom."

He smiled a little self-consciously.

" 'Love yourself, go within, cultivate a relationship with the inner self,' the Ram said.

"There were times when I would just think about something, and notice the next day that it happened."

He had read my book *The Power of Alpha Thinking* and had found it helpful in explaining the far-ranging powers of the subconscious mind.

"By working with my intuition, recalling the Ram's advice about improving one's attitude, I had gone through a healing process. I stopped blaming myself, JZ, and the Dialogues. Oddly, I had never blamed Jeff. I saw now that I had become a secondary concern in my own life, I had been afraid of change—any change.

"Once I realized this, I knew how to make my life better. The more I related to the intuitive self, to my true inner feelings, the more comfortable I was with myself and the more open my life became.

"A year after JZ and I parted, I ran into Trish casually at a horse show. I had not dated anybody at that point. Consequently, I was amazed at my intense reaction to her, equally amazed that I should have this reaction."

He had time to think about it. Trish, a corporate manager, had already planned a trip abroad. After she got back, Mark got in touch with her, and they made plans to see each other.

He smiled as he recalled that first date.

"Was there anything special?" I asked.

"I had planned on taking her to dinner. And I lay awake one whole night anticipating our being together. I couldn't understand why I was so nervous and excited. I had never had this feeling before. And yet underneath all the nervousness, there was a glow that promised a new tomorrow. I could hardly wait for the next day to dawn. As my mind turned to thoughts of where we should dine I suddenly heard a small voice saying, 'You have dined with her many times.' "

I looked at Trish to see how she was taking this.

She was smiling, too, and there was a gleam in her eyes.

"Had you a feeling then," I said, "that you had known Trish before?"

His brow furled for a moment.

"Yes," he decided. "I felt we were continuing what had gone before."

They were free now to exercise feelings and remembrances they had not had the opportunity to explore before.

They looked radiantly happy, and I wondered what their secret was.

"We don't concentrate on trying to make each other happy," Mark said. "We are both very independent and find this attractive in each other."

I was reminded again of what Gibran had said in *The Prophet* about two independent columns standing straight, not leaning on one another, to form a firm foundation. Had the Prophet not also said: "Let there be spaces in your togetherness."

The next time I saw them, they were engaged and planning to be married on a mountaintop.

"Why a mountaintop?" I asked.

"We want to be married," they said almost together, "somewhere enduring and ongoing, not in a mere building that crumbles with time."

I smiled.

"And you really believe you are eternal soulmates?"

They clasped hands and silently looked into each other's eyes. They had given me their answer.

CHAPTER 11

The Chinaman Rings a Bell

I t all began with the Chinaman—Yan Ling by name. Barry saw him first, and then Elizabeth. They had known each other for five years and almost from the day they met the Chinaman was of supreme importance to them. Not that Barry spoke of him incessantly. He didn't, only when there was a crisis in their lives; once when they considered breaking up and Elizabeth carried herself with a heavy heart, again when he spoke, as he often did, of the narrow line between life and death.

"I don't believe in death as people know it," Barry said. "It is a time to rest and prepare our souls for a new and stronger joust with life."

It helped, Elizabeth felt, that they had seen each other's faces long before they met. And so when their paths brought them thousands of miles to meet, it was as if they had always known one another. As if everything that had gone before was but a preparation for this union.

Like so many lovers they met seemingly by chance, though Elizabeth knew there was no such thing as chance, not in matters of the heart. There was light in Barry's eye, as though he had been expecting her for a dozen lifetimes. He took her hand, wrapped it gently in his, and said very simply:

"I was told I was going to meet you."

She looked at him curiously. She felt comfortable with him, magnetically drawn without knowing why, for it was not until later, in acknowledging her love, that she connected him with the face she had visualized years before.

"Who told you?" she asked.

He squeezed her hand, not answering, not ready yet to tell her about the Chinaman.

They had met at a casual dinner party in Hollywood and with other people about there was no opportunity for an intimate exchange after so dramatic an impact.

It seemed the most natural thing in the world for them to form a partnership. Elizabeth had been living in Los Angeles, putting together two pieces for *Billboard* on the emergence of women in music, and working on producing animated films. And Barry, an Australian, had done documentaries on aboriginal life. And so they worked together, and later on lived together. Barry wanted marriage, but Elizabeth felt their only commitment was to each other. No piece of paper could alter that.

They were on the brink of great projects, a feature film in China, another in Australia, and then, without any real warning, these plans were thrown into disarray. For in September of 1982, the hardy soul who thought death the other side of life, passed over in his sleep, while Elizabeth was in the next room reading. He was forty-four.

Elizabeth was inconsolable. She did not feel sad for Barry so much as for herself. Barry had talked of death as he would of taking a walk. "The gods won't let me die," he said, "until I finish what I came here to do."

Though we were friends, I had not seen Elizabeth for five years, not since she had come off a shattering romance with a man who had never made a commitment. For though divorced, he had never made a secret of his love for his ex-wife.

"Can't you see," I said at the time, "that it never had a chance?"

She gave me a mournful look. "But I saw his face as well, long before I met him. Didn't that mean anything?"

"Perhaps," I said, "the one relationship prepared you for the others." She was twenty-eight then, with a delicate beauty that looked like it could hardly weather a summer storm.

"Yes," she said, "Barry was truly my soulmate. His only

concern, as I see now, was for me. Yet he was so vital, so youthful, so brimming with expectations, that I don't understand why he decided to go."

I looked at her sharply.

"You mean he took his own life?"

"Oh no, nothing like that. But I remember him telling me he was ready, the Chinaman had done that for him."

I gazed at the pale, exquisite features, shaded with sorrow, and said severely, "You're not ready."

"I wish I were." She sighed. "If only I knew what to do."

"Did Barry give you any direct intimation of his passing?" I asked.

Her marble forehead furled into a frown.

"Just a few days before he passed, he told me, 'Have no fear. We will meet again.' "

The Chinaman, years before, had told Barry all this, when Barry was flying in China as a mercenary for the Chinese Air Force. And since he had also told him he would one day meet Elizabeth, there was no reason to disbelieve him now.

I was curious about the Chinaman. He had crept into her conversation inadvertently almost, but her mind seemed elsewhere.

"I had a dream about him," was all she would say at this point, "before Barry ever mentioned him to me."

"Are you sorry you didn't marry Barry?"

She smiled. "We were as married as anybody could be."

He had proposed not long after they met.

" 'Ferret,' he said, 'we're getting married.'

"He always called me Ferret, he had two pet ferrets when he was growing up, and they were always digging holes. He called me Ferret because I could always dig things out of him."

Her eyes were a little dewy.

"I just looked at him and smiled and thought, 'This guy doesn't even ask me.' He picked up the phone and called my mother in Merritt Island, Florida, and told her. He invited my brother and a bunch of other people to our engagement party and it was kind of a joke, because I still kept saying, 'Barry, you never asked me. Maybe I don't want to get married.' But it was really a fun time, and we got a lot of mileage out of the idea. But he had been married, and his divorce wasn't final. He had to wait a year before he filed, and the year wasn't up yet. So I said, 'First of all we can't get married because you're not divorced.' And he said, 'Okay, I know that. So we get married a year from now, but that's no reason we can't celebrate.' I said, 'All right, we'll see what happens in a year.' But a year later, when he had his divorce he saw it wasn't necessary. We were irrevocably bound together, so much in tune that we nearly always knew what the other was thinking."

She may have been drawn to Barry by some subconscious remembrance of a distant past. But it was his spiritual strength, his unfailing belief in their destiny that made her realize they were intended for each other, and that her earlier love had appeared only to make her appreciate more fully the depths of Barry's love.

"Of all the love I have to give," Barry told her, "I give you all."

They were incurable romanticists.

Their first Christmas together, when everything had gone wrong in a business way, and they had lost whatever money they had, he barely had enough to buy some flowers, which he sent with a poem to "The most beautiful person and love ever to enter into my present life. To whom I wish all she wishes for herself."

"Yan Ling," Barry wrote, "spoke of the strict testing of us. He knows it all—he knows—he knows."

I was no judge of poetry, but the sincerity was clear, even though it appeared somewhat in debt to Kipling.

The first morning of creation wrote what
The last dawn of reckoning shall read.
This I tell you in my predestined plot of
Dust and soul. Time unveils mystery
And yet that mystery to me is known.

I had no idea at this point what the Chinaman meant to either of them, but it did seem strange she should dream about the same man Barry had spoken to in China, without previously knowing about him.

"Was there any message?" I asked.

She shrugged, obviously coming to a decision. "I don't know. I'll just tell you the dream."

Elizabeth's eyes glowed and the depression that had taken

hold of her seemed to dissolve into an aura of golden light. "I was having this dream about a decision I had to make in my life, when the dream suddenly changed and I found myself with Barry on a train in China. I could tell where I was from the way people looked and dressed. I could gaze out the window and see the hills go by. I had the impression we were on a very urgent trip. We were going to see a Chinaman far across the mountains. We had to cross the mountains to get to him. Yet, while we were on the way, he kept appearing and talking to us. He was no ordinary human—he was as splendid and radiant as the sun, glowing with an immense light. At the same time, he was warm and gentle and wise and loving. He was the most wonderful being I had ever encountered. I felt it was Barry who was taking me to see him, for I sensed a very close rapport between Barry and the Chinaman. They seemed to be old friends. In the dream I was blind, not visually, but I knew my eyes were to be opened soon, and I would learn his connection to us and with it was a sense of impending doom."

When she woke up, she was profoundly moved. She looked about her quickly and saw that she was alone but for Barry. "I knew somehow there was a strong message for me and Barry and that Barry knew this personage." She kept turning it over in her head, wondering how Barry could be involved when it was her own little dream. Yet the conviction persisted.

She couldn't get back to sleep, she shook the sleeping Barry a few times, crying, "Damn it, who's the Chinaman?"

Barry immediately awoke. He looked at her, and said, "How do you know about the Chinaman? I've never told you about him." And then he said something that baffled her even more. "But I have been expecting you two to meet."

As she told him about her dream, he nodded. "Yes, I knew he would come to you sooner or later."

Both prided themselves on their contact with reality. And yet there was something not quite realistic about their perception of the Chinaman. Barry turned on the light, and sat up in bed talking at some length about his recollections.

"As he described him for me," Elizabeth said, "it fit in exactly with my own mental picture. Barry said that when the man walked he left no impression on the grass. Yet, when

Barry walked beside him, Barry saw his own footprints. It was very strange."

As Barry talked, she listened avidly, for she was eager to know all about the Chinaman. Barry had flown in Australia, and in China, working with young Chinese fliers and helping to write a flight manual for China's budding airforce. He had been flying alone over a deserted area in China when he spotted the Chinaman for the first time on the ground below. There was no sign of anybody else for miles. He seemed to have come out of nowhere. Just moments before, Barry had seen what looked like an oasis, and short of water decided to land his plane and investigate. As he looked about him, he saw the Chinaman standing by a well. The wind was blowing strongly, and Barry's hair and shirt billowed in the wind. He had trouble keeping his balance. But as he looked at the Chinaman he noticed his hair and beard were untouched by the wind. He opened a conversation, and they exchanged names. They talked on for a while and Barry got the impression the man was a great and good teacher. They parted with warm regards and the Chinaman said he would see him again one day soon.

Elizabeth was thrilled, for she had the same impression of the Chinaman in her dream. He was somebody to be reckoned with.

The Chinaman disappeared, to return later, when she and Barry were experiencing a crisis in their relationship, when she felt he was dominating her—even to telling her what to eat, wear, and do.

"I was questioning," she said, "whether our relationship was good or bad for us and trying to decide whether we should stay together. That night in a vision or dream I saw these four levels of Barry and myself and then all of a sudden, the four of him and the four of me became as one. They were like different levels of thought, finally merging into one. We were back in the center of the Earth. Barry reached his hand for mine and asked if I was ready and I said yes. I wasn't afraid because I knew I had control. We walked hand in hand into a tunnel.

"And as we walked through the tunnel there emerged a totally different world with all these people who weren't people, and they were timeless to me, existing at a higher level of consciousness. The Chinaman was there and I sat beside him, and in an atmosphere of incredible harmony I was given a great deal of information. There were books, papers, and pens, but no one was using them. The thoughts were flowing and the people knew what I was thinking and I knew what they were thinking and the visions started to speed up in time, and yet through it all Barry and I were still in our physical bodies.

"I can't say I awoke, for I was awake but in a trance state, and it was dawn. I was still very troubled. I was trying to understand my vision. Everything in it kept telling me I could not leave Barry. Something bigger and more powerful than myself was telling me that Barry and I must stay together, no matter how difficult it got. I sat there and knew I had made the choice centuries ago. Suddenly I knew Barry was on his way to my apartment at that very moment even though I had no reason to expect him. Five minutes later he knocked on my door. He already knew my decision. The Chinaman had told him."

And so the crisis passed, with their differences resolved, and their moving in together.

By this time I wondered what the Chinaman had to do with it all. Who was this Yan Ling that moved so fitfully in and out of their lives? And why did they listen?

"Was there really a Yan?" I asked.

She frowned.

"Barry said he saw him on several occasions."

"And you didn't question it?"

"Oh, I did, but he said the people in the villages told him they had seen Yan many times. He was known far and wide as a sage."

She had questioned Barry many times.

"Did you see his physical presence?" she had asked. "Was he external to you?"

"Yes, we talked together," Barry replied. "I asked him many questions and he answered me as well."

"Are you sure he wasn't a manifestation of your own mind?" she demanded.

"I keep telling you the village people saw him and talked to me about his wise sayings. Nobody was surprised when I asked about him."

As she frowned now, she suddenly seemed to age. She was like a chameleon, changing her aspect with her moods. Yet when she spoke of Barry and the Chinaman, she seemed like a carefree teenager, with the weight of the world taken from her shoulders.

"The Chinaman told Barry many things," she said, "and these were manifested in Barry's handwriting. I had a similar experience. After the Chinaman spoke in my dream I would start putting it down and I felt as if my hand was being guided."

Elizabeth had not heard from Yan for a while. And then, abruptly, he made his presence felt. Barry had been in London for two weeks, and she had been feeling low. She was in the kitchen that day, standing at the refrigerator when her knees buckled. She could barely make it to the bedroom. "All my energy had left me. I was on the verge of passing out, and as I lay there trembling, the face of Yan appeared.

" 'Do not be afraid,' he said. 'Your illness is temporary as are all things in this human existence. You will decide of your own choosing which existence shall be yours and for how long. I know of your journey and I am ready for you. But it is not time.' "

Energized and replenished, Elizabeth scrambled out of bed and feverishly wrote down everything Yan had ever said. She had come to where Barry and Yan were speaking together, and the phone rang. It was Barry from London, and he was very excited. He had, by chance, stumbled across Chinese friends in London, and they had discussed collaborating on a film in China. She was excited as well and recognized again how Yan's presence was interwoven with theirs. But, of course, Barry's death ended the project.

She had a sense of impending doom from childhood, and wondered if Yan could help with that. Two weeks before Barry's death it had come back with a renewed force, leaving her depressed and empty. She had a premonition of his death.

"Don't leave me," she cried.

"I'm not going anywhere," Barry smiled.

He had no concern for himself. He ventured casually into sections of the city where other people feared to go. She would warn, "Somebody will kill you." And he would smile and say, "That's their problem. I am ready. Yan has known that for some time."

Barry spoke at times of the Higher Self. Until one day, Elizabeth asked:

"Exactly what is this Higher Self, Barry?"

He thought for a moment.

"It is the essence of the human spirit," he said finally, "which, in attaining, man finds himself closest to God."

After his death she kept thinking of whatever related to his passing. Once he had said, "No man knows where he dies." He had pointedly not said *when*. And then he would say with a laugh, quoting, "Age shall not weary thee, as we who are left grow old."

He would speak of Jesus and His death at an early age. "He will always be young and vibrant, remembered by the slim, broken body He offered to the Cross, a supremely commanding figure that would never grow old."

Barry had asked to be cremated, in keeping with his belief that the body was leaving him, not he it. He and Elizabeth would join again in another thousand years, he promised. She should not mourn for this was but a wink in the eye of time. They had thought of the Chinaman as the Wayfarer and Elizabeth chose a funeral chapel, the Wayfarer, for Barry's memorial service. They had always liked Scottish things without knowing why. And so Elizabeth arranged for Scottish music, dear to both, from a tape of the Royal Scots Dragoon Guard. As the bagpipes swelled with the stirring chords of "Going Home" and "Amazing Grace," Elizabeth had a few last words for her departed soulmate. "True memories are not of mind and body but those that remain forever written on the soul."

Tender thoughts of what had passed between them flowed through her. She remembered the touch of his hand and lips, his constant questioning of his own purpose, the wonderful conversations with and about the Chinaman. And, above all, Barry's concern for the harmony of the soul. In the beginning, Barry had asked: "What is more important, material existence or the soul?"

"My soul, of course," she replied.

He had smiled. "And what is this soul?"

"It is the connection," she said, "to everything you are or have been, and will be, in relation to a Higher Power."

And this Higher Power—in meeting it one day would she know then what life and death were all about?

He smiled very mysteriously. "Ask the Chinaman," he had said.

As the music they loved flowed through her she thought of what Barry had said of the continuity of life. "What's the hurry?" he would say. "We have eternity." And then he would smile, always that smile. "The gods won't let me die till I finish what I have come here to do." He pressed her hand and looked deeply into her eyes. No other words had to be spoken.

In the beginning, when she was unsure of their destiny, he had quoted from Yan, lines that had given support to their years of sharing.

> Be patient, son of the Sun [Barry was a Leo, an astrological sign ruled by the sun], whisper a gentle breeze,
> For it is a gentleness your flower is to be.
> Nourish her for this is your strength
> She holds. For **she** too believes in me.

There had been another side of Barry, one she loved as well. She laughed as she recalled his first efforts to get her to move in with him. He had perhaps one nip too many that night, and she could hear him in the street below, crying in a voice that would have raised the dead.

"I know you're there, Ferret. Come on out."

Many windows flew open, and she was sure the landlord was happy to see her go.

As the last of "Amazing Grace" died away, she remembered Yan's final injunction to Barry:

> The answer to life is not death, my son of Sun.
> Life is to be, you are here, and in that
> You have your answer.
> And as your garments be still.
> From this you will know."

Yes, she sighed, Barry's garments were now as still as Yan's had been. God bless dear Barry—till they met again.

I still had no sense of the Chinaman's reality. He seemed to be everywhere with Barry, as if he were a part of him. And now that Barry was gone, Elizabeth still saw the Chinaman, once on the crest of a hill, standing alone, leaning a little forward, as if beckoning.

Two months had gone since Barry's death and though she missed him terribly, she was gradually adjusting to the notion that he had responded to his destiny.

That first week had been traumatic. "I felt my life was over and it was time to go. I picked up the phone to call my mother in Florida and explain this to her. And suddenly I realized I was being thoughtless and unkind to people who cared for me, oblivious of any heartache I might cause."

She gave a little sigh. "If only I knew what Barry had wanted me to do, if only he had given me a sign."

I recalled how Barry had so mysteriously spoken of their meeting again in another thousand years.

"Would you," I said, "be regressed into a past, perhaps a thousand years past, that may have influenced and molded your present?"

"Anything," she said, "anything that might give me a clue."

Articulate and sensitive as Elizabeth was, Boris found her a responsive instrument for digging into the past—a true Ferret.

"Go back to the relationship that bears on the present experience," Boris enjoined, putting her into a light trance.

She paused for a moment, her face a picture of serenity, before she began, haltingly, to describe a rugged countryside she thought to be Scotland. "I see people," she said, "but I don't know who they are."

"Do you see any familiar face?"

"Not to my present mind," she replied, again with hypnosis's curious dichotomy of time.

"I suggest," said Boris, "that you put whatever you want to see on the screen of your mind. Visualize yourself—your mind and body—in this Scottish period. Describe truthfully and accurately your condition at this time. Let us begin with the present stage of that life. How old are you?"

Her voice held a hint of a Scottish burr.

"Thirty-nine or forty."

"What are you doing?"

"I am designing a fortress for a man I know, and the people around me are bringing in the stones."

"Are you close to this man?"

She nodded, and he asked: "Are you married?"

She shrugged. "The marriage ceremony is not important. A simple verbal contract is binding in the Scotland I know. There are many people I see now. They mostly work on the fortress, and there are a few of my clan. I am the only female and I am working with the people who carry the rocks from a nearby quarry."

Even then, I remarked with amusement, she had no feeling for marriage. I was likewise amused by her concern that her Scottish name be spelled properly. She made it Broldywn, and thinking she had inadvertently misspelled it, I transposed the y and the w. Rigidly, she corrected me. "I certainly know how to spell my own name," she said tartly.

Her lover then was Kenneth, a good old Scottish name. It was toward the end of the eleventh century, a period when knighthood was in flower.

This would have been about the time of William the Conqueror who, in 1066, successfully invaded England from Normandy, and of the legendary Scottish kings, Malcolm, Duncan, and Macbeth, to be immortalized by Shakespeare centuries later. It was a time when Scots were fighting Scots, and the English, Normans, and any others threatening their independence.

"What did this man of yours do?" Boris asked.

"He protected his interests and those of the people on his land."

As was common in the Scotland of that time, there was a blood feud between clans, and Elizabeth's lover was being urged by his henchmen to attack a rival clan.

"When he would not kill their leader," she said, "his own men plotted against him."

He left one day with a kiss and embrace to go out and do battle. She knew he would never be back.

Her voice hung sadly for a moment.

"I waited despondently and two days later they came back and told me. And they brought his body.

"He had told me not to cry for him, and I put my tears away. I felt helpless, knowing I couldn't change it."

After her lord's death, the castle became a memorial. "I went on with the designing work, and the construction took fifteen years."

And then her work fulfilled, she died. Now perhaps for the first time she would understand the feeling of impending doom which had accompanied her recurring dreams and nightmares in this life. For always in these dreams she had seen the ocean crashing against massive stones like those quarried in Scotland centuries before for the great castle.

She was still under, speaking now in a muted voice, as though slipping from one time frame to another.

"I had no joy in the building," she said. "I kept on because it had to be finished."

Boris thought he saw a connection.

"Are you not aware," said he, "that there is more for you to do in this life? That may be why you brought up the building of the past."

"Wasn't it symbolical?" I cut in.

"Yes, but symbols are often reality."

"I don't know what it all means," she said. "But I do know I'm not going to die yet. There's a further purpose. Some building Barry would want me to do." Suddenly, she started to sob, taking us quite by surprise, for her voice had been dispassionate until then.

"I don't know if I can face another life wondering if he will be killed again."

Boris and I exchanged glances. So the Scot was Barry, and Barry was the Scot, Kenneth. Theirs was one continuous life together.

"Enjoy your life," said Boris, bringing her back. "You will awaken to joy in your heart. That old feeling of impending doom will have vanished, never to return."

After her tears, Elizabeth had been lying passively on the couch. At Boris's words, her body stiffened and her back arched sharply. And then she slumped back with a sigh.

"Did you feel your body jump?" Boris cried, as she sat up, blinking. "That was an involuntary discharge of stress. You just rid yourself of your depression and despair. It left body and mind. You are now free."

Elizabeth broke into a radiant smile. "My heart's no longer in the Highlands," she said. "I am out of Scotland and all the darkness and despair I knew there.

"As you were bringing me out," she advised Boris, "my mind kept spinning through time, and I saw Barry as plainly as I ever had. Whether it was reincarnation, genetic memory, or just imagination, it was more real than any reality I have known. I could hear Barry distinctly telling how our love brought us back to each other."

"I was drawn to this life by you, my love," she heard him say. "And you were drawn by my love for you. We must free ourselves, so you are free to be with another. Leave nothing undone that you have the will to do."

He was not holding on to her. That was clear.

I saw Elizabeth a week later, and was amazed at the change. The heaviness about her eyes was gone. Her face glowed. In a sweater and slack suit that looked like a jumper, she seemed a saucy teenager. I could hardly credit the transformation.

"The weight of centuries has been lifted from my mind," she enthused.

She was free at last, free to love and be loved into eternity, whether by Barry or some other embodiment from the past, or perhaps even to begin a new experience.

Her life spread out tantalizingly into a boundless vista. "I'm liberated for the first time," she cried, "and I'm eternally grateful to Barry."

But what of Barry? Why had he come so dramatically into her own life, only to leave it so fleetingly, before his own purpose could be discerned?

She smiled, and the age-old mystery of woman lurked hauntingly in her eyes.

"But don't you see? He came to me, so that I would know the Chinaman."

"And the Chinaman, what of him?"

She smiled. "He is still very much around me—and Barry. He will never leave us, for now I understand, as Barry did, that it was our purpose not only to find each other, but ultimately the Chinaman as well."

I had always thought death a mourning for those we loved who had gone on. But as I looked now at Elizabeth, and saw the new resolve in her eyes, I knew there would be no sad songs for her.

"Will you see the Chinaman again?" I asked.

"Of course," she said, "whenever I am ready." She seemed supremely confident.

"How will you know him," I said, "now that Barry is gone?"

Her face lighted up like the morning star.

"I already know him," she said. "He is no longer in some

obscure Chinese desert or riding outside some nightmare of a train."

I was not sure what she meant.

"I have found him," she said. "And he will never leave me."

My face must have shown my surprise.

"And where is he?"

"Not far from me," she said. "Nor you."

She smiled and it was a smile full of grace.

"The Chinaman," she said softly, "is my Higher Self, and he guides my destiny." Her eyes glistened. "And one day, when I am ready, he will lead me back to Barry."

She was ready to climb the mountain.

CHAPTER 12

A Psychologist Ponders a Soulmate

She made no secret of what she wanted to know. I would have liked to have known as much myself, for if we could do together what she asked, we could very well be on the way to solving the riddle of life itself. She had been very much in love with the singer Dick Haymes, and they had vowed to join one another in the afterlife, if, as the Bible promised, the last enemy to be vanquished was death itself.

"I have to know what Dick was thinking just before he died," she said in a voice of great urgency. "Whether he still cares."

I gave her an uneasy glance. She seemed quite normal. And beautiful. Frankly, I had not expected to find anybody as fresh-faced and lovely in her middle years. There was a subtle sensuality in the sea green eyes, which Haymes must have found intriguing, and a golden look that belied her name.

"So you are Dianne de la Vega!"

"Yes," she murmured. "My husband was Spanish, I am Anglo-Italian myself."

She loved talking about Haymes. That soon became apparent. He had been dead for three years now, and yet his memory lingered, warm, compelling, seeming to jump out at her from the other side. She could not forget him. In her many years of marriage she had not known the ecstatic happiness she had experienced in fourteen glorious months with the much-married singer. There had been only one sour note, in the dwindling weeks of his life, when he was dying of cancer.

"Even though I know people often push their loved ones away when they are dying, I still felt the pain of his rejecting behavior, though the last few days at the hospital were beautiful."

She paused, her eyes misting over for a moment, then said with a return to her earlier urgency:

"I need reassurance of his love, some understanding of those last weeks."

Though she was in a scientific discipline, a consulting psychologist, she believed like Longfellow that "Dust thou art, to dust returnest, was not spoken of the soul." And so, too, had Haymes believed, as an early follower of Yogananda, founder of California's Yogic Self-Realization Center.

He had said they would meet in eternity together, and she had believed, for that, too, was what she desired. But she was still here, pining, anxious for almost any sign of his continuing devotion, believing in the Jungian concept of synchronicity, apparent coincidences occurring as though destined when two hearts beat in harmony.

I had no idea what any regression would turn up, but we had already found that the subconscious mind turned up truths that lay buried under the accumulations of time.

The challenge delighted Boris. He loved the abstract, the esoteric, and the apocryphal, and he certainly had all of that here.

"How," I asked, "can we know Dick's mind by regressing you?"

She gave a little shrug, but Boris's eyes gleamed.

"We will find a way," said he.

He put her in a deep trance, and began questioning her about the relationship from its onset. She had been sitting around a recording studio, waiting for a friend, when she heard Haymes's voice boom out from a recording room with "A Grand Night for Singing." Never before had she heard such a happy blend of tone and resonance. "It was a perfect sound," she said. "It sent a chill through me. Without knowing him, I knew the singer was on the same wavelength as myself."

They met later, briefly. The next morning she got a call,

from her friend, inviting her to a party Haymes was giving with Jerry Van Dyke, a comedian, like his brother, Dick Van Dyke. Haymes was obviously smitten. He sat next to her all evening, then asked if she would go home with him. She shook her head, trembling inside like a schoolgirl. She was too emotionally affected. He kept calling, and she finally made a date for dinner, thinking she now had her emotions under control.

She was so nervous that evening she could hardly get ready. "Here I was a psychologist, counseling people on their love problems, and a friend had to iron my skirt and comb my hair out for me."

They sat by the fireplace, candlelight playing on the table. Throughout the evening, he kept giving her searching looks, then finally blurted out: "Didn't we meet before in another lifetime?"

She didn't know what to make of his remark. Paradoxically, she knew very little about him, even as she trembled at his touch. She knew he had been married, but not six times, to a string of Hollywood stars including Rita Hayworth, Joanne Dru, Nora Eddington, and Fran Jeffreys. Not that it would have made any difference, for she was convinced they had known each other before and were fated to be together again.

As time passed, they discovered they were magically in tune, knowing what the other was thinking, and doing, even apart. It was frightening but exhilarating, for she had always dreamed of a romance like this. And just when she had reached an age when she thought it was out of reach, it was happening.

She had been regressed before, and though she regressed patients herself, taking this shortcut to pinpoint deeply buried conflicts, she had never deliberately foraged into past-life remembrance. Occasionally, unbidden, a patient would slip into a subconscious experience which dovetailed remarkably with the present life pattern. And it was all as real as any recollection of childhood.

Why, she asked herself, if one recollection was true, should another be false? Long before she met Richard, she had herself regressed into a past life, and didn't quite know what to make of the result.

"It was a wonderfully dramatic story," she recalled for us now, "of an Atlantean woman who fell in love with a married man, whose ambition was greater than his love. He headed the

Governor's Palace Guard, and was married to the Governor's daughter. We had been living together openly, but after I bore him a child he felt threatened, and he left me rather than give up his position."

In her grief she had gone to the main temple to pray, and then, despairing, had thrown herself on a dagger on the temple steps. She had been lying in a pool of blood, surrounded by horrified onlookers, when he arrived on the scene. Instead of succoring her, his face hardened as he looked at the scandalized crowd. Angrily, he picked her up, and carried her lifeless body to her mother's door.

I had to smile to myself, for, in a sense history had repeated itself. Again she appeared to have been rejected by a lover, though this time her own death and not the other's signaled the rejection.

I had not heard many tragedies summarized with such analytical sophistication.

"Why would you have killed youself?" I asked.

She smiled.

"I was a silly woman, I suppose, so overcome with grief I couldn't bear the thought of living without him."

She had the feeling this lover was Richard, but she had no wish to push it at him. The only life that really counted, as Edgar Cayce said, was the life you lived now. With the present, she told herself, you retrieved the past, and influenced the future.

It was fun being in love, when love was an end in itself, to laugh and jest like teenagers. They discovered they were a lot alike. Once she playfully asked what she looked like to him, and he took her by the shoulders, peering into her eyes, and said, "Like somebody I know very well—myself."

"Actually," she said, still in trance, "we had the same bone structure, and coloring, the same way of looking at people. We were counterparts. We liked the same foods, the same entertainment, the same people. We could have been the flip side of each other."

"Didn't you consider him a risk, with six marriages?"

She replied with a psychologist's insight.

"Nothing matters except what's going on at the moment between people in love."

She seemed to be the tonic he needed. Her love gave

him the strength to stop smoking and drinking. His spirits renewed, he plunged into his career with a burst of enthusiasm amazing in a man sixty years old. "I'm livelier than Bing Crosby [who was dead]," he would laugh, "and I don't have Sinatra's skinny legs."

There were problems, of a karmic nature perhaps. "Our feeling was so intense that almost anything we did together triggered some traumatic remembrance out of the past."

He was sometimes difficult, volatile, temperamental, hurting from the cancer consuming him even then. But she had one advantage the other women he loved didn't have. She was a psychologist, and she understood his moods. "When he and Rita had an argument, it usually wound up with one of them storming out. I always stayed. Generally, he was unmanageable only when he drank. I treated him like a patient I loved better than anything in the world. I'd say, 'You must be hurting very badly to be so angry.' That would throw him off. He was used to anger arousing anger. His anger would ooze away. 'If I've offended you, please tell me what it is,' I'd say."

She would take his hand. " 'It doesn't matter what you do or say, I will never stop loving you.' He would subside then, and sometimes he would cry. He would go off by himself and later he'd say, 'You know, that's the way I feel about you. I'll always keep loving you.' "

There were no barriers between them, no boundaries. "He had been impotent. I convinced him it was purely psychological, and he should think only in terms of loving, not of sex." The first evening they were together, they had no trouble. "And never thereafter. It was like we had always been this way."

She had thought about soulmates, in particular and in general. "Millions of people are looking for a soulmate, hoping for some magic fulfillment, and yet some people just can't stand the thought of loving somebody, then losing them. They can't bear the pain, grief, rage, the feeling of abandonment, and so they back off. That's where courage comes in. Shall it be a whole loaf or half a loaf?"

She had reached for the whole loaf. "How else can you know a soulmate? You have to be willing to go through a lot. But it opens you up. It's a wonderful madness, ecstatic, agonizing, but still wonderful."

As a psychologist himself, Boris thought it time to appraise another psychologist's thinking.

"You mention vulnerability," he said, "the letting go of the ego. Yet often people think they've met a soulmate, confusing it with infatuation. I have a client, a young woman, who is a giver. The man's the taker. Yet she tries to make a soulmate thing of it because it validates an otherwise shallow relationship."

De la Vega replied, "He obviously wasn't open enough to share the experience. He was blocked off. There was something karmic keeping them together, but he was afraid to look inside himself, or into her, to learn what her dependency was. They settled for half a loaf."

What did this specifically have to do with soulmates?

"Everything," said Dianne, "for when two people are on the same frequency, regardless of the differences, they are no longer closed off. They have opened each other up and are ready to share the infinite joy love can bring."

Boris frowned.

"So why in all this infinity did you almost freak out when Richard died?"

"I lost contact. But one day, I woke up to his singing, 'The More I See You, the More I Love You.' And that brought me back."

"Couldn't that have been an illusion?"

She was sitting up on the couch now, rubbing her eyes.

She smiled. "It was on the radio. But, still, isn't all life an illusion?"

This had been one of her favorites which he had sung for her on his last tour, just before his collapse. She had taken him back to California with her, and he died a few months later. The following day she found a red rose on her doorstep with a card which read:

"In memory of love." He had asked a friend to deliver it.

"I desperately needed that message to affirm our continuing love," she said, sighing the least bit. And then there was a lull, and she would lapse into a depression all over again.

She had felt his presence heavily one day, when she was debating a trip to Israel. "Generally, I didn't look for messages. But this time I asked for a sign.

"Distinctly the impression came back, I saw the date clearly; 1987. Of course, this was pretty subjective and I realized that. But that night a friend took me to a movie, *Diner*. In the movie there was a scene in a beauty parlor, and I thought I heard Richard singing in the background. The song was 'Where and When.' I waited for the credits to make sure I hadn't dreamed it up."

There were other songs with a special meaning for her. She would be thinking of him, turn on the radio, and break in on Haymes singing, "For You, For Me, Forever More."

Was this coincidence? She thought not. There was a vast synchronicity that argued nothing was by chance. All one's associations, parents, kin, teachers, companions, lovers, husbands, wives were in a certain place for a certain purpose.

Shortly before his death, Haymes, thinking of writing an autobiography, had an idea his subconscious mind might provide a key to his relationships with his past wives, particularly Hayworth, whom he had found something of an enigma. He asked Dianne to regress him.

No aspect of the human experience surprised her. So she sat by calmly when her regression of the singer spontaneously took him back to Atlantis. But there was a growing wonder when he became the very lover she had loved so desperately she could not live without. His recollections matched and exceeded hers. His ambitions had fared well. After her death, he rose in power, becoming head of the Atlantean armed forces, and then supreme ruler, after his father-in-law's death. With his wife, he brought up the son who grew up hating him for his mother's death. In the end there was retribution. At the peak of power, when he had everything he wanted, he was assassinated, fatally stabbed, ironically, by that very son.

Dianne spoke of it so matter-of-factly it was difficult to grasp the full extent of the Greek-like tragedy that lay behind these few words.

"Karmically," I asked, "would you say Dick Haymes had to pay for his blind ambition? That is, of course, if there's anything to any of this."

She shrugged.

"I don't think we pay for anything. I discussed this with Richard many times. We just keep repeating our patterns. When you get hurt enough, you begin to look at yourself closely and you wake up to a different set of values."

Granted life's continuity, had she any difficulty forgiving her Atlantean lover?

"Not at all, I was partly to blame. I could have waited, and not involved him." She gave a rather hollow laugh. "It almost reminds me of what I went through at Dick's death. I just zapped out. I tried different psychologists, but they were hopeless. The worst were the ones trained to help cancer patients and their families. One of them told me it was just as well Richard was going to die, because if he lived, he probably wouldn't love me anyway."

The regressions had not yet established what Dianne had wanted to know—why Dick Haymes had apparently rejected her during his last five weeks, not wanting her with him as they had been before.

Boris, thinking Dianne mediumistic, from her apparent closeness to the singer's spirit, now revealed the plan he had almost from the beginning.

"Let us try to channel Haymes through her," he said, as I shook my head. "Don't you see, she's a natural medium?"

I looked at him doubtfully.

"Why not," he said, "perfectly normal people, as we know, pick up on others, their secret thoughts and ailments, and whatever else, through the power of the subconscious, the alpha brainwaves. You wrote about it in *The Power of Alpha Thinking*."

And so Boris regressed Dianne for a final time. But this time, her subconscious was linked to that of the late singer, and the questions were put to her as though she was Haymes himself. It was something new, something I had never heard of before, outside of the spiritualist world, but then all of this was new to me before I explored any of it.

"Why," Boris asked of the sleeping de la Vega, "did you, Richard Haymes, appear to push away your soulmate, Dianne de la Vega?"

I had observed mediums go through a change of voice many times, and half-expected Dianne to respond in a gruff male tone. But her voice was the same, soft and dulcet, clearly feminine. She spoke clearly, without hesitation.

"Because I loved her so," came back the response. "I couldn't bear to see her suffer. Her grief overwhelmed me. I wanted to go, but the grief she manifested, whenever she visited me, was so strong it kept me from going. And so, as I lay there, dying, knowing it was only a matter of time, I was in constant conflict.

" 'Don't come in here if you can't keep your face straight,' I'd tell her. She would try but she couldn't quite manage it. She would get up to leave so I wouldn't see her sorrow, and I would call her a coward for leaving. What she hadn't realized then was that I had never stopped loving her. Her grief triggered mine and the emotional drain on top of my physical pain was almost more than I could bear. It reminded me of a song I used to sing:

> Though there be rain
> And darkness, too,
> I'll not complain.
> I'll see it through."

Boris looked at me triumphantly over Dianne's prone body.

"That's it," he said. "She kept repeating her pattern. She wallowed in grief, and neither lover liked it."

I smiled as he brought her back.

"Tell her what it was all about—one psychologist to another."

As she came to, he explained.

"Richard apparently came through you," he said. "He told us there was no rejection, only a manifestation of his love. He was staying on because of you, and his time had come. He needed to go."

She looked at us thoughtfully.

"It makes sense, but he never mentioned it, not even in the recent messages he sent me, so I don't know what to believe."

"What messages?" Boris cried.

"In automatic writing," she said, unabashed.

"Why," we asked almost in unison, "didn't you ask him what you had us find out?"

"I didn't ask anything. I only wrote down what came through me."

The automatic writing filled in certain details lacking before. For this, she said, was Richard speaking:

"I sit next to her now, only she doesn't see me. I put my

arms around her, only she doesn't feel them. I know now what it is like to be ignored. She used to say, 'There are times when I am with you I feel I don't exist.' Funny all six of my wives said the same thing.

"She used to come to me every night after work, usually late but she'd be there. She'd wait so patiently for me to take her hand. She'd lie next to me in bed—I knew she wanted me to hold her—and I didn't. She loved to have me hold her. Sometimes she'd ask. I would for a few minutes but not too long. I let her go before she wanted me to.

"I'm here in the spirit now and she's there in her body. Sometimes I think I'm getting through to her. She stops her tears for a moment and listens. I'm singing to her right now. It's the song I sang to her in my last performance in Detroit. 'The More I See You, the More I Love You.' "

I had never encountered so fantastic a story, and yet it still fascinated me, coming as it did from a psychologist trained in separating illusion from reality.

Dianne saw him last in Cedar Sinai Hospital in Los Angeles the day before he died. He looked around, a wan smile on his face, and said:

"Where's Dianne?"

As she leaned over him tenderly, he took her hand, and spoke his last to her.

"I love you," he said. "Drive carefully."

I had seen Dianne on March 14, 1983, almost the anniversary of Richard's death, when she again mentioned Haymes speaking through her, and singing a song or two in the gloaming.

She sighed through her tears, paraphrasing a song long a favorite of theirs.

"I'll never stop loving him. Death has not separated us. We made a promise and by God we shall keep it. We shall see it through."

I climbed into my car that evening, pondering all the strange realities—and unrealities—that had been thrust on my numbed consciousness. And heaving a bewildered sigh of my own, I twirled the radio dial, stopping at the Los Angeles Music of Your Life station, WPRZ (1150 on the dial). A deep, resonant voice was singing an old melody. I listened idly at first, not recognizing the voice, but liking the song. It was strangely familiar, having a haunting quality:

Though there be rain
And darkness, too,
I'll not complain.
I'll see it through.

And then, with a start, I suddenly realized I was listening to the all but forgotten voice of Dick Haymes.

I only wished Dianne had been there to share it. It was an old favorite, and the message was loud and clear.

For Haymes was singing, as he had a hundred times before:

"I'll get by as long as I have you."

CHAPTER 13

Togetherness

They did everything together, so naturally they wanted to be regressed together. There was no reason for it given, and none was asked, for it was more revealing to come on the answer as we hoped out of their own subconscious minds. I had admired the work of John Ericson, from the time I had first seen him on the Broadway stage in *Stalag 17*. And though, like many actors, his career was in a period of lull I could sense he was on a comeback. He was not at all concerned. As we talked, he threw his arm affectionately around his wife, Karen, a capable actress in her own right, and said with a fond smile:

"We have been together for so long that we treat adversity and success as the twin impostors they are."

This was somewhat puzzling, for they had only been together ten years or so, the marriage being John's second, and Karen's first.

"Oh, no," he said, "we go back a lot longer, for we have known each other always, of that I am sure."

And so it seemed when they met that first time on a plane bound from Los Angeles to San Francisco.

"As a youngster," John recalled, "I avidly read the Prince Valiant comic strip, and fell in love with the Princess Aleta with the long blonde hair and the beautiful face with the turned-up nose. But, of course, as I grew up I realized it was a boyish fantasy."

And then on a routine plane trip, he looked across the aisle, and there she was, Princess Aleta, complete to the blonde hair and smiling blue eyes, even the turned-up nose. "Only," he laughed, "more beautiful than Aleta ever dreamed of being."

There was an overwhelming feeling of having known her before. It came over him in waves. As with so many great moments, there was a turn to the banal and the trivial to gloss over an emotion one was not quite ready to cope with.

"Can I buy you a Coke?" he asked.

Karen recalled the incident with a smile. "The Cokes, of course, were free."

I could see she liked to tease him. But in a moment she turned serious. "I was very low, vulnerable at the time," she said. "I had just ended a close relationship, and I didn't feel strong enough to go through that again. So I drew off a bit at first."

But the magnetic attraction was there, as it had been for Dianne de la Vega and others. And she soon found that John didn't want anything of her, except the opportunity to give, to love without measuring his devotion, to love for love's sake. He seemed to have the faculty of saying and doing the right thing at the right time, at this emotionally low point in her life. He gave her the reassurance she needed.

She looked at him now, the tears came to her eyes. "He was always warm, always unselfish. He seemed to know exactly what suited my mood. He didn't care how I looked or acted. He didn't try to remake me. He was patient, he cared about what was happening to me. Most of the men I knew only cared about what I looked like. I had the notion John would have cared for me if I looked like the Princess Aleta's grandmother."

They had things to say about their relationship that were neither trite nor pat. Not everything was perfect, beyond improvement, or it would have been painfully dull. "There have been lacks in other persons which bothered me, but never with Karen," John said. "She likes books and music. I did very little reading, except for scripts and the Hollywood trades. But it didn't matter to me. Whatever she did was easy for me to go along with."

Karen joined in, with a laugh. "I was always dragging John to places like concerts and museums, and the next thing you know he would be enjoying them."

They had something together that marked nearly all the soulmate unions I had come across. They didn't have to speak, yet the communication was there. "I could be in a room or driving with Karen and not say a word," said John. "But we'd be picking up each other's thoughts. This interplay keeps us stimulated. I pick up things from Karen and integrate them into my life. It helps round me out. We keep growing because of what we give each other. If you keep communication going, you're bound to grow. And you see the other person growing right along with you."

Oddly, as though this oneness expressed itself in the physical as well, their features had come to resemble each other's, even to the jaw and chin line. They looked enough alike to be brother and sister, though John was some years older.

"After I got to know John," Karen said, "I felt like we had been related before. I used to tease him and say we were twins in the past."

"Oh, so you believe in reincarnation?"

She shook her head. "It has nothing to do with reincarnation. Nobody has ever given me a valid explanation. I just had this feeling about him."

I mentioned genetic memory, as quite separate from reincarnation. "For instance, a dog can swim, without learning how. It goes back to his origin. It's in his genes. He knows instinctively, so we call it instinct, and yet it doesn't explain it."

She nodded. "Some things, though, we don't remember. Some animals make very poor mothers, like certain animals in the zoo. The chimpanzees and many other animals there don't even feed their offspring. They don't know what to do."

There was a note of disdain in her voice, at the thought of any mother behaving so indifferently.

John nodded sympathetically.

I envied them for not needing anything or anybody but themselves. I could see how neatly one offset the other. The same questions, the same observations, trembled on their lips. And one had the feeling that no matter who answered the question the reply would be the same. They were in "sync," as the saying goes. But still the similarity in features was not in expression alone, not defined purely by an attitude or posture. There was a likeness that may have formed not from one brief period of thinking alike, but from a long continuity which had nothing to do with a genetic legacy. There was a warm, abiding closeness, which affected others about them, and which obviously kept growing, as they said, as distinguished from infatuation whose fire blew itself out.

They looked as if they belonged together, not unlike Prince Valiant and the Princess Aleta. John, tall and lean, athletic, with rugged Nordic good looks, and Karen looking in her blonde loveliness as if she had just floated out of a fairy tale.

Watching as they held hands, I wondered what they were looking for. How could it be any better than it was?

"Neither of us has been hypnotized before," said John, "and we thought it might throw some light on a few things."

Karen nodded in quick assent.

"It could be disappointing," I said, "for life, unlike a play or movie, is not always neatly tied together at the end."

An errant thought struck her.

"Suppose I can't be hypnotized, and nothing comes out?"

"It always does," I assured her, "particularly with somebody like Boris. He seldom misses."

Boris had joined us by now. "It's not me," he laughed. "Everybody has a story, and a past, and they pick out the highlights meaningful to them."

Obviously, they looked on our little experiment as a novel adventure in which they could share together whatever they gleaned from it.

They took to Boris, and that was a help. A rapport between hypnotist and subject was important, even though he was but a catalyst, and they did it all, out of their reaching into a past apparently as infinite as the Universe.

"Have you had any specific memories?" Boris asked, as a prelude to putting them under.

Karen's eyes lighted up.

Not long before, she had gone through a holistic program at the Edgar Cayce regeneration clinic in Phoenix, Arizona, directed by the husband-and-wife team, Doctors William and Gladys McGarey. As her eyes closed, during a meditative session invoked by classical music, she had gone into a spontaneous regression. It was a new and frightening experience. Suddenly, she found herself in medieval Spain, victim of a murderous attack by an assailant she could not quite identify because of the overwhelming impact the whole scene had on her emotionally. She had tried to escape to save a child she was bearing, but it was killed as well. "This regression and my reaction to it," she said, "was as real as anything I had ever experienced. When I came out of it, I was out of breath, panting as though I had been running, breaking into a cold sweat. My heart was pounding furiously, and I wept inconsolably. I felt melancholy, with a deep sense of loss. I finally had to stop the meditation. I couldn't bear to remember any more."

Just talking about it seemed to shake her up and it took her a few minutes to compose herself. I wondered where she was coming from. There were no children now, so I saw no immediate relevance.

"John has two children by a previous marriage, both grown. We have none together."

She seemed very casual about it.

They were completely supportive of each other and their careers. John had starred in such films as *Bad Day at Black Rock*, with Spencer Tracy, *Rhapsody*, with Elizabeth Taylor, *Green Fire*, with Grace Kelly, and the television series *Honey West*, with Anne Francis. All this was in the past, and Karen kept assuring him the future would far surpass that past. They were not competitive. John spoke raptly about how great Karen had been in *The Boston Strangler*, in TV and on the stage in *The Crucible* and *Cat on a Hot Tin Roof*.

Though we had dealt with actors on several occasions, there had been no inclination on their part to dramatize the regressions dug out of their subconscious. The situations were dramatic enough, but were often minimized in the telling, since they were devoid of graphic sequence, plot, or denouement. All this, we felt, said something for their spontaneity and authenticity.

Boris let Karen and John decide whatever past experience was of consequence to them. They were stretched out comfortably alongside each other, within touching distance as he put them under. They seemed completely at ease, conscious throughout of the other's presence, sometimes answering simultaneously, and nearly always in "sync."

There was a long silence, then Boris asked:

"Where are you, Karen?"

She answered slowly:

"In a garden. There are trees around, a park, or woods." She burst into laughter. "He's wearing not much, some fig leaves, and I don't have much more on myself. He's standing there and he's gorgeous."

"Does he look like John?"

"The man does, but I can't tell if the girl is me. I can't quite see her face. Her hair is reddish blonde, not like mine."

"Remember," said Boris, "you don't necessarily look the same. It's the soul, the spirit, not the body we're dealing with."

I interposed:

"But wouldn't they look the same to each other, if they're coming out of a soul experience with one continuous life?"

Boris looked at me doubtfully.

"It really doesn't matter. For all we know, they could be Adam and Eve."

Time was of no concern to the young lovers.

They were standing together, their bare thighs touching. "I feel physically turned on," she said. "I know we're not supposed to be feeling like we do."

He stood eating nonchalantly a piece of fruit he had picked off a tree. "We're talking a bit, my leg still against his, and there's a nice cozy feeling. There's a gentle breeze, and the sun is shining. It's pleasantly warm. There's an intimate feeling, like you have with someone after you've made love with him."

John's head came up a little. "I have very light eyes, haven't I? Kind of water blue or gray."

Karen, smiling:

"You look younger then I've ever known you. You don't have any love handles."

Boris pinched the fleshy part of his waist over the hips.

"Love handles," he whispered.

Before anything further could develop they parted. She was left by herself, sitting on a marble bench, staring out to sea. She gave an impression now of abject loneliness.

"I still don't know it's me," she cried. "It doesn't exactly look like me."

"How do you know it's John?"

"He looks like John."

"But how would you know unless the woman on the bench was you?"

"I know," she said firmly, "from looking at him."

They had been younger then. John was eighteen, and she fifteen.

They seemed young for what they had apparently been doing, recalling the French axiom that the more things seem to change, the more they remain the same—whatever the time period.

Under hypnosis, John spoke now with feeling.

"We were together then, and before, we'll always be together."

It was a wonderfully romantic notion, but he did little at the time to make this wish materialize. For he took off in flight, never to return to his young inamorata.

"They'd kill me if I went back," he explained in a strained voice. "I'll never see her again." And he never did.

Theatrically, all this left much to be desired, for the world loves a lover, and dotes on his surrendering all for love, even life itself. Surely, John and Karen could have fashioned a likelier scenario had they made it up.

But Boris felt something had been gained.

"At least," said this old cynic, "they broke the ice."

Soon they were in another experience that offered more promise. Karen was older now, married and pregnant.

With a quiver of expectation I noted the time and place—medieval Spain. She had been in the throes of an emotional convulsion when this spontaneous recall hit before at the McGareys', and now we had some explanation of her breathlessness and agitation, her heart pounding as though her chest would burst. For here she was running for her life, having been set upon by dangerous marauders in the courtyard of a dark, gray castle. Quickly, she darted into a secret passageway, and ran up a spiral staircase to escape the threatening danger. She heard angry voices, and knew they were directed at her and her lover.

"Your lover?"

"Yes," she said, "I had pleaded with him to leave, but he insisted on coming back with me."

She had entered the castle to draw the men away from him as from herself. But there was no escape. She was racing down a long, dark hall, gasping for breath, holding her stomach, as though to shield the child she was bearing, when one of the men overtook her. He flung her to the floor and with one swipe of his sword dug deep into her body. She groaned a little, fighting unconsciousness, as the blood seeped through her beautiful white gown.

Her voice was agonized now.

"My dress was red with blood. I was dying, I had lost so much blood. I thought of my child, knowing it was dying as well. They had killed us both."

And then, as we listened enthralled, picturing the life ebbing out of this poor creature, the lover she had sent off dramatically reappeared, too late to save her, but in time to avenge. With one bound he leaped on her assailant, stabbing him furiously until he fell mortally wounded.

Karen's voice was now so feeble it could barely be heard.

"He picked me up tenderly," she whispered, "and carried me into a little room, kissing my eyes, my lips, my hair. He laid me down on the bed and bent over me, sobbing. My life's blood was oozing out of me. The room was swimming darkly before my eyes. He whispered a few words and with a last effort I reached up and touched the face I loved so much. I felt his tears warm on my face as he kissed me goodbye."

Boris's pity turned to horror.

"You mean he left you to die?"

She sighed, as I recalled how he had left her before.

"There were footsteps on the staircase, and I motioned for him to go. They would have killed him."

The men burst into the room, infuriated that their quarry had already fled. They vented their wrath on her, shouting threats and imprecations she didn't even hear.

She was so weak her mind was floating. "It was as if I were under ether or some similar drug. They were all very much there, with their angry cries and gestures, yet remote at the same time. I kept thinking in my grief, 'They've killed my baby.'

"Though I was dying, one of the men was struggling to get at me. But the others held him back, telling him I was as good as dead."

It was rather confusing. There was the lover who ran off, and the mysterious stranger, so irate he was ready to attack a dying woman with child. Obviously, he was a man betrayed, in a country where honor was dearer than life.

"Whose child was it?" I asked.

Karen's eyes were still closed, but her brow lifted in surprise.

"Why, it was John's, of course. He was my lover. We had been planning to leave together that very day."

We hadn't quite pieced the fragments together.

Boris liked things neatly in place.

"Was that your husband trying to get at you?"

Suddenly, the energy drained out of her. Her hand came limply to her eyes.

"Yes, my husband," she sighed. "It was John I had always cared for. And now he is gone. We are all gone."

Her voice faded off.

Boris and I exchanged glances.

How did she know it was John?

With almost her last breath she explained.

"I just knew. When he held me it felt just like John. He was bigger, heavier than John was before, more like he is now, tall and well-formed."

And the husband? We could only speculate that she had married without love, against her will, not uncommon in that day and age. There was no point to questioning her. She had all she could of this life.

John had remained silent, as if spellbound.

"Do you remember any of this?" I asked.

He shook his head and went off on a tangent, as though it was all he, too, could handle.

"I never got back," he said, woefully. "She died. There was nothing to come back for."

Boris smiled.

"That's called blocking."

After three or four sessions, we were on to nothing significant, and the logical assumption was that not all lives were exciting, memorable, or meaningful. First, there had been an unfinished love, too fleeting to consummate in marriage and family. Next, a horrifying experience in which John and Karen had evidently had an illicit affair, ending in a horrible nightmare, with a young wife and mother murdered and a helpless child deprived of life before it could be born.

"Does it ever get anywhere?" I wondered aloud to Boris.

"There is a pattern," he said.

I gave a hollow laugh. "Where?"

"Their love was always aborted."

"Twice," I said, "but now they're happily married. What are they looking for?"

Boris's eyes flashed. "We'll find out," he said confidently. And so we plunged ahead.

We came next to an Indian land, where the passage of events was gauged by the sun and moon, and nobody knew what year it was, for the history of their world was all in the mind until the white man came.

She was Raven then, a dark-haired Indian beauty, consigned to the arrogant young warrior, Two Rivers, who because of his fighting prowess had the right by tribal custom to pick a bride from all the unwed beauties of the Indian village. Raven soon made it clear she wanted no part of an obnoxious Two Rivers.

"He was always stunting, not because he was brave, but to gain attention. He would ride his horses into the ground. Indians were supposed to respect animals, but he was cruel."

As we came on the scene, she was not sure how he would treat a child she had rescued from the ruins of a village destroyed by white soldiers. She had found a tiny baby, frightened and sobbing, in the midst of a bloody shambles. "People are crying and dying all around me. I don't know what to do.

"The baby is so pathetic. It needs me. She's crying. She's hungry and I don't have any food. I don't know what to feed her. She's so little. And I can't find my parents. They either ran off or they're dead. I'm tired, confused, so thirsty my throat is parched. I can't think straight. But I must do something for this poor baby."

I could almost see her looking down and fondling the child.

The thought struck Boris and myself simultaneously. Karen had lost a child and now had found one. With all the destruction, her parents missing or dead, her own confusion and fatigue, the child was her first concern.

The village had scattered under the attack by the soldiers. Afraid they might return, she collared a stray horse, and rode off, picking up the trail of the Indian survivors, finally finding them where they had made camp.

There was one bit of good news amid the disaster. Two Rivers, true to her thought, had taken flight instead of making a stand. And with him vanished the prospect of unhappy marriage.

Several years passed. She had not married, and she still had the child. She kept her close, troubled that the tribe had not accepted them. Even the Chief, her friend, gave only a grudging welcome to the child.

"They don't care about us," Karen cried. "They don't care what happens to my little girl and myself."

The Chief made a point of being friendly, hoping to influence the others. But it didn't change anything.

"He tries to help us, but the people don't want us."

Her voice held a mournful note.

But why? Boris and I exchanged puzzled glances.

And suddenly it was resolved for us, in a simple expression of fact.

Karen had paused, as if trying to carefully phrase what she was about to say.

"She still remembers some English."

It was a motherless white child she had been raising, perhaps the relic of a wagon train. The tribe obviously held the girl's presence responsible for the raid by the soldiers, bent on rescuing her.

The pressure kept mounting to give up the white child. Even the Chief added his voice. "If you do not give it up, the soldiers will come back one day and take it anyway," he warned.

She ultimately surrendered, telling herself the child could never grow up properly in an alien environment.

With a sore heart, she watched the soldiers march off with the child, who was sobbing unrestrainedly, her soul wrenched by the parting.

There was a tear in the Chief's eye as well.

"All that is left," he said, "is for us to die in dignity."

And so again she died young, without fulfilling herself. John had not been there to comfort her—or had he? Who was the Chief, could he possibly have been John?

John had remained silent throughout the ordeal. And Karen, questioned, could only say: "He was much older, and very wise. He helped me, and he cared. I never knew why."

And now we came to the strange land of Azu, stranger even than the lost continents of Atlantis and Lemuria. It was cast in the fuzzy prehistoric period, the age of the caveman.

The land had been rocked by a massive volcanic eruption, and only now was painfully recovering.

Karen and John were among the few survivors.

"Where," asked Boris, "is Azu?"

John replied, with a shudder.

"In the land of the black rock, which you find in a stream, huge and hard."

"Sounds like a pleasant place," said Boris cheerfully.

John's teeth chattered. "Brr, it's cold," he shivered.

"And what is your name?"

"Ara," he smiled, as Karen cut in:

"That's very nice. And what's my name?"

"Ganew," he said, spelling it out.

"I like your name better," Karen decided.

Boris persisted.

"Are you of dark skin, John?"

And again Karen replied, laughing a little:

"He's hairy."

Boris's lips curled. "What else would you expect of a caveman?"

John assumed the leader role. He had been outside a cave they called home, and now proudly announced:

"I'm going inside to my fire."

She was exiting but he imperiously ordered her to remain.

"Stay," he cried, "the mountain is coming. Wait till the black clouds and the thunder roll away."

Their lives moved without incident. They foraged for food, and hugged the fire for warmth. They enjoyed each other and then one day, adding a bit of excitement, a child was born. For the first time Karen had both her own mate and a child born of him.

Even Boris was gratified.

"We should congratulate Ganew of Azu."

But misfortune dogged the new mother, even in her moment of fulfillment.

Just as we were sharing their happiness, John's voice was raised in anguish, from outside the cave. It was a heartrending cry that brought her instantly to the mouth of the cave.

"Ganew, Ganew," he cried, "where are you?"

"I'm here," she responded reassuringly. "I'm all right."

"It's the baby," he shouted.

"The baby?" Her voice quickly reflected his alarm. "What about the baby?"

"The baby is dead," he screamed. "Dead."

"Dead?" Her voice broke. "It can't be."

"It was the animals," he came back, "the mammoths, they trampled her."

"That can't be," she repeated in shocked disbelief. "They're too big, they can't get in the cave."

By this time he was a nervous wreck. "Listen more, woman," he cried. "You talk too much. The baby got outside. Somebody put her there." There was an accusing tone in his voice.

Karen's voice trembled. "But how could it happen? Who took the baby out? Was it you?"

She looked around her, still in shock, still hoping to see the child.

"Why was the baby alone?" he demanded.

"She wasn't alone. I didn't go anywhere."

His voice was hard. "The baby was dead, and you were not with it."

"I didn't leave it," she said. "Where could I go?"

Her voice was suddenly subdued, with a great sorrow.

Even as my senses reassured me Karen was reclining comfortably in Boris's studio, I saw her standing half-naked in a dark cave, her eyes turned in a dumb, animal appeal to the primordial mate who had fathered her child.

"Come," he said, with a last look for the trampled child. "We must go somewhere."

She was inconsolable.

"Do we just leave her?" she cried. "Shouldn't we cover her up?" I could see her wringing her primitive hands in a mother's helpless gesture. A low moan escaped her and her voice broke. "I don't want the animals to eat her up. Please, can't we bring her into the cave and bury her?"

He was adamant, obviously afraid the animals might be on a rampage.

"Come," he said, "we must get away."

We never did find out how the baby had gotten out of its secure home. Obviously, it must have crawled out as her mother was busy elsewhere.

The years passed without lightening her grief. They stayed together. But there were no more children. And she no longer enjoyed his frolicking in the streams, fishing with his bare hands, nor hunting in the fields. She stood by impassively, not sharing any of his pleasure.

"What's wrong, Ganew?" Boris asked.

Her voice was full of pathos.

"I don't have the baby."

"Do you feel that Ara might have taken the baby outside with him?"

She shook her head in misery. "I would never have done it," she said, in a bare whisper.

At this point, John mumbled something to himself. It was a strange tongue, with a certain jungle rhythm to it. Three little words I had never heard before, very much like:

"Keara, neara, seara."

Karen's head bobbed a bit.

"Keara, neara, seara," she came back in a surprised tone.

Whatever it was, it seemed to satisfy her. We were given no explanation. Perhaps it was too intimate to discuss. We left it at that, and swiftly moved back to the present.

Boris expressed my own unspoken question.

"What is it you are both seeking? Is it a child you want? Have you wondered, John, why you have had no child with Karen in this experience?"

It was Karen who answered.

"I had certain physical problems, but I don't see it as a barrier any longer."

"Have you and John discussed why there is no child?" I put in.

She nodded. "Yes, I had surgery, so I could have a child. Either that or adopting. Either way, it's our child by choice."

And why not? As Raven, the Indian maid, had she not adopted a child on her own, not of her own race, giving her up finally when she had no choice?

"I always wanted a little girl," said Karen, sadly.

"Do you feel a child is vital to your relationship?"

"John is the important thing in my life. But I'd always planned on children."

"It was a girl you wanted?"

"I'd take either one. A boy like John would be great."

John returned the compliment.

"A girl would be nice, reminding me of Karen."

Suddenly the drollness of the situation struck me, with

its swift passage from an incredibly mordant prehistoric experience to a somewhat sophisticated modern discussion of family
planning.

I wondered if there was anything more they wanted to
know.

John, still under hypnosis, replied in a questing voice:

"I was always looking for something, always moving about,
always searching, not quite sure what it was."

"And in this lifetime, what was it you wanted to know?"

"I would love to contact the one mind, the one God, the
Universal Intelligence, and love through it. To know what God
wanted of me."

It was a thought I knew that many of us had in our
lifetimes.

His mind again delved back into the past, as I wondered
whether he might indeed have been the Indian chief Raven
respected so much.

"People should study the American Indians," he said.
"He knows of being at one with his God and having the strength
to overcome his enemy with love. We have to think of each
other more. Our society is too me-oriented."

We had all heard how a sick crumbling society—our
own—was heading for a terrible catastrophe. But nobody seemed
to believe it. For nothing was new, the old values of force and
might, greed and lust, still prevailed wherever one turned.

John seemed to read my thoughts.

"We must live and love together, but still keep our own
individuality, constantly questioning our actions, doing unto
others, as we would they do unto us."

I had heard this before, spoken two thousand years ago
by somebody greater than any of us. And now we were in a
New Age, and who knew but what the next few years might
bring a hopeful change.

It was time now for Boris's analysis of our travels through
Azu, Greece, medieval Spain, and the Indian lands.

"You have come a long way," he told our two soulmates.
"Your misfortune with children set up a block, which your
awareness will now dispel. You are free now to develop spiritually to any extent you wish."

I could see Karen's lips tremble, parting a little, and I
leaned forward to catch her response.

"Our baby, our baby," she sighed. "I want her so much."

CHAPTER 14

Looking at the Stars

The astrologer Signe Taff had said they were very special—soulmates, if she had ever seen any. "You can just look at their charts and see how their Saturns are so well-aspected, and Saturn, you know, is the planet that tells us about soulmates."

What was also so special was that they were brought together by a dog, Caesar, who was part wolf, and that she, Peggy Polk, was some twenty years older than her partner, and neither a glamorous movie star, nor as well off economically, nor as successful, as he.

"You must see them together," said Signe, "to know how special they are." And so, with their acquiescence, a little tea was arranged.

When I arrived he was outside in the court, smoking, for Signe did not permit it. I knew immediately it was he, though I had not seen him before. He was tallish and rugged, youthful-looking with a mop of reddish blonde hair. He gave me a pleasant smile and followed me into Signe's home.

We all soon got acquainted. I even met the dog, through a picture. He was huge and formidable-looking, weighing some 160 pounds, and Nolen Roberts explained rather proudly that Caesar had been sired by a 190-pound timber wolf with a Mameluke mate. So much was made of Caesar because he was a key to the relationship. Normally, Roberts explained, Caesar could not be petted or played with, nor would he permit anybody but his master to touch him. And because of his size and pedigree, his owner had been careful to obedience-train him personally. He always came when Roberts called or whistled, and he would sit quietly for twenty-four hours or more in one spot if Roberts commanded him to do so.

Peggy, fortunately perhaps, knew none of this as she sat leafing through a book in a shaded park in Beverly Hills. She was a doctor's aide, and frequently took her lunch hour reading or watching the birds. Suddenly, she felt a cold nose nuzzling her hand, and as she quickly turned she saw this half-wild animal of the north looking up at her inquiringly. She reached out and patted his head, and she could almost see him purr. He pushed forward a little so she could pat him again. Meanwhile, she heard a whistled command, and looking up, saw a youngish man with a thick crop of hair firmly calling the dog. The dog looked up, started toward him, and then came back, to be caressed again by Peggy, before reluctantly returning at his master's imperative whistle.

"Never before, and never since," said Roberts, "had he approached a stranger, not to mention allowing one to touch and fondle him." This was not the way of the timberland.

But the dog, being more primal, more sensitive than mere mortals, may have known something they did not yet know—that his master had found his mate.

Roberts, an Englishman, a theatrical producer—who had wandered the world as he willed, skiing here and sunning there—was a free soul. He had never married, nor stayed long with anyone, taking his pleasure as he found it. As he came forward now and claimed his dog, his eyes quickly met Peggy's. They may even have remembered subconsciously, for as Peggy was to say later, she felt with a surge of excitement somehow she had always known him. And yet, while her heart leaped, she felt sadly that it couldn't be. She was old enough to be his mother, with three adult children. How could he find her attractive? He was so young and vital. But, surprisingly, after chatting awhile, he asked if she would have lunch with him. There and then she did something she had never done before. She gave a stranger her telephone number, while not really believing he would call.

That night she looked into the mirror with special care. The face that looked back was still lovely, still showed plainly the unmistakable beauty that must have been hers as a young woman. She was still beautiful, but in a different way, her marble features illuminated by an inner glow, her eyes soft with a touching humility and a concern for others. She had achieved maturity and with it a warm wisdom, with which she tried to put a new perspective on her life. She was lonely since her divorce six years before. It had not been easy. She had always led a rigidly structured life, born into a conservative family, which maintained the stringent Puritan ethic. She was not dramatic or glamorous, or rich. She was middle-aged, the romantic years were behind her, she told herself ruefully, and the phone was not ringing off the wall. Her children were at an age where they were busy with their own lives. Her friends were either married or trying to get married. "Go out and meet people," they advised, "join singles clubs, a country club, do something." She could do none of these things. It was not her style, she was too conventional, too introspective, and, quite frankly, too shy. One night, when the loneliness got especially heavy, she found herself sitting on the edge of her bed, praying tearfully:

"God, just send me someone who loves me for myself."

On the other hand, Nolen Roberts seemed like the answer to a maiden's prayer, the man with everything. She was sure he was just being polite, that he wouldn't call, but she reckoned without polarities, the tug that inexorably brings two people together, regardless of differences in age, race, creed, or class. For he did call, wonder of wonders, and asked her to join him for lunch. Over the table, he eyed her curiously. Stimulated, charming, vivacious, responding to his vibration, she looked so lovely she seemed ageless.

He hesitated for the barest moment.

"By the way," he said, not intending to be abrupt, "how old are you?"

She wouldn't tell him.

"I was afraid," she said, "that he might get up and run away."

Instead, almost perversely, she asked his age.

He was just short of thirty, but he wouldn't say.

"I was afraid," he said, "that she might think it a barrier."

They had been together for nine years now, and as I sat across from them, watching them unobtrusively hold hands under the table, I sensed a oneness, a unity, that I had seen in few couples. He had the reticence of many Englishmen, and had consented to see me only to please her. She was not only proud of their union but felt their example might give heart to many divorced or middle-aged women like herself who were beginning to feel outside the mainstream of life.

She looked over at him fondly. "I can't begin to tell you what knowing him has done for me," she said. "Ironic as it may seem, he has been my teacher. He took me out of this structured, sheltered, arid world I was in, and gave me a strong sense of who I was. Because of the importance he attached to me, he gave me a reflected sense of importance."

She had seen the changes in herself in the changed attitudes of the people around her. To her busy children, preoccupied with their lives, she was no longer just their mother, but an individual, a person to be reckoned with, having ideas and thoughts and dreams of her own.

How had he done this? He modestly pushed the question off on her. "He gave me a sense of freedom," she said, "which I had never had before, and so I was able to free myself for the first time in my life of all those foolish inhibitions I had nursed so long."

There was an easiness in the way they spoke about each other that I liked. They were completely open, they had no secrets from each other, or from us. It was merely a matter of asking the right question to tap the right answer.

How deeply committed were they?

The smiles they exchanged were an eloquent answer.

But we lived in a conventional world that espoused marriage, and they had not married. Was that not the usual commitment of couples professing their depth of love?

"Is there any reason," I asked him, "that you and Peggy have not married?"

He looked at me silently for a moment.

"We would be doing that for others, not ourselves. We do not require that."

She nodded her approval, referring to him fondly as Robert.

"Robert has always been a free soul," she said. "He left

home early to be on his own, and over the years formulated his own values and priorities." She smiled. "Actually, my newborn freedom is only a reflection of how he has lived his life. He has the Aquarian outlook, of unbridled love and humanitarianism. He doesn't conform for the sake of conforming, nor does he march to the beat of another's drum."

To somebody like myself, married twice, marriage had always seemed the supreme commitment between man and woman. But this was my own reality, shaped earlier in life by conventional standards and a desire for family. Yet as one thought about it, why sacrifice something as precious as freedom which could only add to a relationship? Shouldn't love be an accretion rather than a giving up?

Peggy and Robert's love was simplified by nature. Even had they wished it, there would be no children in this match. And yet I had the feeling, had the possibility existed, it would still have made no difference. Many spoke easily of free souls, but these, I felt, were truly free souls, and they were enjoying every moment of it. In the give-and-take of their relationship, there was no place for bickering or argument. She was happy to defer to him, and he to her. They grew through ideas they exchanged, as with freedom, not through activities, or hobbies, or whatever it was that people did to free themselves from boredom.

"We don't have to do the same things," she said, "as long as we think the same and have the same values."

He had been so quiet that I had no feeling of knowing him. To prod him a bit, I asked if he thought the marriage certificate just a piece of paper. He merely smiled and shrugged, and I got the idea that my opinion of what he thought was of no great consequence to him. He was polite, civil, courteous, but he was not about to debate something that had a different significance for each of us.

I still had no clear idea how deep his feeling ran.

"Do you believe you have found your soulmate?" I asked.

A twinkle came to his eyes. He reached out and patted her arm, a natural impulse which, I was sure, had taken place privately a thousand times and more.

"She's like a mother to me," he laughed.

Her eyes gleamed in a smiling response, and she waved her hands in a disclaimer to this obvious bit of humor.

"He knows more than I ever shall," she said.

I knew that Peggy believed in reincarnation, for we had discussed this before. But I had no idea where he stood on something so momentous, and yet controversial, causing some to scoff who had no better alternative but a dark hole at the end of a tunnel.

"Yes," he said, "I do." His eyes narrowed, and for the briefest instant he seemed to be somewhere else.

"I had a dream many years ago, the same dream for six months, in which I had a distant and vivid sense of having lived before. It was a disturbing dream. I didn't see any faces, only treading feet on the cobblestones, mine and others' as well. I had an impression of the eighteenth century, surreys and horses' movement and pre-Victorian dress as though all this connected with something very significant in my life. But, gradually, the dream diminished and it never came back."

As one who lived with the present, Nolen had put it out of his mind. But the two often spoke of the lives experienced together in the past. As for the future, Peggy was a free soul now, and she faced a vast horizon unafraid. She wanted no commitment but what they had, just as Elizabeth Barrett Browning had said long before, "If thou must love me, let it be for naught. Except for love's sake only."

And the answering call came clearly.

"I love thee to the depth and breadth and height my soul can reach."

Peggy put it very well herself in a few lines of verse she had written:

> Long, long have you been with me.
> The sun rose in other dawnings,
> The moon glowed splendidly in other nights,
> Other springs, other summers, other falls—
> All were ours.

After meeting the pair, noting their togetherness, I thought it rather anticlimactic to review their astrological charts. But Signe pointed out that long before she saw them together she knew they were soulmates from these charts.

I had written a book about astrology. But it was always somebody else's astrology, somebody else observing the planetary aspects in such a way that they could often predict the course of a person's life. I knew that certain planets stood for certain things, along with the Moon and the Sun. Saturn was the teacher and lesson-maker, the disciplinarian; Jupiter, the planet of plenty; Uranus of change and innovation, Venus of love, and so forth. They were all universal forces, and who was I to say they had not cosmic influence when they were much greater, if more distant, than our highly affecting Sun and Moon. We all knew what they could do, the Sun causing flowers and crops to thrive and grow, keep our bones straight, and tan our hides. The Moon, in its fullness, making the tides rise, until they enveloped our ocean homes, likewise causing the body fluids to expand until they brought on dramatic swellings and hemorrhages during surgery. And though I didn't know his reasoning, I took Keppler's word for it, when this most famous of astronomers said that planets in transit directly affected the lives and emotions of the people of the earth.

So I was not surprised when Signe mentioned that Saturn, the teacher, played an important role in identifying soulmates. Saturn was invariably strongly aspected in each lover's chart, that is, in conjunction, meaning in the same sign, or in opposition, signifying not opposition, as being against one another, but complementary, in positions directly across from each other. Signe worked out her soulmate aspects from both a primary chart, familiar to every astrology student, and the secondary chart, which was almost unique with her, and rather technical, based on what was known to astrologers as the Arabic parts.

But even so, why should Saturn be so special for soulmates?

"The planet Saturn," said Signe, "represents our karma, the carry-over from the past, and the conditions we put on others and ourselves. It represents that portion of ourselves we must deal with in dealing with others. Consequently, as the karmic planet, it governs our aspects with those we love, for these are the people we obviously have the most karma with— the most to work out from the past."

Where the Saturn aspects were strong, soulmates were stimulating as well as demanding, bringing out the best in us. "In these romantic relationships we have more incentive to let go of our bad habits and attitudes and allow the other person to be as they are. But it's often a struggle, for the very desire to please often makes us hypersensitive. The only ones who can push our buttons are those we deeply love. People marry those they have the most Saturn ties with, then wonder why the relationship is often so trying (actually challenging). Where there is this strongly aspected Saturn to that degree people have problems in a relationship because of the strictures and conditions they put on the other person."

The Sun and Moon also had a vital role. "In a woman's chart the kind of man she gets involved with is represented by her Sun, and her own relationship to that Sun energy within her, as reflected in her chart. In a man's chart, the woman he gets together with is represented by the Moon, the Moon energy within himself.

"Peggy and Nolen's charts have very powerful Saturn ties to the Sun and Moon. Peggy's primary Saturn sits on Nolen's Sun and Moon in a T-square position reflecting many past lives together. Her Sun and Moon are on his North Lunar Node, an important destiny aspect when coupled with a strong Saturn. His Mercury, enhancing communication, is on her secondary North Lunar Node. And his Saturn sits on Peggy's Venus and Mercury, meaning he would teach her, as we now know, about a love not structured, not traditional, but spontaneous, with the flow. His being born on a full moon reflects a certain conflict in energy which is stabilized by her Saturn T-square aspect with his Sun and Moon. Expressed in everyday living this accounts for an enduring, mutually satisfying relationship."

In the technicalities of astrology, I was a little lost, but there was something she had said that impressed me far beyond any astrological delineation. "When people were drawn in love, they began to eliminate the conditions they put on that love. No longer were they concerned with the traditional ideas of others, but stood for unconditional love."

We had seen the hippie movement and the so-called sexual revolution of the Sixties, and now the New Age and the counter-revolution that were to glorify the quest for a spiritual monogamy.

So what could astrology do? How did one break out of these Saturn strictures that could put a damper on love? "I am planning a class on soulmates," said Signe. "Maybe you'll find your answers there."

There were some fifty in the class, predominantly women,

with a scattering of men. They were of all ages and persuasions, and some had little pads, to jot down the magic words of astrology.

With Signe's permission, I asked how many believed in soulmates. Every hand but three or four went up. When I asked how many had already found their soulmates, the hands dwindled to five or six. I then asked how many thought their lives would be wonderfully transformed by finding their soulmates. The response was not quite what I expected. Only three or four hands went up.

Why so eagerly await a soulmate, I wondered, and then expect so little?

But the question would have to wait, for the teacher was ready now for her class. She was to talk about Saturn, its opportunities and restrictions, and how the latter could be overcome in the quest for unconditional love.

"Saturn," she said, "represents that which We give power to in the outer world. Now all of us here, in this earth plane, are working on clarifying our relationship to God. And so what is God? All the great spiritual teachers tell us God is love. So the more we are of love the more we are of God."

It was a nice thought, and it had little to do with astrology, or so I thought.

"So what keeps us," said Signe, "from being more loving? It is the conditions we put on things, the restrictions. We are saying, 'I will love you if you only behave this way. I will love you if you are of the light.' So, how do we learn not to put conditions on love?"

Everybody's head perked up.

"Saturn gives the warning signal," she said. "It tells you when the situation is restrictive, and then you know that you have to relax and give more, stop thinking of all those restrictions you put on love. For unless you break out of these Saturn strictures, which are, paradoxically, part of the same Saturn ties that brought you together, the relationship won't be a happy one, even though it may continue.

"As you get to know the other person better, gaining confidence in the relationship, you often make known your wants, sometimes in the form of demands. And that is what you have to watch. For love is giving not demanding. Whatever you put out comes back to you. Saturn tells you that. And getting to know yourself, which is what astrology is all about, works like a mirror, helping you to know the other person. We are always more trusting of a known quantity. And trust so often becomes the basis for an unconditional love. If we want this love for ourselves, we must put it out there ourselves."

I thought of what the essayist Christopher Morley had said about the successful person being one who lives the life he wants to live.

It didn't seem like much, but as I looked around, how many were doing that?

"Remember," Signe was saying, "the purpose of life is growth. We are not here to be the loveliest or the happiest but to grow. Every person we know well represents some facet of our being. You don't necessarily have karma with that individual but with that facet of yourself that the other individual reflects. The majority of people who get married have a Saturn tie. Now the thing about Saturn ties is that if you get a divorce or you part before you have learned the lessons you were supposed to learn, you are going to meet up with it again. However, it may then be more difficult to work out because you have already established an escape pattern. People in a Saturn-tie relationship generally blame the other person for any problems they need to surmount in themselves. It is best not to abruptly end these relationships, however stormy the going, but to let them go gradually, doing your best, and letting the relationship be what it wants to be."

It was inevitably my turn again with the class.

"So why," I finally got to ask, "doesn't a soulmate radically transform one's life?"

Many hands went up.

"As Signe said," put in an attractive woman of thirty or so, "soulmates are growth relationships, and there's a lot of growing pains in loving somebody as you want to be loved. It's not all strawberries and cream."

"Do you have a soulmate?" I asked, wondering where she was coming from.

"Yes, but it took a while for us to grow together, even though we recognized each other from the beginning."

All this sounded painfully laboring to me. I had the eternal hope, built on solid fantasy, that the Princess Aleta would materialize in all her beauty and purity, as she had for John Ericson, and take me by the hand into the golden sunset.

I wondered how many had the same fancies as myself, how many idealized the dreamed-of relationship beyond anything that was humanly possible or likely? And so I kept inquiring as I had all along:

"And what, Madam, is your idea of a soulmate?"

"Someone I've loved, and been loved by in the distant past, and whom I will love again."

Thinking of the ever-practical Russ Michael, I asked:

"Do you think there can be more than one soulmate relationship?"

An honest frown ruffled her forehead.

"I don't know."

Another young woman, also professing a soulmate, came to her help.

"It's a matter of loving unconditionally. You have to cast out your doubts, your fears of being hurt, you have to let yourself go. In spite of the things that sometimes drive you up the wall. As I see it, you are one, but for some reason, from the past, you had to separate and do things apart, so you could appreciate each other more when you came together again. If I had met this person ten years ago, I wouldn't have been ready. I had some growing by myself to do first."

"Are you happy?" I asked.

She smiled, and no other answer was necessary.

Soulmates obviously were not as special in some minds as they were in others.

"What is the value of a soulmate?" I asked.

Virtually everybody in the room raised their hands, and yet nearly all had been married, divorced, or involved in some relationship that hadn't worked out.

In the sea of femininity a man rose, and immediately commanded attention. He had a serious face, and his words reflected this gravity.

"To me the value seems to be in the increased understanding. Philosopher John Locke said that understanding is the highest human quality even though it may still be limited. So the only way to get beyond these limits is to develop some other, outside force greater than our own understanding. That's what a soulmate means to me. It's an eternal reality, an aspect of a dual inner reality, which we can't reach by ourselves, without an interacting love that invokes extradimensional realities which we didn't even know existed."

There was a momentary lull as we all digested this, and then a woman slowly rose. She was attractive without being beautiful, neatly attired without being fashionable, neither young nor old.

"When two people have a relationship," she said, "they create a new powerful energy which becomes a special entity with a force of its own."

The man who had invoked philosopher John Locke jumped to his feet.

"That's what I was saying. It's as though a new boundless energy with its own identity had formed out of them."

The discussion had turned into a forum on soulmates.

"There are things you have to accomplish together, even if you don't stay together," the woman said. "It could be the working out of things from the past. It might have been pleasant to have stayed on longer in my case, but I don't feel, karmically, we could have put a whole life together."

She laughed ironically.

"Though we're no longer together, no longer married, the vibrations of love are still there, and we learned a lot together. We parted when we had no more to give each other."

"You meet your soulmate, and you still have problems," said Signe. "Sometimes a new set of problems, worth working out because it brings you closer to that unconditional love we all want, even if one partner is ninety and of a different race. Regardless of the turmoil and trauma, the other person makes them aware of a part of themselves previously missing."

Somebody recalled that the great cellist Pablo Casals, ninety, had taken a much younger wife, and added a new dimension to his music.

"Even at his age, he felt a new freshness and energy."

So why, in view of experiences like this, hadn't more of them expected their soulmate to magically transform their lives?

The woman with a broken marriage acknowledged that the prospect of eternal closeness frightened her. "Why not allow the other person to be as they are?"

"But you can," said Signe. "They change of themselves,

wanting to be what you want of them." She smiled. "If it frightening how can it be your soulmate?"

"I gained," said the other. "I was more alert, more aware constantly forced to confront myself. And so, I grew."

"It's too bad you didn't grow together," said a sympa thetic Signe.

"I was under stress. But my ability to understand change completely. We were like two mirrors. So in seeing his weaknesses and strengths, I saw myself as well, and worked on correcting these faults in myself. But it still didn't remove the contention and make everything wonderful."

Signe was young, attractive, and idealistic. I could sense certain disappointment at an apparent disinclination to stick out a karmic relationship, even as I recalled what Nikki Schever had said of the excessively intense relationship she had found so little comfort with.

"Wasn't he increasingly kind and considerate?" asked Signe.

"I gained self-confidence," the woman said, "something I never had before."

Astrology, Saturn, and Saturn ties had been momentar ily eclipsed.

"So why did the marriage end?"

"We were hypersensitive about each other. But through a couple of really incredible fights, we got to the bottom of things and understood why we were at loggerheads."

Signe shook her head, incredulously.

"And yet you separated?"

"But the relationship didn't end. It's still continuing though we live 2,000 miles apart and it's been five years since I've seen him."

Signe's eyes widened.

"And how long were you married?"

"A year and a half."

"And you still think he's your soulmate?"

"Yes, by your definition. We both grew, acknowledging we had to finish what we had left uncompleted from the past. But there was just too much karma."

It seemed to me that she might have tried harder.

"What was the point of it all?" I asked.

She raised her eyebrows in surprise.

"It's not instant Campbell soup," she said. "Once these changes come over you, once your understanding increases, then it becomes a part of your attitudes and directions. You're a better person for it."

So with all these changes why hadn't they reaped the promised rewards of a greater togetherness?

She shrugged.

"It depends where you're coming from. And, as Signe said, I try to think things out, instead of going by my feelings. A lot of the thinking about soulmates is in reverse. You don't necessarily make yourself ready to find your soulmate. But in finding your soulmate, you make yourself ready for life. And I believe that's where I'm at."

But how about this love eternal that soulmates make so much of?

"You've done what you had to do, and you go on," she said. "And you're both better for it. Your lives are easier and take on new meaning separately."

Signe had been listening intently, nodding or shaking her head every once in a while, as I thought back on what Elizabeth Clare Prophet had said about letting go.

"You can be lovers without being soulmates," Signe observed. "There's a mystique between soulmates, establishing not only their connection with themselves, but with the Universal Force."

The woman smiled.

"I am ready for a new and greater adventure. That was his gift to me. I shall always love him for it."

CHAPTER 15

Regina

I had just finished my talk on soulmates, and was sifting through questions when she rather timidly approached the speaker's table. She handed me her card which said, Elizabeth Watson, Professor of Philosophy.

She looked very young to be a professor, and much too pretty. She had good features, dark straight hair, a rosy tint to her skin, and she was black.

She gave me a pleasant smile.

"I was interested in what you had to say about this New Age of soulmates breaking down all the traditional distinctions in race, creed, and color."

"And in age," I said, "don't forget that."

"That was never a problem," she said. "We're the same age."

She was thirty-two but looked considerably younger, married to a biochemist.

"White on white," she said with a laugh. "From North Carolina, of Norwegian ancestry, and college in Utah. What could be more white?"

She came from Birmingham, where the black and white population was more polarized than in most cities. There may have been certain minority defensiveness, but she soon made it

lear that her family and herself had always been militantly
roud of being black.

By now people were beginning to swarm about the table,
nd she was looking around uncomfortably.

She gave me a helpless look.

As I remarked to myself on her subdued good looks, I
ouldn't help but wonder why she was unburdening herself to
total stranger. But I knew there was something, something
nore than just another interracial marriage.

"How about coffee?" I suggested.

She hesitated a moment, then nodded.

And so we arranged to meet an hour or so later.

She was prompt and punctual, as I imagine was a prac-
ice of hers. She must have been singularly well-organized to be
professor in a school of higher learning at her age.

We had a discreet corner of the coffee shop to ourselves.
had speculated the marriage might have run onto the rough
hoals of intolerance and prejudice.

"Oh, no," she said, with amusement, "we've been mar-
ied for nearly twelve years, and have enjoyed total acceptance.
Our families expressed concern, pointing out the difficulties,
ut they turned out for the wedding just as though it was what
hey had ordered."

They had no problem socially, most of their friends
eing of liberal persuasion, with similar interests intellectually.
t had been a broadening experience and there was nothing
bout it she would change. There was a reason for meeting
im, for falling in love, for marrying. As she looked back she
new it was inevitable. And yet had anybody ever told her she
vould marry a white man she would have laughed in his face.

"I had never even thought of dating a white before
neeting Philip. It wasn't considered in the black culture I came
ut of. It just wasn't done."

I looked at her speculatively, noting the irony behind the
hell-rimmed glasses.

I felt like asking, "Well, what happened?" but instead
nquired politely, allowing her her own pace:

"How did you meet?"

"I had just entered graduate school, and it was all very
new to me, as anybody could see. My only interest was my
tudies and my degree. I was walking down a hall, drinking in

this new experience, when we almost bumped into each other He stopped me, and started talking, and I thought what doe this white man want of me? I felt I should walk off, bu something held me. He was new, too, in the graduate school and we talked about that for a while. But I finally drew off, a little confused, wondering what kept me talking to him."

That day she kept thinking about him, angry that she couldn't get him off her mind. The following evening she attended an open house for new graduate students. There were two hundred students milling around, only a handful of them black. She found herself looking around for him, chatting with some of the others, while his eyes were roving around the room. Their eyes finally met, and he rather hesitantly picked his way toward her. They were drawn to each other, yet afraid of rejection.

"I had made up my mind I wouldn't speak to him unless he spoke to me first," she laughed. "And I learned later that he had the same idea himself."

They spoke diffidently at first, a little awkward with each other, then warmed up as they got into their reactions to their new life in the city and the university. They were careful not to touch on anything personal. She was fascinated, without knowing why. And this troubled her as much as his being white.

"What do I see in him?" she kept asking herself.

He was tall, muscular, pleasant-looking, with blue eyes and blond hair. A honky, if she ever saw one. There was nothing compelling about him, and yet she was compelled. She found herself thinking, "I wouldn't be this drawn if he was black, yet here I was in a new school in a new city, preoccupied with this white man who had no place in my world."

It was apparently an antagonistic attraction. She found herself alternately resisting yet irresistibly drawn. She knew she had to straighten out her head, for her work was suffering and here she was an honor student, setting an example for others of her race with the ambition to make something of themselves.

I was surprised at the extent of her feelings, for in the course of her education she most certainly had been subjected to whites of liberal persuasion who had readily responded to her well-bred good looks.

There was obviously more here than met the eye, some psychological quirk, dating from childhood perhaps, some rebuff or slight, some act of discrimination that had left its mark on the subconscious, that part of the mind that always remembers.

At the start, she moved warily, forever conscious of the racial difference, which she then considered an irrevocable bar to an enduring relationship. He seemed so open, so kind, so thoughtful, that she thought there must be a trick to it, the white man's devious game, to triumph over the hapless black one way or the other. But there was never a wrong note, never a flaw in his deportment, almost as if he were trying to make up to her for all the wrongs ever visited by the white man on the black.

After a while she found her suspicions receding, then to her wonderment found that his feeling was so deep that he wanted to marry her. The thought was even more shocking than her first realization that she was drawn to him. She didn't take the proposal seriously, but as she thought about it, she was filled with a strange sort of excitement, as though contemplating an adventure in forbidden waters. There was her family to overcome, and his, but they loved her and hopefully would understand.

She laughed now as she thought about it.

"How could I expect them to understand when I didn't? It was crazy, mad, for somebody in my position, but it was something I had to do, I felt that so strongly, as though impelled by some outside force vastly stronger and more knowing than myself."

I still didn't know what she wanted of me, and found my mind wandering to my flight-time out of Cleveland. Interracial marriages, while not commonplace, were still not that rare, particularly in the sophisticated liberal milieu in which she traveled.

"It seems like a model marriage," I said, for want of anything better to say.

"Oh, yes, we have our individual interests and mutual interests, and we give each other space. That's important. We have a three-story home, one story is his, one mine, one ours, as our moods or work dictate."

As I checked my watch, her eyes followed mine.

"There's more to it," she said hurriedly, "but I don't quite know where to begin." She paused and the dark eyes sparkled behind their glasses. "But I do have one question." Her brow lifted a little. "Exactly what is a soulmate?"

Apparently my talk hadn't made that clear.

"Someone you feel you've always known, who you feel a close, compelling affinity for, whose life you want to share."

"Even if they've done something terrible to you."

"Well, that would establish the law of karma, something from the past you have to work out this time around."

She looked at me doubtfully.

"Must you believe in reincarnation?"

I shrugged. "It could be something else, something we don't even know about, a spiritual or genetic memory bank perhaps, but reincarnation seems the plausible explanation."

She had not thought much about reincarnation—it had seemed weird and far out—until recently, when she attended a seminar on past lives given by hypnotist Dick Sutphen.

I looked at her in some surprise.

"You must have had some reason for going."

She hesitated for a moment, and I could see she was trying to formulate her thinking.

"It had to do with a lot of things, emotions and feelings about the past that I couldn't quite understand."

And it had something to do with her marriage, but again she was hazy and uncertain, not as specific as she might have been.

"I had been thinking about Philip and myself, how our being together, loving one another, even after all these years, seemed to develop as much out of our differences as anything else."

This struck me as rather curious.

She quickly explained.

"I felt after a while that Philip's being white, and me black, had something to do with the intensity of our feelings, causing a great deal of interacting. It did a lot for our thinking and our caring to know we loved each other enough to throw aside the life that had been laid out for us. It helped our growth. It made us think about things we ordinarily wouldn't have. I saw the whites as people like myself, and Philip gained some insight into the black people. We were broader and better for it."

She had experienced all this without losing any interest

in her own background. She had always been fascinated by that tragic family figure, her great-aunt Regina. She lived in the Mississippi delta country around the turn of the century. A woman of singular beauty, her name had been a byword even in the white community, where the mixture of the races was forbidden by Mississippi's old miscegenation laws.

Elizabeth Watson's eyes shone as she spoke of Regina. "She was a woman of great virtue, and pride of race, from what I was told, and though pursued by many men, she never succumbed, for she was never tempted. However, there was one suitor, a white man of some wealth, who kept after her, following her from place to place, not dissuaded or discouraged by her being married, or her indifference."

I could see that Elizabeth was affected by her own story. Her eyes were limpid now, with the least suspicion of a tear. Her face had lost its composure. She seemed to be reliving Regina's experience.

"Couldn't she have called the police?" I asked.

"In Mississippi, at the turn of the century?"

Her voice was incredulous.

"She must have done something."

"What could she do—a black woman in a world where blacks weren't people? They were powerless, her friends, her family, her husband. Nobody dared raise a hand to a white man. But she stood him off, making it clear that even if she hadn't been black, she wouldn't have anything to do with him.

"His anger mounted. Finally, one day, as she drew away in disdain, he picked up an axe that had been lying around and in a burst of temper struck her with it. Her beautiful face was destroyed. She died moments later."

As Elizabeth finished her story, I could see a grimness I had not noticed before.

"And what happened to the man?" I asked.

"He was never prosecuted, but he became his own executioner. Stricken with remorse, he kept pleading with Regina's family for forgiveness. They never gave it."

She had felt closer to the dead Regina than to anybody in her family, thinking of her as a noble, if tragic, symbol of her race.

"Even as a child, I felt connected to her in some special way, without knowing why. I knew exactly how she must have felt, and a lot of my feelings about whites came about through empathizing with her."

She gave an eloquent shudder.

She seemed to have the details at her fingertips. But why wouldn't she, when the incident was so reflective of an ugly past that had its shock waves even today?

She had not told me what had happened at the Sutphen seminar which had featured a training in self-regression, a form of self-hypnosis.

It had been a notable experience. By the simple expedient of expanding her consciousness, developing the visualization process which had opened up the memory bank of the subconscious mind, she had been able to stir up ancient memories. And while she had no proof of their validity they had given her cause for thought.

"Did any particular memory especially affect you?" I asked.

She nodded, frowning over her coffee.

"Yes," she said, "I saw myself as clear as day, in a plantation setting I would never have imagined. I saw this beautiful black woman, dusky, but still lighter-skinned than myself, moving through the fields of cotton like a black goddess, serene in the pride of her own presence. I saw a man approaching her, and the black people working in the field look up in alarm, for he was a white man, and there was a grim, menacing purpose in his stride.

"He had no eyes for anybody but her, moving to within a few feet of her, and barring her passage. There was a brief exchange of words, her voice full of scorn, and his face flushed. His voice rose angrily and his hand raised as if he were about to strike her and then . . ."

The picture broke off abruptly, as if in a bad dream the dreamer could not tolerate in its total reality.

"And what did you make of it?" I asked.

She smiled, a look of satisfaction on her sensitive face.

"There was no doubt in my mind. The experience was as vivid and real as anything I had ever known. I, Elizabeth Watson, was my great-aunt Regina."

I had half-expected this. But who was the white man, had she any inkling of him?

Again she hesitated.

"Wouldn't it be somebody with something to atone for in this life? Somebody I could come together with on a more equal footing, who I could forgive, without appearing to, just by my dealing with him."

"You mean accepting him?"

She sighed. "Something like that."

"And who may it be?"

She shrugged.

"I thought you would know," she said, rising with a graceful little movement. "You spoke about karma, and our living by it."

I cursed myself for my obtuseness as it suddenly came to me who she meant. It explained a number of things, including the masking of an old feeling she had dared not admit even to herself.

"Have you forgiven him?" I asked.

She gave a mysterious smile.

"A long time ago. Or we wouldn't be married today."

CHAPTER 16

The Hypnotist Hypnotized

Dick Sutphen had regressed thousands of persons into the past, and taught thousands of others to regress themselves. Invariably, with a few modest exceptions, they had picked up on past lives, with or without soulmates, and these recalls had been validated to an astonishing degree.

Sutphen had made a name for himself in hypnosis and reincarnation. As the author of *You Were Born Again to Be Together*, and *Past Lives, Future Loves*, he advocated regressions which were not mere glorifications of the ego but utilitarian in nature. So often they explained in one or two dramatic sessions troublesome divisions between couples. "In all my work in this area," he reported, "I have found only a few cases where I have been unable to establish a past link between present lovers."

The explanation of so many marital problems was often only one past-life away, providing a pathway to wisdom and understanding. A frequent complaint was a lack of sexual compatibility, even between men and women who looked upon themselves as soulmates in other respects. One Sutphen subject, a youthful businessman, married four years, had been concerned by the frigidity of his otherwise doting wife. "Our sexual relationship is a nightmare," he told Sutphen. "It is unsatisfying for both of us. My wife has never experienced an orgasm, and I feel not only frustrated but inadequate."

Sutphen regressed them into a period in Colonial America. They were together again and the marriage had been a happy one until the wife was attacked and raped by three marauding strangers in her husband's absence. Although she was blameless, her husband, instead of sympathizing, considered her ineradicably blemished, and would have nothing more to do with her physically. There was a twofold traumatic impact, which, Sutphen felt, had buried itself deeply in her memory bank, reflected in her present frigidity.

"She had brought into this experience not only the negative effects of the traumatic assault, but subconscious resentment of her husband because of this painful rejection in their previous life."

So why, resenting each other, had they been brought back to so uncomfortable a situation?

"They have this opportunity," Sutphen said, "as do so many soulmates, of rising above the past through manifesting a love and wisdom they had not shown before. If he acknowledges this past lack, as he himself described it, compensating with a new patience and understanding, the underlying resentment will in all likelihood disappear, along with her inexplicable distaste for sex. They now have the knowledge. The choice is theirs."

Sutphen interested me, not only as an authority, but personally as well. I had been instrumental in his meeting a young lady he was convinced was his soulmate. He was confident they had many life experiences together, accounting for the rapturous feeling that struck them on sight. She, too, though twenty years younger than the forty-five-year-old Sutphen, was so enraptured that she floated off to Hawaii with him, with their respective children, in a brief but glorious honeymoon independent of marriage.

Both were already in the process of divorce, so I felt no qualms about being the innocent party that had brought an unlikely soulmate into their lives. All I did was introduce them. Nature did the rest. I was not even aware when lightning struck, and it remained for Dick to fill me in via a published account.

"Often, upon first meeting someone," he wrote, "I sense

a bond with them and like and trust them immediately. Much more rarely, I have been intensely attracted to an individual upon first meeting, having such a strong reaction that I'm almost unable to respond. I can only recall this happening to me about three times in my life. The last time was a couple months ago to a beautiful young woman named Tara. We both took one look at each other and immediately felt the bond. Neither of us has been the same since."

Sutphen became pardonably philosophical. Only a few months before, a psychic whose predictions had always been accurate had described a "beautiful, lean, dark lady" to soon come into his life. Tara McKean certainly fit this bill, with a mind as agile and trim as her body.

They were joining their lives with a swiftness that took my breath away. They had so many common interests that it truly seemed as if this prospective marriage was made in heaven. Tara, who had been living near Seattle, put her horses on a van and shipped them from Washington to Sutphen's ranch home in Malibu. Dick's five-year-old son and Tara's six-year-old boy were already like brothers. There seemed nothing lacking. It seemed only too perfect, for Dick was a catch himself—handsome, youthful, successful, universally admired by the thousands who sought him out trying to find a soulmate.

As Dick had told so many, it was impossible to avoid one's destiny. All one could do was go with it, learn by it, and grow. These were the magic words, learn and grow. To know one's destiny was to understand one's life. What free will we had was our response to events so abruptly and unceremoniously thrust into our path. If Tara had not been visiting from Washington, had I not known Sutphen, and had he not invited me to a party that we only went to at the last moment, then that meeting certainly would not have occurred. But there was no doubt in Dick's mind it would have happened another way, the bond between them being so powerful.

As Dick had explained:

"Relationships and the concept of destiny manipulating us on the chessboard of life have always been my primary interest. I know that shared past lives are the prerequisite for an important relationship in this life. People appear to come together by an unseen plan. Their union is often a reward, structured for them to learn or teach together, sometimes to support each other in a shared purpose or mission, recalling Edgar Cayce's 'Like a glove slipping onto a hand, like a tenon into a mortice.' "

The scantily educated Tara, unknowledgeable about the metaphysical field, fit smoothly into Sutphen's lifestyle. Soon, she was flying around the country, participating in all his seminars, offering him advice so sound it startled him that he had not thought of it before. So astonished was he by the impact of this twenty-four-year-old novice on his highly complex life that he decided to do what he was teaching others to do—a self-regression, with Tara at the heart of it.

"If Tara and I have been together before," he told himself, "I want to go back to the most important lifetime we shared, one influencing present events more than any other."

More quickly than any student, he slipped into his meditation. The setting was perfect, a psychic center, known throughout the world, the Valley in the Mountain, Sedona, Arizona. As he gazed at the red clay mountains, a wave of serenity came over him. His pulses stilled, his breathing slowed rhythmically, and he peered beyond the veil that keeps most of us prisoners in a mundane world.

As he closed his eyes, he perceived a scene completely new to him. "With my sharpened awareness, I saw vividly a ridge sloping down to the sea. It overlooked a bay and many small boats anchored below. Along the ridge there was a latticed walkway, and about every hundred feet a tall, decorative archway. Halfway down the ridge the walkway became a circle, obviously a viewing site for the bay below. I was strolling down the pathway with a beautiful young woman—Tara. When we got to the circle we were holding each other. We were very much in love."

He had sketched a picture, not only showing the path, but her hairstyle, neatly tied in the back by a decorative comb.

In his regression he got another image of the topmost portion of South America. "Venezuela. Later, by looking at a map I had a very strong feeling of the Maracaibo area by a huge bay."

It was the mid-nineteenth century. They were in a Spanish style house with formal high ceilings. "I had the impression she lived there. We were having a discussion. I wanted her to leave with me, for an assignment I had elsewhere. We loved each other, but I refused to pass up a golden opportunity. I wanted her to love me enough to choose my life. But she, as stubbornly, felt we could do better under the protective wing of her wealthy and influential family. We became very sad, knowing we were about to lose one another."

And so they did, parting sorrowfully, to perhaps find each other at another time and place.

On meeting Tara, Dick had the feeling of having not only known her before, but of some unsatisfied yearning between them. Was this time to round out a chapter ended more than a hundred years ago? He found it odd, too, that Tara, whose maiden name was the Scottish McKean, was dark and Spanish-looking, with all the verve of a passionate Latin beauty.

While bowled over, he was mature enough to realize it might be an infatuation that could leave him pondering that old adage about youth serving youth. A few days later he asked Alan Vaughan, an associate and a leading psychic, to give him a reading, which might cast light on his past-life excursions. Without telling the psychic anything of his own regression, he arranged the session, with Tara and one other present.

Tara, too, had questioned the juggernaut that had hit them both. Vaughan, in trance, picked up on this. "Beautiful stranger, greetings," he said. "Tara, any questions about why you are together?"

Predictably almost, there were several experiences together. One in Mongolia, another in Rome, then Mexico, Nova Scotia, and finally, South America. Strangely enough, or perhaps not so strangely, if it was a valid recall, Vaughan tuned into the earlier parting.

"Was there matrimony, you ask? No, there should have been but there was not. There was a beautiful moment, in a garden, tropical scents. You bid goodbye. You, Tara, a beautiful maiden. He an earnest, young military adviser. Tears were shed. You, Tara, said never more will I become so upset with my emotions. You married another man. He married another woman. You never saw each other again."

So much for love's sweet dream. Now after centuries of uncertainty, of cross-purposes that divided and agonized them, they had nothing blocking the road to happiness but themselves. But neither, at this time, the psychic said, had yet made the necessary inner commitment.

Vaughan counseled:

"So look to your past and find what is more agreeable and foster that in your relationship. You, Richard, have investigated relationships because you realize that you have messed up so many of them. That is why you want to make them better. You are sensitive to other people in profound ways. You give them love, but you do not want love back. You give them understanding, but you do not want understanding back. That would defeat your purpose of staying free, so that you can give yourself to the many."

From what I knew of Dick, the substance of the reading was correct. He had been married three times, with many relationships interspersed, and now, with a possible fourth, would he "mess up" again?

I was struck by the corroborating South American life, and equally intrigued by a Mongolian experience where the sex roles were reversed, with Tara the man and Richard the woman. In this rather wild and wooly experience, the male Tara seduced the then-female Richard, and produced five babies whom he (Tara) abandoned when he went off to battle. Richard (the maiden) brought up the babies alone. For the warrior (Tara), loving power more than his mate, never returned.

I found this change of sex confusing, and sometimes humorous. But life was prone to play these little tricks on us. To teach us, presumably, how the other shoe fit.

This struck Richard as a form of reverse karma. "I have the five children now," he said, "and Tara has come back."

He was grateful she was back since he was a man, and as the French say, "Vive la difference."

To experience the past, it was not necessary to accept reincarnation. Just as a cell remembered, so could the brain. "Obviously," said Dick, "these memories stirred out of the past. When you see an effect, there is a cause. Your entire life—your mental state, health, relationships—all are effects. But somewhere in the background, in this life, or before, there were provocative causes. You may not remember this consciously because it would probably be so painful it would cloud your freedom of choice in this life."

But the events were there, shaping the subconscious, waiting to be invoked as a signpost to the past and future.

"The meeting of soulmates," he went on, "is predestined

for their soul's growth. As a troubled relationship sharpens the awareness, the unlearned lessons from the past begin to surface, since all learning is a process of remembering the past."

Tara had never been regressed before, and was rather uneasy about it. However, she had the normal feminine curiosity and wanted to round out the equation.

As it turned out, she was a good subject. It was only a matter of minutes before Dick had her under. She spoke in a measured, yet uneven tone, as if groping for a period when they were together. Her breathing was steady and rhythmical, indicating she was in a light trance. Suddenly, she began to describe the house Sutphen had described in his regression. This house, too, had broad terraces and overlooked the sea. She saw herself strolling with the Richard that was, just as he had, and saw that same impasse, as they stood looking help-lessly at one another. But she went further, her voice barely a whisper. "I cared for him, but I was not in love, not then. I could not go with him. My heart would not let me."

And so there it was, an explanation that would satisfy anybody who had ever loved. It was not the thought of leaving home that had saddened and dismayed her, but the prospect of giving up that home for a man who could not match what she would be leaving.

There were other past experiences, in the prehistorical period, when they dwelt together in caves, and carried spears, their only protection against the predatory animals and people of the plains and hills. They ate what they could off trees and bushes, or the flesh of animals less formidable than themselves and the dappled fish out of the tropical streams.

"I carried his spear," said Tara, her voice strangely muted, "and we made love. But I didn't love him. I never loved him."

So there was Tara, never in love with Dick, but mated to him all those times because of his dominant force. Had that karma again imposed itself when with the magnetic force of his personality he had swept her off her feet? Obviously, they had much to work out.

As before, Tara had divided loyalties, but, finally, having to choose once again between her family and Dick, she chose to go off with him and never looked back.

"I truly love him," she said, as the thought of any part-ing brought tears to her eyes.

And as for Dick, he echoed valiantly:

"This time, it's forever."

Obviously, there were changes in both, forged out of the past, which gave them a new appreciation of what they meant to each other.

"Everything I am," she said, "tells me we are finally together at the right time and place."

Still there were lessons to learn. But how else was one to learn from the past, unless he knew that past? And there was no simpler way, said Sutphen, than to regress oneself, hardly a difficult process.

"All hypnosis is self-hypnosis anyway," Sutphen observed. "All I do is teach people to alter their state of consciousness, give themselves the suggestion that will evoke the memories dormant in the same genetic makeup responsible for their ability to think, talk, walk, breathe, and reproduce themselves."

He was happy to pass on the pointers he found useful in teaching others to regress themselves.

"The subject should lie down in a dark warm room, without light and distracting noises. His clothes should be loose, free of belts and buckles, and other restrictions. He (or she) should remove shoes, and anything that may impede the natural circulation and rhythmical breathing. Concentrate on deep, slow, rhythmical breathing for five minutes, helping mind and body to relax. Keep the mind a blank, but don't consciously block anything out. You are in control at all times. You never lose consciousness, but only alter it. You pass from beta brainwaves to alpha and theta, an exchange that takes place naturally twice a day when you go to sleep and wake up. There is nothing strange or mysterious about the process. All you are preparing to do is tune into that part of the mind, the subconscious, which governs the memory. You speak to yourself softly, in a slowed cadence, without necessarily uttering a word.

"Do not resist, for nobody can achieve the altered state against his will. In this state, in light trance, you will be aware of your immediate surroundings. Don't let that deceive you. You are under."

Visualization was a simple process. Anybody could do it. More than ninety-five percent of those regressed had past-life experiences.

"After the breathing, the subject closes his eyes, and

begins a countdown, from seven or ten, as he prefers. He sees himself descending on an escalator, even deeper and deeper, until he sees himself in a black tunnel. He passes through that tunnel, coming out clear-headed and open, altered on all levels. All hypnosis involves the narrowing of the attention to one point. In this instance the subject visualizes a familiar household scene, perhaps the bathroom, picking out each article and perceiving it up close, not just letting the mind's eye wander over it.

"Concentrate on a moving scene, an Indian on horseback, the ocean surf rolling onto the shore, not just seeing, but perceiving in every detail. Listen for the Babbler inside your head, perceiving different sounds, the barking of a dog, the grinding of brakes, the patter of rain on the roof. As you do so, you will visualize the pictures associated with these sounds.

"In this altered state you become relaxed to the point of losing awareness of your body. You are open to suggestion and able to relive any event. Although you remain aware, to some degree, of outside noises, they will not distract you.

"As you see things, speak up and verbalize them. Let a tape recorder run, if you like, so you can play it back later. After you have become visually oriented, you are floating into an alternative alpha-theta state. As you allow your mind to drift, you are ready to flip back into time, and with the greatest of ease. Trust your own input, confident the past will emerge."

The induction, as I knew from my book *The Power of Alpha Thinking*, was a simple procedure. The alpha mind, as in dreams, functioned like a motion picture as Elizabeth Watson had discovered in tuning into her great-aunt Regina.

"With the visual mind now wide open, but under control, suggest it revert to a past-life situation very meaningful to this life. Trust that the answer will come. Think of yourself as a mind, for in reality this is what you are. You do not have a mind. You are a mind. You are the sum total of all your experiences from the beginning of time.

"If pictures form to which you do not relate, move to events vital to your condition, throwing some light on the person you want to know about. The subconscious will do as you tell it. Repeat aloud, as I have, that you are completely open to suggestion, able to relive any true event—narrowing your attention to this event. It will happen."

Just as it happened, I suppose, to Richard and Tara.

CHAPTER 17

The Deeper Call

Reaching into the seat pocket, I pulled out a copy of the United Airlines magazine. I started turning the pages, and came to a story about realtor Donald Trump. He was young, attractive, and rich. At thirty-six, he was redoing the skyline of mid-Manhattan, and making millions in the process. He controlled upwards of a billion and a half dollars of choice properties. And like Trump Tower, a magnificent edifice thrust high into the sky on Fifth Avenue, he stood for the opulent elegance of a Big Apple staging a dramatic comeback.

I began the article two-thirds of the way out of Chicago and had it finished before we dropped down at La Guardia. Trump was always doing something big, a towering Grand Hyatt Hotel in the heart of New York or a gigantic $200 million casino in Atlantic City. There was nothing too vast for this sensitive man with the facility of putting together deals that baffled other men. And there was an extra blessing. God had granted him a beautiful young wife, who was his helpmate, overseeing the details of his projects, picking out the bathroom fixtures, and selecting the designers.

It all seemed so perfect, the epitome of the American dream, a success story no different from many others, except that its hero appeared more reflective, more modest, wondering almost to himself if "it was too much, too fast."

I was reminded of Elvis Presley at twenty-eight, having achieved fame, wealth, undreamed-of success, yet feeling empty inside, looking for some spiritual guidance, some deeper purpose to rekindle his zest for living. But there was no hint of ennui or discontent in the Trump saga, only the flush of success, with ever new worlds to conquer. As I was about to toss the magazine aside, my eye slipped to the last paragraph. And something stopped me. A new dimension had suddenly been added.

"What does it all mean?" Donald Trump asked, looking down on the skyline he had helped mold. His face turned "pensive," in the words of his interviewer, and he added softly, as if to himself:

"Life is what you do while you're waiting to die."

The reporter, thrown off for a moment, suggested that Trump may have been "suffering from postconstruction depression."

My own reaction was quite different. I would have speculated that Donald Trump, having made his mark in the world of commerce, had in a moment of illumination sensed there must be something beyond the mundane, something that explained our being here and the tasks we set for ourselves, something he had not quite reached.

Obviously many more would think as Donald Trump but for the fact that few attained his success so readily, and so kept striving for goals they might not find fulfilling once attained.

Edgar Cayce had said there was one continuous life, one soul, one great love for that soul, though other karmic relationships could be as vital if not eternal. He had regressed himself many times and described names and places from the past, which were subsequently unearthed on investigation. For myself, I had observed countless regressions in which everything provable seemed to dovetail, but I was still more impressed by the emotional links between people than by any validation of dates and names. The past, after all, could be seen psychically, just as the future so often was.

Cayce had said it very well, I thought, when asked if it was the individual destiny to be united with some special soul.

"Know rather," he said, "that the soul is the soulmate of

the Universal Consciousness than of an individual entity, accounting therefore for its growth."

He had put a lot in a few words, pointing out that the growth we have mentioned so frequently did not specifically come out of the interaction exclusively of the two, but of their interaction, as a unit, with the Creator. Their horizons grew as they drew others into an orbit extending their growth to the outer boundaries of the Universe. And so we had the trinity of consciousness, which Signe's class had spoken of.

Without one's soulmate—twin soul, companion, or karmic —life, said Cayce would be less than negligible. But one must prepare: "Be in that position that when the complement of self in the opposite sex appears, thy heart, thy mind, thy body will recognize same. For without that complement, the self will be as naught and become nil."

A classic example had existed in his own experience and that of his son. With a soulmate wife, Hugh Lynn Cayce was able to wander the world spreading his father's work. Without her support he might never have taken that first step.

"My dad was my inspiration, my wife my strength."

Obviously if one person lived before then all have, for there is a universality, as St. Paul said, in the human condition.

The past, and all its wonders, was as near as the individual's subconscious.

"When regressed," said Dick Sutphen, "everybody comes up with a past life."

Did that mean that all were suffering from subconscious delusions, or rather experiencing an emotional linking of import not only to another person, but to a past which illuminated the present and presaged the future?

When Susan Strasberg and Patrick Flanagan described their togetherness in Egypt and Rome, I was not so much affected by Flanagan's perception of the pyramids, as by a love story which held shades of sorrow and joy, exciting moments of history as well as banalities, and all the grasping and invidious, great and noble qualities man manifests in his struggle to justify an existence he can make what he wills. For in his striving, in his ceaseless seeking of the immortality of love, he finds a door to his own immortality.

Like General Patton, who made no secret of it, Susan had misty memories of a Roman experience, which shaded her behavior in this life, making the Eternal City almost a second home, tantalizing at times, forbidding at others. "At least," she said, "I discovered why lions weren't my favorite animals."

I was disappointed when relationships didn't work out, for this exchange of love not only uplifted my own spirits, but others' as well. But I had not given a long life, even at its peak, to the Susan Strasberg-Patrick Flanagan idyll, for both obviously were coming off past-life experiences that had not bound them tightly together. But Susan was still the gainer.

"Patrick helped me," she said, "to distinguish between a true and lasting love, and a love aborted in the past, and now concluded with this experience. I learned what I had not learned before. I had to heal the past, getting rid of old resentments, before I could find a lasting love in the present. I am ready for my twin soul now."

Those who loved in the past had hopefully come back to rebuild on that past. There was a connection from that past in the same assortment of characters, and a few new ones as well. Actress Terry Moore was to find her Irish groom in the Jewish cabdriver she visualized as that groom. And, ironically, she had come into this life in the Mormon faith that had a century ago become a way of life for that groom. Only through her regressions which had taken on so much reality could she explain the stormy relationship with Howard Hughes. But her disputed marriage, affirmed by his blood heirs years after his death, finally gave her the financial independence denied her by Roger Elliott and provided by Hughes in posthumous retribution.

Providentially, a poor man had as good a chance of finding a soulmate as a rich one. Less affected by the material, he might be inclined to attract by his own innate qualities. And less involved with wealth, he would be less preoccupied with what he had so little of. Like a homely woman he had to sharpen whatever qualities of the mind and spirit he had to attain his soulmate. But there was no good reason why the economic classes couldn't merge, once it was established wealth was not an issue in love.

Accustomed to wealth, Terry had reached out for the man she thought Jonna reborn, not once pausing to reflect that for a second time she had preferred a penniless mate. "Jerry's smile," she said, "did more for me than Howard's billions—just like it had before."

I could not imagine Peggy Polk caring whether her Robert had a dime, for brought up in relative wealth she had seen how it ruled people rather than being an instrument of happiness. And, of course, with the Cayces, father and son, it was never a consideration, for there was—literally—nothing to consider.

I marveled how it all fell into place, even to Tara McKean's having abandoned five children with Dick Sutphen in a previous experience, only to find her returning now after he had fathered five children with other mates.

"You would almost think," said a startled Sutphen, "that there was some recognition here of a karmic debt."

I didn't question their being soulmates—karmic soulmates perhaps. But the thought passed through my mind that they had moved too far, too fast. Not because they had defied conventional prudence—soulmates were always doing that. But because they had not heeded the lesson of their pasts. The pattern of the regressions was all too clear. They had been together many times. Yet in the experiences I had noted, like the rest, they had never developed a lasting love. Something of their karma, or circumstance, had kept them from a realization of that special togetherness. Again, as in her subconscious experience in South America, the stumbling block appeared to be Tara's excessive devotion to her family. On a visit to their home in Alaska, she seemed to cling to them inordinately, or so Dick thought. But love triumphed over this crisis of divided affections. And in this instance, the experience of the past played a part as Tara—having suffered through the South American standoff—now opted for love and marriage.

"I saw my mistake in time," she said, "and did not repeat it."

Nearly every soulmate relationship I looked into seemed to thrive on coincidence or synchronicity, from the chance meetings of astral mates: Peggy and Robert, brought together by a dog; Savilla and Burl Schilling, drawn into each other's space by a commonplace wish to stop smoking.

"I am convinced," said Savilla, "that I picked up my habit not only to bring me to the man who would cure me of smoking but to reaffirm my belief in the continuity of life."

And yet none of this was coincidence because of its very incidence and the recurring bonds that reflected a universal design. Some of these unions appeared inevitable, as that of Monaco's Prince Rainier and Hollywood's Princess Grace. She had found her soulmate, choosing this obscure head of a petty principality over the captains of industry and distinguished nobility because of an intuitive feeling, supported by a psychic's impression, that she would one day be a princess.

I recall her telling me, at her cinematic peak, of a psychic who had accurately foretold every detail of her brilliant career, when she was still unknown. But then she had laughed as she airily added, "But, of course, she was wrong about one thing. She said I would be a princess one day."

Her eyes sparkled, but I could sense the undercurrent of seriousness in her voice, and I was not surprised when she met and married her Prince.

We had shared a lively interest in the Unknown, and only recently she had looked into some serious research on psychic healing, which she had hoped to bring to the attention of some nursing nuns, concerned with the power of prayer in healing.

Shortly before her untimely death, she had appeared at an award ceremony honoring her playwright uncle, George Kelly. Friends were struck by a new mystique, a sense of peace, as though she were on the verge of something great and wonderful.

"She has had it all," one observed at that time. "What is there left for her?"

No force was greater in the soulmate quest than the power of the mind, shaped by its heart's desire. Just as Robin Blake, Holly Markas had been impressed by Terry McBride when he spoke at her church in Huntington Beach, California. But hers was a more personal interest as well, for as his speech continued she was excited by the realization they shared the same reverence for peace, joy, and love. She listened avidly as he stressed:

"Write down what you want, see it, know it—and go for it. Everybody wins."

As she listened to him, she felt that he was speaking directly to her, and her heart responded. She did nothing about it, for she did not know what to do, though her mind kept coming back to him, long after he had gone on.

She knew she would see him again, and sure enough, a short time thereafter he gave a motivational talk to a realty group to which she belonged. She took two friends with her, not telling them anything, but wondering what their reaction would be.

Midway through the talk, one friend said, "You are perfect for each other. He represents everything you believe in. Have you written him down?"

It was not till then that she realized that she had to use the tools he had offered if she were to bring him into her life.

"So I wrote him down, meditated about being with him, to where I could feel his presence."

And he felt her presence as well. For within a short time he called, and wanted to see her. They had been together for only a few hours, talking at random, when he turned to her and said, tears in his eyes:

"God has sent you to me."

And with her heart full of love, she nodded. For she had known that from the first day she saw him.

Their love reduced their fears, and made them face each other and themselves. "I can't put off being who I am anymore," wrote Holly. "You have allowed me to remember that I am as magnificent as you, that the wall I have hidden behind isn't necessary anymore. Thank you, thank you, for your presence and for the love you have brought into my life. My love is a celebration and you, my love, are my song."

They were married three months later.

This was no more a coincidence than Peggy and Robert, or Savilla and Burl. For each time a thought had gone out expressing a desire, the Universal Intelligence that governs us all had overseen its fulfillment. There was nothing esoteric about it, it was a simple everyday demonstration of the power of remembrance in the implementation of Universal Law.

Edgar Cayce and Elizabeth Clare Prophet both spoke of twin souls working, learning, growing together, to serve God and their fellow man. The deeper people searched within themselves, the more they made of themselves, the greater likelihood of finding a soulmate.

There was an essential goodness, a lack of cynical sophistication, a freedom from deception, chicanery, betrayal, a love of not only their soulmate but their fellow human. In loving one person, mellowed by that love, there was a kindling of love for humanity.

I thought of Elizabeth Watson, forgiving a sin out of the past, terribly real in her own experience, serving to break down age-old hostilities which kept a world teetering on the edge of disaster.

"In loving one man," she said, "I realized we were all pretty much the same clay. As I stopped thinking in terms of black and white, I could see the altered consciousness in others about me. The thought that reduced one prejudice could eliminate others as well. We were all connected, that lesson I learned and hopefully am passing on."

The world was the sum of its parts, a macrocosm of endless microcosms in which spiritual love was a potent and transcending force. I had found the story of Burl and Savilla particularly inspiring. Mysteriously intriguing, largely unvalidated except for their regressions and memories, it was still a heart warming demonstration of the immortality of love.

"We knew from our love," said a serene Savilla, "that we had loved before, this was but another interlude in the laboratory of life. I had much to learn, and Burl was there, properly aged and seasoned, when I was ready."

They seemed the ideal prescription for soulmates, supportive, loving others out of their love, taking strength out of a Universe and a God which had given them enduring love for Burl perhaps as a final gift for remembering so long and so well. Out of their remembrance—subconscious, genetic, past-life—had blossomed a love that defied tradition. The pluses were hers—youth, money, beauty. But with one moment of illumination, love's alchemy had miraculously transformed them both.

"I had this secret yearning," Burl had recalled, "but as the years passed, the dreams of youth vanished as well. And then Savilla appeared to show me that faith should never flag, that it was never too late to dream."

Soulmates were special, I found, because they wanted something special. They knew that without this special love their lives had no grace or purpose. Yet, they were humble in their quest, putting no price on love, only a value.

I thought of Nikki Schevers's wistful smile that day in the restaurant in Pacific Palisades, and wondered what had come of her. She had been so beautiful, so young, and so alone.

As if in answer to my thought, she called.

"I am getting married," she announced.

The wedding took place in Yosemite National Park. The groom was handsome, loving, a few years younger, but mature, just what she had been waiting half a lifetime for. They were married by his father, a minister. There was no honeymoon, for as with so many of the soulmates, every day was a lovefest.

Once before she had thought she had met her soulmate. But the impact had been so strong, so electric, they were unable to relax together. "After a while we couldn't think of anything but how we felt and how we affected each other. The tension of just being together, of nervously reacting, drained me completely and yet it was so compulsive I kept thinking we belonged together. But it was all an illusion out of the past."

Yet it had its purpose, as all soulmate relationships do.

"I was better able to appreciate my husband. There was an easiness about our relationship. We didn't have to say or do anything, there were no rules or boundaries. He didn't believe in everything I believed in, but he did believe in my being my own person. He was not into the metaphysical, but he didn't question my interest, and he listened. We seemed to grow through the growth we allowed each other."

She had no doubt he was her soulmate.

"I knew the moment he walked into the restaurant. But I had to let him find out for himself and that took a while. I knew he could not be hurried. I remembered, and I was waiting for him to remember." She smiled. "Not that it really mattered. For we are building new memories every day."

The multiplicity of soulmates, I found, disturbed some perfectionists.

I had been speaking on soulmates at a seminar, when a young woman protested.

"I don't want to be told that after I find my soulmate I may lose him."

With any growth, I explained, she might well go on to a new and greater relationship.

"I want it to be perfect," she said, "particularly when I've been waiting around several lives for it to happen."

"Don't wait," I said, "open your heart and your mind."

Nature being what it is, we have all had romances of some degree. So what makes a soulmate so special, not only as a love interest, but in affecting the fabric of one's life?

"We're living in an unstable world where we all need

support," said our hypnotherapist Boris Bagdassaoff. "With our world caving in on all sides, it takes a very special relationship to provide a compensating love. These are not ordinary times, they call for special people, working in a very extraordinary way."

This was all very fine, but how was it to turn around a world hellbent on destruction? "That," smiled Boris, "is what the New Age is all about."

Love and growth. You grow to love and love to grow, and in this process merge with the Universal Intelligence. Carl Jung spoke of synchronicity, events coming together for a specific purpose, even that of soul development. And a developed soul, sensitized by a soulmate relationship, was sharply attuned to its purpose. In time, the ardor of soulmates, becoming almost a physical presence, should emerge as a decisive force, transforming hate into love and war into peace.

It all seemed unrealistically Utopian. Christ had preached as much and been taken to the Cross. And now there was talk of a new Christ consciousness, of a Christ reborn in the bosom of soulmates pledged to a universal love.

It began with two people, then millions, scattered around the globe. They were, as Boris said, the foundation for the vaunted New Age. There was an affinity nothing could shake, a communication vibrating across a room or a broad expanse, always with shadowy memories of other times and places.

We were all adventurers, embarked on a greater quest than Columbus ever dreamed of. Suddenly, the Universe seemed to merge with our own thoughts and goals. We were exalted, often without knowing why, for we had found the mate the Creator destined for us. And the world had now become our precious preserve.

I was sure the Creator had no prejudices against any of his creations. As I listened to Shirley MacLaine that day in Tacoma, I saw, as she did, no reason why homosexuals should be excluded as soulmates. "Why in the world," Shirley had asked, "should they alone be barred from eternal happiness?" The Ram had argued that soulmates were a by-product of natural law. "And part of this law is a love expressing itself in the perpetuity of life."

But, supporting Shirley, Edgar Cayce, the personification of reincarnation, had spoken of sex changes from one lifetime to another, and of the righting in the present of old indulgences and aberrations.

There were no fixed patterns, for age was no barrier, nor race, color, creed, until it seemed at times as if the Creator was sending out lovers to do battle for a just world.

I had described our soulmates as I found them, especially those who made a statement of their love. But I did not object when others, professing such a love privately, still refused to publicly proclaim it for fear of ridicule.

"But you and your soulmate believe in reincarnation," I said to a famous star, publicized for just about everything but what she presumably believed in.

"Yes," she said, "but what will the Bible Belt think?"

I had not expected a quick metamorphosis in realtor Donald Trump, for I knew that one had to have a metaphysical experience himself before he laid his mind open to the untracked wonders of the infinite. Consequently, I was amused by reports that his restless spirit, ever seeking new diversions, had led him to buy a professional football team and dicker for a baseball club as well. How long would it be, I wondered, before this man of vision became bored with these playthings?

When I first met Elizabeth Prophet I was intrigued that she had accomplished so much herself, only to find that she had been influenced by a dead husband's thoughts and dreams, his energies taking life in her. He lived on in what she attained. Her mind had put his face on the mirror, her heart told her what that meant, her resolution established what they had visualized together.

Neither prudish, nor against sex, she felt the answer lay in balance. "You decide that balance, by what you want of your life. You are the best judge of what you are getting."

She urged a cautious discrimination, sparing one the hollowness of love for sex's sake. For without love, sex was like ashes, offering no prospect of a rewarding tomorrow.

I could hardly believe Joan Hackett was gone. She was so alive and animated, so involved as we discussed her quest for her soulmate. As I sat with a throng of others in the church where the last rites were observed, I felt that her unquenchable spirit had left the body that lay before us in a sealed casket. The priest had a message from her which he read with a break in his voice, for he had known her for many years and loved her for her faith and integrity.

The message was for all in the church and beyond, for her friends and those she had never met.

"Let there be no sorrow," she said. "We will meet again one day in a place where there are no goodbyes."

She would now be a companion of the Lord.

I had seen immortality in action, not only in the amazing recall of Taylor Caldwell's historical novels, but in the expressions of love's continuity manifested by the people we regressed. For these regressions, supplemented by spontaneous recollections, embodied vivid and vital experiences which resolved the uncertain gaps in so many lives.

Under hypnosis, I had been told, the individual clearly saw the truth, not the fanciful truth, nor the subjective truth, but the absolute truth, because the subconscious mind was so closely in tune with the Universal Intelligence. So when a hypnotized Terry Moore saw the faces of Howard Hughes and Roger Elliott merge, her heightened awareness told her they were one and the same, just as Jerry Rivers was the Jonna of long ago.

I was struck by the exalting changes I saw in Terry and others who had been touched by a love they knew as eternal.

I thought of Elizabeth Bell, frail in person, but strong in spirit, who still kept herself serene, looking always for the Chinaman who was her higher self, not leaping into the jaws of death to join Barry, but finding strength in the knowledge that she had known her soulmate and he was still hers.

I thought of Dianne de la Vega, looking for a message in every song Dick Haymes had ever sung, happy in the thought he was communicating with her, and she with him, holding within herself the reality of an echoing melody that would never fade.

I thought of Gertrude Cayce, patient, courageous, a soulmate to a very special man; and of Sally Cayce, the soulmate of a very special son. I saw Sally in her chair musing with a dewy eye, having known a love she knew to be immortal, and which reflected the immortality of all who ever loved.

And I could hear her say, with a twinkle in her eye, "Don't feel sorry for me. Don't you know that we were all together many times before, and we will be together again?"

Epilogue

I had never seen Tara more beautiful. The mist shimmered in her eyes, and as she turned her head toward Richard and promised him all the treasures of "my mind, my heart, and my hands" I could not help but think of the time in a distant land when they had come so close to the altar and yet loved not quite enough to take the final step. There had been regret later, voiced out of the past, and one wondered why they had even met then, if it was only to deal with another chapter in frustration.

But now with the gleam in her eyes, and the answering glow in Richard's, as they became Mr. and Mrs. Richard Sutphen, they had finally achieved the fulfillment that had eluded them through all their misadventures.

They had asked if they could marry on my deck overlooking the blue Pacific, and it had been a gratifying experience for me, since I had brought them together. It seemed to me that they had been through enough of a crucible to understand what was expected of their love, to know, once and for all, that they were true soulmates.

I was pleased as I listened to the minister, a jovial spirit named Dave Van Hooser. For even without knowing the background, he had made a soulmate ceremony of it.

"Remember," said the minister, "that love between man and woman will be perpetual only as it is pure and true. Let your love for each other lead you to broader and fuller living. Then shall your hearts live, not to themselves alone, but shall go out in tenderness and helpfulness to your fellow man."

Later, as the guests commingled about the happy couple, I asked Tara what she had been thinking about as the knot was finally tied.

She looked at me blankly for a moment, as if her thoughts were ages away, and then she smiled.

"Yes," she said, "it does seem like a completion of all that has gone before."

I was not about to speculate on how much of their subconscious experience had stirred out of the past to influence the present. It was enough to know that nothing happened without a reason, and that no mischance occurred without casting its ripple, however tiny, on the sea of life.

"Whatever a man soweth, that shall he also reap," as the Apostle Paul once said.

I no longer thought of love or emotion, or the remembrance of these things, as something temporary or permanent, successful or unsuccessful, but more as a lesson or stepping-stone in the development of the individual.

Hence, I was not surprised when any of "my" soulmates separated on the verge of a union.

Even before Patrick Flanagan and Susan Strasberg, now thoroughly into her writing and metaphysics, had painlessly parted, and she had taken to the road to perform brilliantly in *Agnes of God*, their separation was highly predictable, written in the currents and eddies of the past. In Rome and Egypt, even Arcturus, as I recalled, there had been no measure of fulfillment, no give or take, that could have brought completion, even with a little more effort or luck. I never had the feeling they were mated, only that they had perhaps come together to facilitate certain events, and then disjoin, leaving each ready for another love.

"We have always been together," said Patrick, looking at the Crystal Lady, Gael Gordon, with a love-light in his eyes.

I restrained a smile.

"It seems to me I have heard this song before."

He thought back and shook his head.

"No jealousy, no grievances, no claims, no commitment, except that of trust and love. Love is its own commitment."

"You mean you don't even argue over who was what in Egypt?"

Gael gave me an almost pitying glance.

"My mother is of the earth," she said, "my father of the sky."

She was a lissome dark-haired beauty, five years younger than Patrick, strong and supple, with hidden fires in her coal black eyes. She was known as the Crystal Lady because she was said to heal people with magic cylinders of quartz. She had given herself completely to him, as he had to her. They had no life, no preoccupation, that was apart from each other. Theirs was indeed a joint mission.

"What we have accomplished jointly," she said, "neither of us could have accomplished apart."

By their own regressions, they had found themselves together in ancient Greece, Egypt, Atlantis, and other distant lands, but never as now. For in this lifetime, they felt themselves chosen to unlock the portentous mysteries of the pyramids, which Edgar Cayce had once said would solve the riddle of the Universe.

They had meditated for days in the Pyramid of Giza, feeling each day an increment in power. On coming out, they fasted for a month, concentrating on the subconscious, as they synchronized the present with the images drawn from the past. And out of this came an explanation of why their relationship was different from the others.

"There was an imbalance in me," said Patrick, "as there is in other people, which I had not been aware of. This imbalance worked against all the other relationships I had. There was a side of me missing, like the errant piece of a jigsaw puzzle. And once I discovered what this was, I had found the piece that completed the picture. I had tried before to find myself in others, seeing bits and parts of myself in their reflections of me. It was a constant effort to fit it all together in some semblance of a design that would explain me to myself."

Gael had been a revelation. "We were counterparts of one another, thinking the same thoughts at the same time. We would write them down and find they matched, though we were often miles apart. It was fascinating to look into my mind and know ˻ ˻s reading hers as well. And even more fascinating to look ˻˻o hers and see mine as it really was. I saw then that we were twin souls, having discharged all our karmic obligations, in this life, and before."

Had he not had misgivings about losing someone he loved?

"Susan and I were both better and stronger for our coming together. We filled each other's special need at that time. When we parted, we were strong enough to strike out for ourselves, Susan with her triumph on the stage, and myself in a search with Gael for a greater meaning of life."

"We have put our trust in God," said Gael quietly, "He will show us the way."

I was still puzzled.

"This imbalance you mentioned. Exactly what is it?"

Patrick smiled as though he had been expecting my question.

"We are all made up inside of male and female energies. And like other men I allowed my masculine side to dominate. Consequently, there was an imbalance in me that I do not believe nature intended. In meeting Gael, and finding my own counterpart, I was able to release the female energies I shared with her, making me a well-balanced person."

In Flanagan's simple grasp of something obviously complex, he may very well have come on a truth that lent some plausible explanation to the precious concept of twin flames.

At any rate, he had come out ahead. He had found, for himself, his perfect love, the lady who out of the past had loved him unconditionally in Egypt, Atlantis, and ancient Greece, and, even more pertinently, I thought, tuned in harmoniously to his every present mood.

"This is it," he said, with an air of finality.

"I hope that you will still be together when this book comes out."

"If it is delayed a thousand years," he said with a smile.

The reincarnationists say we have all known many people before and so have a variety of relationships to work out. Additionally, new relationships are constantly launched to bring out those vital facets of a person hitherto untested.

I thought of all this as I sat in the living room of Holly Markas McBride's home in Corona del Mar. She was a different Holly from the one I had known a year before. She was radiantly aglow, and yet she was separated from the man she had so ecstatically thought her soulmate.

It had been rough at first. She had been bewildered and

hurt, wondering miserably what had gone wrong, bitterly blaming herself and her lack of judgment.

As we talked my eye lighted on a wall plaque, prominently placed.

"If the world gives you lemons, make lemonade," it read.

She noticed my look and smiled.

"That about sums it up," she said.

She had realized, believing in the Almighty, that it had all happened for a reason, even if she didn't know the reason at the time. "I could go forward, growing out of the experience, or wallow in despair."

She looked back, only to look ahead. She considered the process that had brought her Terry. "There was nothing wrong with Terry's teaching. I had just applied it improperly, not knowing that I was limiting myself. I had programmed a certain person—Terry—and I got him. What I should have done, as I look back, was to have programmed an ideal life situation."

"But," she shrugged, "then I wouldn't have had the growing experience with Terry."

At first she had felt slightly ambivalent. "How could I have thought that Terry and I were soulmates, when now we were no longer together? I meditated long and hard, questioning my own beliefs, and the concept of soulmates itself. I arrived finally at an image of twin spirits, put together at a certain time for a certain reason, what some refer to as synchronicity. As I thought about it I realized Terry had been my perfect teacher. Our divorce, even more than our marriage, had made it necessary for me to crawl into the very core of my being, and my relationship with God Himself. I had been so full of myself before, my home, my cars, my real estate business, my ego. All of this suddenly palled, and I realized that love, with a recognition of its connection with God's Universe, was all that really counted. I was a child of God, understanding at last that abundance came through knowing your oneness with the Universe."

She had gone away for a while to think these things out, putting the mainstream of her life behind her, and with it the realities that had so largely documented it.

"Giving up old belief systems can be very painful. It's not easy to let go of the old, comforting ideas, even when we realize they have been self-limiting."

So far, it seemed to me, we had not come to grips with the immediate problem.

"Do you have any idea," I asked, "why your marriage broke up?"

She smiled, without bitterness.

"Yes," she said, "or it would not have been a soulmate experience. I have profited out of it. People who love can't help but gain within themselves."

She saw I was still waiting. Her girlish face lit up, its radiance embracing me in its warm glow.

"I had to surrender something to come to the truth. I gave up the fancy that a relationship with 'the perfect one' would make me happy. I now saw that all along I had been searching for a person outside myself to validate me, to confer on me the approval I thought I needed. But now, in my adversity, I turned to this wonderful universal powerhouse we know as God. In renewing this faith of my childhood, I saw that I was restoring my faith in the God-awareness inside me. It was a belief in something larger than myself that was still not detached from me. It gave me a peacefulness I had never known before, a confidence and trust in the dynamics of change, for like others, I found, I had always resisted changing my cherished concepts and attitudes. I was ready now to go with the flow, to move to another level of consciousness."

That was all very fine, but how did it work? Was there another soulmate in the offing? And how could she be sure when she had been so sure before?

She laughed. "I am not the same person. I see things as they are, not as I would wish them to be."

As I looked at her, I thought of the soulmates I had met, the ecstasy and the agony, the fulfillment and the disappointment.

"Every day," she said, "begins with my new affirmation."

It was a very simple one.

"I am happy and confident in the anticipation of my own God-given good, and this I know to be my truth."

I couldn't resist one last question.

"Is there anybody on the horizon?"

She smiled.

"I can see him," she said, "as if he were standing before me in the light of the noonday sun."

I sighed to myself.

"And whom the Lord gives hope," I recalled a wise man once saying, "He gives all the blessings of love."